MW00592675

COLLECTED WORKS OF
WILLIAM BUTLER YEATS

CONTENTS

FOUR YEARS

FOUR YEARS 1887-1891.

I

At the end of the eighties my father and mother, my brother and sisters and myself, all newly arrived from Dublin, were settled in Bedford Park in a red-brick house with several wood mantlepieces copied from marble mantlepieces by the brothers Adam, a balcony, and a little garden shadowed by a great horse-chestnut tree. Years before we had lived there, when the crooked, ostentatiously picturesque streets, with great trees casting great shadows, had been anew enthusiasm: the Pre-Raphaelite movement at last affecting life. But now exaggerated criticism had taken the place of enthusiasm; the tiled roofs, the first in modern London, were said to leak, which they did not, & the drains to be bad, though that was no longer true; and I imagine that houses were cheap. I remember feeling disappointed because the co-operative stores, with their little seventeenth century panes, were so like any common shop; and because the public house, called 'The Tabard' after Chaucer's Inn, was so plainly a common public house; and because the great sign of a trumpeter designed by Rooke, the Pre-Raphaelite artist, had been freshened by some inferior hand. The big red-brick church had never pleased me, and I was accustomed, when I saw the wooden balustrade that ran along the slanting edge of the roof, where nobody ever walked or could walk, to remember the opinion of some architect friend of my father's, that it had been put there to keep the birds from falling off. Still, however, it had some village characters and helped us to feel not wholly lost in the metropolis. I no longer went to church as a regular habit, but go I sometimes did, for one Sunday morning I saw these words painted on a board in the porch: 'The congregation are requested to kneel during prayers; the kneelers are afterwards to be hung upon pegs provided for the purpose.' In front of every seat hung a little cushion, and these cushions were called 'kneelers.' Presently the joke ran through the community, where there were many artists, who considered religion at best an unimportant accessory to good architecture and who disliked that particular church.

II

I could not understand where the charm had gone that I had felt, when as a school-boy of twelve or thirteen, I had played among the unfinished houses, once leaving the marks of my two hands, blacked by a fall among some paint, upon a white balustrade. Sometimes I thought it was because these were real houses, while my play had been among toy-houses some day to be inhabited by imaginary people full of the happiness that one can see in picture books. I was in all things Pre-Raphaelite. When I was fifteen or sixteen, my father had told me about Rossetti and Blake and given me their poetry to read; & once in Liverpool on my way to Sligo, "I had seen 'Dante's Dream' in the gallery there—a picture painted when Rossetti had lost his dramatic power, and to-day not very pleasing to me—and its colour, its people, its romantic architecture had blotted all other pictures away." It was a perpetual bewilderment that my father, who had begun life as a Pre-Raphaelite painter, now painted portraits of the first comer, children selling newspapers, or a consumptive girl with a basket offish upon her head, and that when, moved perhaps by memory of his youth, he chose some theme from poetic tradition, he would soon weary and leave it unfinished. I had seen the change coming bit by bit and its defence elaborated by young men fresh from the Paris art-schools. 'We must paint what is in front of us,' or 'A man must be of his own time,' they would say, and if I spoke of Blake or Rossetti they would point out his bad drawing and tell me to admire Carolus Duran and Bastien-Lepage. Then, too, they were very ignorant men; they read nothing, for nothing mattered but 'Knowing how to paint,' being in reaction against a generation that seemed to have wasted its time upon so many things. I thought myself alone in hating these young men, now indeed getting towards middle life, their contempt for the past, their monopoly of the future, but in a few months I was to discover others of my own age, who thought as I did, for it is not true that youth looks before it with the mechanical gaze of a well-drilled soldier. Its quarrel is not with the past, but with the present, where its elders are so obviously powerful, and no cause seems lost if it seem to threaten that power. Does cultivated youth ever really love the future, where the eye can discover no persecuted Royalty hidden among oak leaves, though from it certainly does come so much proletarian rhetoric? I was unlike others of my generation in one thing only. I am very religious, and deprived by Huxley and Tyndall, whom I detested, of the simple-minded religion of my childhood, I had made a new religion, almost an infallible church, out of poetic tradition: a fardel of stories, and of personages, and of emotions, a bundle of images and of masks passed on from generation to generation by poets & painters with some help from philosophers and theologians. I wished for a world where I could discover this tradition perpetually, and not in pictures and in poems only, but in tiles round the chimney-piece and in the hangings that kept out the draught. I had even created a dogma: 'Because those imaginary people are created out of the deepest instinct of man, to be his measure and his norm, whatever I can imagine those mouths speaking may be the nearest I can go to truth.' When I listened they seemed always to speak of one thing only: they, their loves, every incident of their lives, were steeped in the supernatural. Could even Titian's 'Ariosto' that I loved beyond other portraits, have its grave look, as if waiting for some perfect final event, if the painters, before Titian, had not learned portraiture, while painting into the corner of compositions, full of saints and Madonnas, their kneeling patrons? At seventeen years old I was already an old-fashioned brass cannon full of shot, and nothing kept me from going off but a doubt as to my capacity to shoot straight.

III

I was not an industrious student and knew only what I had found by accident, and I had found "nothing I cared for after Titian—and Titian I knew chiefly from a copy of 'the supper of Emmaus' in Dublin—till Blake and the Pre-Raphaelites;" and among my father's friends were no Pre-Raphaelites. Some indeed had come to Bedford Park in the enthusiasm of the first building, and others to be near those that had. There was Todhunter, a well-off man who had bought my father's pictures while my father was still Pre-Raphaelite. Once a Dublin doctor he was a poet and a writer of poetical plays: a tall, sallow, lank, melancholy man, a good scholar and a good intellect; and with him my father carried on a warm exasperated friendship, fed I think by old memories and wasted by quarrels over matters of opinion. Of all the survivors he was the most dejected, and the least estranged, and I remember encouraging him, with a sense of worship shared, to buy a very expensive carpet designed by Morris. He displayed it without strong liking and would have agreed had there been any to find fault. If he had liked anything strongly he might have been a famous man, for a few years later he was to write, under some casual patriotic impulse, certain excellent verses now in all Irish anthologies; but with him every book was a new planting and not a new bud on an old bough. He had I think no peace in himself. But my father's chief friend was York Powell, a famous Oxford Professor of history, a broad-built, broad-headed, brown-bearded man, clothed in heavy blue cloth and looking, but for his glasses and the dim sight of a student, like some captain in the merchant service. One often passed with pleasure from Todhunter's company to that of one who was almost ostentatiously at peace. He cared nothing for philosophy, nothing for economics, nothing for the policy of nations, for history, as he saw it, was a memory of men who were amusing or exciting to think about. He impressed all who met him & seemed to some a man of genius, but he had not enough ambition to shape his thought, or conviction to give rhythm to his style, and remained always a poor writer. I was too full of unfinished speculations and premature convictions to value rightly his conversation, in-formed by a vast erudition, which would give itself to every casual association of speech and company precisely because he had neither cause nor design. My father, however, found Powell's concrete narrative manner a necessary completion of his own; and when I asked him, in a letter many years later, where he got his philosophy, replied 'From York Powell' and thereon added, no doubt remembering that Powell was without ideas, 'By looking at him.' Then there was a good listener, a painter in whose hall hung a big picture, painted in his student days, of Ulysses sailing home from the Phaeacian court, an orange and a skin of wine at his side, blue mountains towering behind; but who lived by drawing domestic scenes and lovers' meetings for a weekly magazine that had an immense circulation among the imperfectly educated. To escape the boredom of work, which he never turned to but under pressure of necessity, and usually late at night with the publisher's messenger in the hall, he had half filled his studio with mechanical toys of his own invention, and perpetually increased their number. A model railway train at intervals puffed its way along the walls, passing several railway stations and signal boxes; and on the floor lay a camp with attacking and defending soldiers and a fortification that blew up when the attackers fired a pea through a certain window; while a large model of a Thames barge hung from the ceiling. Opposite our house lived an old artist who worked also for the illustrated papers for a living, but painted landscapes for his pleasure, and of him I remember nothing except that he had outlived ambition, was a good listener, and that my father explained his gaunt appearance by his descent from Pocahontas. If all these men were a little like becalmed ships, there was certainly one man whose sails were full. Three or four doors off, on our side of the road, lived a decorative artist in all the naive confidence of popular ideals and the public approval. He was our daily comedy. 'I myself and Sir Frederick Leighton are the greatest decorative artists of the age,' was among his sayings, & a great lych-gate, bought from some country church-yard, reared its thatched roof, meant to shelter bearers and coffin, above the entrance to his front garden, to show that he at any rate knew nothing of discouragement. In this fairly numerous company—there were others though no other face rises before me—my father and York Powell found listeners for a conversation that had no special loyalties, or antagonisms; while I could only talk upon set topics, being in the heat of my youth, and the topics that filled me with excitement were never spoken of.

IV

Some quarter of an hour's walk from Bedford Park, out on the high road to Richmond, lived W. E. Henley, and I, like many others, began under him my education. His portrait, a lithograph by Rothenstein, hangs over my mantlepiece among portraits of other friends. He is drawn standing, but, because doubtless of his crippled legs, he leans forward, resting his elbows upon some slightly suggested object—a table or a window-sill. His heavy figure and powerful head, the disordered hair standing upright, his short irregular beard and moustache, his lined and wrinkled face, his eyes steadily fixed upon some object, in complete confidence and self-possession, and yet as in half-broken reverie, all are exactly as I remember him. I have seen other portraits and they too show him exactly as I remember him, as though he had but one appearance and that seen fully at the first glance and by all alike. He was most human—human, I used to say, like one of Shakespeare's characters—and yet pressed and pummelled, as it were, into a single attitude, almost into a gesture and a speech, as by some overwhelming situation. I disagreed with him about everything, but I admired him beyond words. With the exception of some early poems founded upon old French models, I disliked his poetry, mainly because he wrote *Vers Libre*, which I associated with Tyndall and Huxley and Bastien-Lepage's clownish peasant staring with vacant eyes at her great boots; and filled it with unimpassioned description of an hospital ward where his leg had been amputated. I wanted the strongest passions, passions that had nothing to do with observation, and metrical forms that seemed old enough to be sung by men half-asleep or riding upon a journey. Furthermore, Pre-Raphaelitism affected him as some people are affected by a cat in the room, and though he professed himself at our first meeting without political interests or convictions, he soon grew into a violent unionist and imperialist. I used to say when I spoke of his poems: 'He is like a great actor with a bad part; yet who would look at Hamlet in the grave scene if Salvini played the grave-digger?' and I might so have explained much that he said and did. I meant that he was like a great actor of passion—character-acting meant nothing to me for many years—and an actor of passion will display some one quality of soul, personified again and again, just as a great poetical painter, Titian, Botticelli, Rossetti may depend for his greatness upon a type of beauty which presently we call by his name. Irving, the last of the sort on the English stage, and in modern England and France it is the rarest sort, never moved me but in the expression of intellectual pride; and though I saw Salvini but once, I am convinced that his genius was a kind of animal nobility. Henley, half inarticulate—'I am very costive,' he would say—beset with personal quarrels, built up an image of power and magnanimity till it became, at moments, when seen as it were by lightning, his true self. Half his opinions were the contrivance of a sub-consciousness that sought always to bring life to the dramatic crisis, and expression to that point of artifice where the true self could find its tongue. Without opponents there had been no drama, and in his youth Ruskinism and Pre-Raphaelitism, for he was of my father's generation, were the only possible opponents. How could one resent his prejudice when, that he himself might play a worthy part, he must find beyond the common rout, whom he derided and flouted daily, opponents he could imagine moulded like himself? Once he said to me in the height of his imperial propaganda, 'Tell those young men in Ireland that this great thing must go on. They say Ireland is not fit for self-government but that is nonsense. It is as fit as any other European country but we cannot grant it.' And then he spoke of his desire to found and edit a Dublin newspaper. It would have expounded the Gaelic propaganda then beginning, though Dr. Hyde had as yet no league, our old stories, our modern literature—everything that did not demand any shred or patch of government. He dreamed of a tyranny but it was that of Cosimo de Medici.

V

We gathered on Sunday evenings in two rooms, with folding doors between, & hung, I think, with photographs from Dutch masters, and in one room there was always, I think, a table with cold meat. I can recall but one elderly man—Dunn his name was—rather silent and full of good sense, an old friend of Henley's. We were young men, none as yet established in his own, or in the world's opinion, and Henley was our leader and our confidant. One evening I found him alone amused and exasperated.

He cried: 'Young A . . . has just been round to ask my advice. Would I think it a wise thing if he bolted with Mrs. B . . . ? "Have you quite determined to do it?" I asked him. "Quite." "Well," I said, "in that case I refuse to give you any advice."' Mrs. B . . . was a beautiful talented woman, who, as the Welsh triad said of Guinevere, 'was much given to being carried off.' I think we listened to him, and often obeyed him, partly because he was quite plainly not upon the side of our parents. We might have a different ground of quarrel, but the result seemed more important than the ground, and his confident manner and speech made us believe, perhaps for the first time, in victory. And besides, if he did denounce, and in my case he certainly did, what we held in secret reverence, he never failed to associate it with things, or persons, that did not move us to reverence. Once I found him just returned from some art congress in Liverpool or in Manchester. 'The Salvation Armyism of art,' he called it, & gave a grotesque description of some city councillor he had found admiring Turner. Henley, who hated all that Ruskin praised, thereupon derided Turner, and finding the city councillor the next day on the other side of the gallery, admiring some Pre-Raphaelite there, derided that Pre-Raphaelite. The third day Henley discovered the poor man on a chair in the middle of the room, staring disconsolately upon the floor. He terrified us also, and certainly I did not dare, and I think none of us dared, to speak our admiration for book or picture he condemned, but he made us feel always our importance, and no man among us could do good work, or show the promise of it, and lack his praise.

I can remember meeting of a Sunday night Charles Whibley, Kenneth Grahame, author of 'The Golden Age,' Barry Pain, now a well known novelist, R. A. M. Stevenson, art critic and a famous talker, George Wyndham, later on a cabinet minister and Irish chief secretary, and Oscar Wilde, who was some eight years or ten older than the rest. But faces and names are vague to me and, while faces that I met but once may rise clearly before me, a face met on many a Sunday has perhaps vanished. Kipling came sometimes, I think, but I never met him; and Stepniak, the nihilist, whom I knew well elsewhere but not there, said 'I cannot go more than once a year, it is too exhausting.' Henley got the best out of us all, because he had made us accept him as our judge and we knew that his judgment could neither sleep, nor be softened, nor changed, nor turned aside. When I think of him, the antithesis that is the foundation of human nature being ever in my sight, I see his crippled legs as though he were some Vulcan perpetually forging swords for other men to use; and certainly I always thought of C . . ., a fine classical scholar, a pale and seemingly gentle man, as our chief swordsman and bravo. When Henley founded his weekly newspaper, first the 'Scots,' afterwards 'The National Observer,' this young man wrote articles and reviews notorious for savage wit; and years afterwards when 'The National Observer' was dead, Henley dying & our cavern of outlaws empty, I met him in Paris very sad and I think very poor. 'Nobody will employ me now,' he said. 'Your master is gone,' I answered, 'and you are like the spear in an old Irish story that had to be kept dipped in poppy-juice that it might not go about killing people on its own account.' I wrote my first good lyrics and tolerable essays for 'The National Obsever' and as I always signed my work could go my own road in some measure. Henley often revised my lyrics, crossing out a line or a stanza and writing in one of his own, and I was comforted by my belief that he also re-wrote Kipling then in the first flood of popularity. At first, indeed, I was ashamed of being re-written and thought that others were not, and only began investigation when the editorial characteristics—epigrams, archaisms and all—appeared in the article upon Paris fashions and in that upon opium by an Egyptian Pasha. I was not compelled to full conformity for verse is plainly stubborn; and in prose, that I might avoid unacceptable opinions, I wrote nothing but ghost or fairy stories, picked up from my mother, or some pilot at Rosses Point, and Henley saw that I must needs mix a palette fitted to my subject matter. But if he had changed every 'has' into 'hath' I would have let him, for had not we sunned ourselves in his generosity? 'My young men out-dome and they write better than I,' he wrote in some letter praising Charles Whibley's work, and to another friend with a copy of my 'Man who dreamed of Fairyland:' 'See what a fine thing has been written by one of my lads.'

VI

My first meeting with Oscar Wilde was an astonishment. I never before heard a man talking with perfect sentences, as if he had written them all over night with labour and yet all spontaneous. There was present that night at Henley's, by right of propinquity or of accident, a man full of the secret spite of dullness, who interrupted from time to time and always to check or disorder thought; and I noticed with what mastery he was foiled and thrown. I noticed, too, that the impression of artificiality that I think all Wilde's listeners have recorded, came from the perfect rounding of the sentences and from the deliberation that made it possible. That very impression helped him as the effect of metre, or of the antithetical prose of the seventeenth century, which is itself a true metre, helps a writer, for he could pass without incongruity from some unforeseen swift stroke of wit to elaborate reverie. I heard him say a few nights later: 'Give me "The Winter's Tale," "Daffodils that come before the swallow dare" but not "King Lear." What is "King Lear" but poor life staggering in the fog?' and the slow cadence, modulated with so great precision, sounded natural to my ears. That first night he praised Walter Pater's 'Essays on the Renaissance:' 'It is my golden book; I never travel anywhere without it; but it is the very flower of decadence. The last trumpet should have sounded the moment it was written.' 'But,' said the dull man, 'would you not have given us time to read it?' 'Oh no,' was the retort, 'there would have been plenty of time afterwards—in either world.' I think he seemed to us, baffled as we were by youth, or by infirmity, a triumphant figure, and to some of us a figure from another age, an audacious Italian fifteenth century figure. A few weeks before I had heard one of my father's friends, an official in a publishing firm that had employed both Wilde and Henley as editors, blaming Henley who was 'no use except under control' and praising Wilde, 'so indolent but such a genius;' and now the firm became the topic of our talk. 'How often do you go to the office?' said Henley. 'I used to go three times a week,' said Wilde, 'for an hour a day but I have since struck off one of the days.' 'My God,' said Henley, 'I went five times a week for five hours a day and when I wanted to strike off a day they had a special committee meeting.' 'Furthermore,' was Wilde's answer, 'I never answered their letters. I have known men come to London full of bright prospects and seen them complete wrecks in a few months through a habit of answering letters.' He too knew how to keep our elders in their place, and his method was plainly the more successful for Henley had been dismissed. 'No he is not an aesthete,' Henley commented later, being somewhat embarrassed by Wilde's Pre-Raphaelite entanglement. 'One soon finds that he is a scholar and a gentleman.' And when I dined with Wilde a few days afterwards he began at once, 'I had to strain every nerve to equal that man at all;' and I was too loyal to speak my thought: 'You & not he' said all the brilliant things. He like the rest of us had felt the strain of an intensity that seemed to hold life at the point of drama. He had said, on that first meeting, 'The basis of literary friendship is mixing the poisoned bowl;' and for a few weeks Henley and he became close friends till, the astonishment of their meeting over, diversity of character and ambition pushed them apart, and, with half the cavern helping, Henley began mixing the poisoned bowl for Wilde. Yet Henley never wholly lost that first admiration, for after Wilde's downfall he said to me: 'Why did he do it? I told my lads to attack him and yet we might have fought under his banner.'

VII

It became the custom, both at Henley's and at Bedford Park, to say that R. A. M. Stevenson, who frequented both circles, was the better talker. Wilde had been trussed up like a turkey by undergraduates, dragged up and down a hill, his champagne emptied into the ice tub, hooted in the streets of various towns and I think stoned, and no newspaper named him but in scorn; his manner had hardened to meet opposition and at times he allowed one to see an unpardonable insolence. His charm was acquired and systematised, a mask which he wore only when it pleased him, while the charm of Stevenson belonged to him like the colour of his hair. If Stevenson's talk became monologue we did not know it, because our one object was to show by our attention that he need never leave off. If thought failed him we would not combat what he had said, or start some new theme, but would encourage him with a question; and one felt that it had been always so from childhood up. His mind was full of phantasy for phantasy's sake and he gave as good entertainment in monologue as his cousin Robert Louis in poem or story. He was always 'supposing:' 'Suppose you had two millions what would you do with it?' and 'Suppose you were in Spain and in love how would you propose?' I recall him one afternoon at our house at Bedford Park, surrounded by my brother and sisters and a little group of my father's friends, describing proposals in half a dozen countries. There your father did it, dressed in such and such a way with such and such words, and there a friend must wait for the lady outside the chapel door, sprinkle her with holy water and say 'My friend Jones is dying for love of you.' But when it was over, those quaint descriptions, so full of laughter and sympathy, faded or remained in the memory as something alien from one's own life like a dance I once saw in a great house, where beautifully dressed children wound a long ribbon in and out as they danced. I was not of Stevenson's party and mainly I think because he had written a book in praise of Velasquez, praise at that time universal wherever Pre-Raphaelitism was accurst, and to my mind, that had to pick its symbols where its ignorance permitted, Velasquez seemed the first bored celebrant of boredom. I was convinced, from some obscure meditation, that Stevenson's conversational method had joined him to my elders and to the indifferent world, as though it were right for old men, and unambitious men and all women, to be content with charm and humour. It was the prerogative of youth to take sides and when Wilde said: 'Mr. Bernard Shaw has no enemies but is intensely disliked by all his friends,' I knew it to be a phrase I should never forget, and felt revenged upon a notorious hater of romance, whose generosity and courage I could not fathom.

VIII

I saw a good deal of Wilde at that time—was it 1887 or 1888?—I have no way of fixing the date except that I had published my first book 'The Wanderings of Usheen' and that Wilde had not yet published his 'Decay of Lying.' He had, before our first meeting, reviewed my book and despite its vagueness of intention, and the inexactness of its speech, praised without qualification; and what was worth more than any review had talked about it, and now he asked me to eat my Xmas dinner with him, believing, I imagine, that I was alone in London.

He had just renounced his velveteen, and even those cuffs turned backward over the sleeves, and had begun to dress very carefully in the fashion of the moment. He lived in a little house at Chelsea that the architect Godwin had decorated with an elegance that owed something to Whistler. There was nothing mediaeval, nor Pre-Raphaelite, no cupboard door with figures upon flat gold, no peacock blue, no dark background. I remember vaguely a white drawing room with Whistler etchings, 'let in' to white panels, and a dining room all white: chairs, walls, mantlepiece, carpet, except for a diamond-shaped piece of red cloth in the middle of the table under a terra cotta statuette, and I think a red shaded lamp hanging from the ceiling to a little above the statuette. It was perhaps too perfect in its unity, his past of a few years before had gone too completely, and I remember thinking that the perfect harmony of his life there, with his beautiful wife and his two young children, suggested some deliberate artistic composition.

He commended, & dispraised himself, during dinner by attributing characteristics like his own to his country: 'We Irish are too poetical to be poets; we are a nation of brilliant failures, but we are the greatest talkers since the Greeks.' When dinner was over he read me from the proofs of 'The Decay of Lying' and when he came to the sentence: 'Schopenhauer has analysed the pessimism that characterises modern thought, but Hamlet invented it. The world has become sad because a puppet was once melancholy,' I said, 'Why do you change "sad" to "melancholy?"' He replied that he wanted a full sound at the close of his sentence, and I thought it no excuse and an example of the vague impressiveness that spoilt his writing for me. Only when he spoke, or when his writing was the mirror of his speech, or in some simple fairytale, had he words exact enough to hold a subtle ear. He alarmed me, though not as Henley did for I never left his house thinking myself fool or dunce. He flattered the intellect of every man he liked; he made me tell him long Irish stories and compared my art of story-telling to Homer's; and once when he had described himself as writing in the census paper 'age 19, profession genius, infirmity talent,' the other guest, a young journalist fresh from Oxford or Cambridge, said 'What should I have written?' and was told that it should have been 'profession talent, infirmity genius.' When, however, I called, wearing shoes a little too yellow—unblackened leather had just become fashionable—I understood their extravagence when I saw his eyes fixed upon them; an another day Wilde asked me to tell his little boy a fairy story, and I had but got as far as 'Once upon a time there was a giant' when the little boy screamed and ran out of the room. Wilde looked grave and I was plunged into the shame of clumsiness that afflicts the young. When I asked for some literary gossip for some provincial newspaper, that paid me a few shillings a month, he explained very explicitly that writing literary gossip was no job for a gentleman. Though to be compared to Homer passed the time pleasantly, I had not been greatly perturbed had he stopped me with 'Is it a long story?' as Henley would certainly have done. I was abashed before him as wit and man of the world alone. I remember that he deprecated the very general belief in his success or his efficiency, and I think with sincerity. One form of success had gone: he was no more the lion of the season, and he had not discovered his gift for writing comedy, yet I think I knew him at the happiest moment of his life. No scandal had darkened his fame, his fame as a talker was growing among his equals, & he seemed to live in the enjoyment of his own spontaneity. One day he began: 'I have been inventing a Christian heresy,' and he told a detailed story, in the style of some early father, of how Christ recovered after the Crucifixion and, escaping from the tomb, lived on for many years, the one man upon earth who knew the falsehood of Christianity. Once St. Paul visited his town and he alone in the carpenters' quarter did not go to hear him preach. The other carpenters noticed that henceforth, for some unknown reason, he kept his hands covered. A few days afterwards I found Wilde, with smock frocks in various colours spread out upon the floor in front of him, while a missionary explained that he did not object to the heathen going naked upon week days, but insisted upon clothes in church. He had brought the smock frocks in a cab that the only art-critic whose fame had reached Central Africa might select a colour; so Wilde sat there weighing all with a conscious ecclesiastic solemnity.

VIII

Of late years I have often explained Wilde to myself by his family history. His father, was a friend or acquaintance of my father's father and among my family traditions there is an old Dublin riddle: 'Why are Sir William Wilde's nails so black?' Answer, 'Because he has scratched himself.' And there is an old story still current in Dublin of Lady Wilde saying to a servant. 'Why do you put the plates on the coal-scuttle? What are the chairs meant for?' They were famous people and there are many like stories, and even a horrible folk story, the invention of some Connaught peasant, that tells how Sir William Wilde took out the eyes of some men, who had come to consult him as an oculist, and laid them upon a plate, intending to replace them in a moment, and how the eyes were eaten by a cat. As a certain friend of mine, who has made a prolonged study of the nature of cats, said when he first heard the tale, 'Cats love eyes.' The Wilde family was clearly of the sort that fed the imagination of Charles Lever, dirty, untidy, daring, and what Charles Lever, who loved more normal activities, might not have valued so highly, very imaginative and learned. Lady Wilde, who when I knew her received her friends with blinds drawn and shutters closed that none might see her withered face, longed always perhaps, though certainly amid much self mockery, for some impossible splendour of character and circumstance. She lived near her son in level Chelsea, but I have heard her say, 'I want to live on some high place, Primrose Hill or Highgate, because I was an eagle in my youth.' I think her son lived with no self mockery at all an imaginary life; perpetually performed a play which was in all things the opposite of all that he had known in childhood and early youth; never put off completely his wonder at opening his eyes every morning on his own beautiful house, and in remembering that he had dined yesterday with a duchess and that he delighted in Flaubert and Pater, read Homer in the original and not as a school-master reads him for the grammar. I think, too, that because of all that half-civilized blood in his veins, he could not endure the sedentary toil of creative art and so remained a man of action, exaggerating, for the sake of immediate effect, every trick learned from his masters, turning their easel painting into painted scenes. He was a parvenu, but a parvenu whose whole bearing proved that if he did dedicate every story in 'The House of Pomegranates' to a lady of title, it was but to show that he was Jack and the social ladder his pantomime beanstalk. "Did you ever hear him say 'Marquess of Dimmesdale'?" a friend of his once asked me. "He does not say 'the Duke of York' with any pleasure."

He told me once that he had been offered a safe seat in Parliament and, had he accepted, he might have had a career like that of Beaconsfield, whose early style resembles his, being meant for crowds, for excitement, for hurried decisions, for immediate triumphs. Such men get their sincerity, if at all, from the contact of events; the dinner table was Wilde's event and made him the greatest talker of his time, and his plays and dialogues have what merit they possess from being now an imitation, now a record, of his talk. Even in those days I would often defend him by saying that his very admiration for his predecessors in poetry, for Browning, for Swinburne and Rossetti, in their first vogue while he was a very young man, made any success seem impossible that could satisfy his immense ambition: never but once before had the artist seemed so great, never had the work of art seemed so difficult. I would then compare him with Benvenuto Cellini who, coming after Michael Angelo, found nothing left to do so satisfactory as to turn bravo and assassinate the man who broke Michael Angelo's nose.

IX

I cannot remember who first brought me to the old stable beside Kelmscott House, William Morris' house at Hammersmith, & to the debates held there upon Sunday evenings by the socialist League. I was soon of the little group who had supper with Morris afterwards. I met at these suppers very constantly Walter Crane, Emery Walker presently, in association with Cobden Sanderson, the printer of many fine books, and less constantly Bernard Shaw and Cockerell, now of the museum of Cambridge, and perhaps but once or twice Hyndman the socialist and the anarchist Prince Krapotkin. There too one always met certain more or less educated workmen, rough of speech and manner, with a conviction to meet every turn. I was told by one of them, on a night when I had done perhaps more than my share of the talking, that I had talked more nonsense in one evening than he had heard in the whole course of his past life. I had merely preferred Parnell, then at the height of his career, to Michael Davitt who had wrecked his Irish influence by international politics. We sat round a long unpolished and unpainted trestle table of new wood in a room where hung Rossetti's 'Pomegranate,' a portrait of Mrs. Morris, and where one wall and part of the ceiling were covered by a great Persian carpet. Morris had said somewhere or other that carpets were meant for people who took their shoes off when they entered a house, and were most in place upon a tent floor. I was a little disappointed in the house, for Morris was an old man content at last to gather beautiful things rather than to arrange a beautiful house. I saw the drawing-room once or twice and there alone all my sense of decoration, founded upon the background of Rossetti's pictures, was satisfied by a big cupboard painted with a scene from Chaucer by Burne Jones, but even there were objects, perhaps a chair or a little table, that seemed accidental, bought hurriedly perhaps, and with little thought, to make wife or daughter comfortable. I had read as a boy in books belonging to my father, the third volume of 'The Earthly Paradise' and 'The Defence of Guinevere,' which pleased me less, but had not opened either for a long time. 'The man who never laughed again' had seemed the most wonderful of tales till my father had accused me of preferring Morris to Keats, got angry about it and put me altogether out of countenance. He had spoiled my pleasure, for now I questioned while I read and at last ceased to read; nor had Morris written as yet those prose romances that became, after his death, so great a joy that they were the only books I was ever to read slowly that I might not come too quickly to the end. It was now Morris himself that stirred my interest, and I took to him first because of some little tricks of speech and body that reminded me of my old grandfather in Sligo, but soon discovered his spontaneity and joy and made him my chief of men. To-day I do not set his poetry very high, but for an odd altogether wonderful line, or thought; and yet, if some angel offered me the choice, I would choose to live his life, poetry and all, rather than my own or any other man's. A reproduction of his portrait by Watts hangs over my mantlepiece with Henley's, and those of other friends. Its grave wide-open eyes, like the eyes of some dreaming beast, remind me of the open eyes of Titian's' Ariosto,' while the broad vigorous body suggests a mind that has no need of the intellect to remain sane, though it give itself to every phantasy, the dreamer of the middle ages. It is 'the fool of fairy ... wide and wild as a hill,' the resolute European image that yet half remembers Buddha's motionless meditation, and has no trait in common with the wavering, lean image of hungry speculation, that cannot but fill the mind's eye because of certain famous Hamlets of our stage. Shakespeare himself foreshadowed a symbolic change, that shows a change in the whole temperament of the world, for though he called his Hamlet 'fat, and scant of breath,' he thrust between his fingers agile rapier and dagger.

The dream world of Morris was as much the antithesis of daily life as with other men of genius, but he was never conscious of the antithesis and so knew nothing of intellectual suffering. His intellect, unexhausted by speculation or casuistry, was wholly at the service of hand and eye, and whatever he pleased he did with an unheard of ease and simplicity, and if style and vocabulary were at times monotonous, he could not have made them otherwise without ceasing to be himself. Instead of the language of Chaucer and Shakespeare, its warp fresh from field and market, if the woof were learned, his age offered him a speech, exhausted from abstraction, that only returned to its full vitality when written learnedly and slowly. The roots of his antithetical dream were visible enough: a never idle man of great physical strength and extremely irascible—did he not fling a badly baked plum pudding through the window upon Xmas Day?—a man more joyous than any intellectual man of our world, called himself 'the idle singer of an empty day' created new forms of melancholy, and faint persons, like the knights & ladies of Burne Jones, who are never, no, not once in forty volumes, put out of temper. A blunderer, who had said to the only unconverted man at a socialist picnic in Dublin, to prove that equality came easy, 'I was brought up a gentleman and now, as you can see, associate with all sorts,' and left wounds thereby that rankled after twenty years, a man of whom I have heard it said 'He is always afraid that he is doing something wrong, and generally is,' wrote long stories with apparently no other object than that his persons might show one another, through situations of poignant difficulty, the most exquisite tact.

He did not project, like Henley or like Wilde, an image of himself, because, having all his imagination set on making and doing, he had little self-knowledge. He imagined instead new conditions of making and doing; and, in the teeth of those scientific generalisations that cowed my boyhood, I can see some like imagining in every great change, believing that the first flying fish leaped, not because it sought 'adaptation' to the air, but out of horror of the sea.

X

Soon after I began to attend the lectures, a French class was started in the old coach-house for certain young socialists who planned a tour in France, and I joined it and was for a time a model student constantly encouraged by the compliments of the old French mistress. I told my father of the class, and he asked me to get my sisters admitted. I made difficulties and put off speaking of the matter, for I knew that the new and admirable self I was making would turn, under family eyes, into plain rag doll. How could I pretend to be industrious, and even carry dramatization to the point of learning my lessons, when my sisters were there and knew that I was nothing of the kind? But I had no argument I could use and my sisters were admitted. They said nothing unkind, so far as I can remember, but in a week or two I was my old procrastinating idle self and had soon left the class altogether. My elder sister stayed on and became an embroideress under Miss May Morris, and the hangings round Morris's big bed at Kelmscott House, Oxfordshire, with their verses about lying happily in bed when 'all birds sing in the town of the tree,' were from her needle though not from her design. She worked for the first few months at Kelmscott House, Hammersmith, and in my imagination I cannot always separate what I saw and heard from her report, or indeed from the report of that tribe or guild who looked up to Morris as to some worshipped mediaeval king. He had no need for other people. I doubt if their marriage or death made him sad or glad, and yet no man I have known was so well loved; you saw him producing everywhere organisation and beauty, seeming, almost in the same instant, helpless and triumphant; and people loved him as children are loved.

People much in his neighbourhood became gradually occupied with him, or about his affairs, and without any wish on his part, as simple people become occupied with children. I remember a man who was proud and pleased because he had distracted Morris' thoughts from an attack of gout by leading the conversation delicately to the hated name of Milton. He began at Swinburne. 'Oh, Swinburne,' said Morris, 'is a rhetorician; my masters have been Keats and Chaucer for they make pictures.' 'Does not Milton make pictures?' asked my informant. 'No,' was the answer, 'Dante makes pictures, but Milton, though he had a great earnest mind, expressed himself as a rhetorician.' 'Great earnest mind,' sounded strange to me and I doubt not that were his questioner not a simple man, Morris had been more violent. Another day the same man started by praising Chaucer, but the gout was worse and Morris cursed Chaucer for destroying the English language with foreign words.

He had few detachable phrases and I can remember little of his speech, which many thought the best of all good talk, except that it matched his burly body and seemed within definite boundaries inexhaustible in fact and expression. He alone of all the men I have known seemed guided by some beast-like instinct and never ate strange meat. 'Balzac! Balzac!' he said to me once, 'Oh, that was the man the French bourgeoisie read so much a few years ago.' I can remember him at supper praising wine: 'Why do people say it is prosaic to be inspired by wine? Has it not been made by the sunlight and the sap?' and his dispraising houses decorated by himself: 'Do you suppose I like that kind of house? I would like a house like a big barn, where one ate in one corner, cooked in another corner, slept in the third corner & in the fourth received one's friends'; and his complaining of Ruskin's objection to the underground railway: 'If you must have a railway the best thing you can do with it is to put it in a tube with a cork at each end.' I remember too that when I asked what led up to his movement, he replied, 'Oh, Ruskin and Carlyle, but somebody should have been beside Carlyle and punched his head every five minutes.' Though I remember little, I do not doubt that, had I continued going there on Sunday evenings, I should have caught fire from his words and turned my hand to some mediaeval work or other. Just before I had ceased to go there I had sent my 'Wanderings of Usheen' to his daughter, hoping of course that it might meet his eyes, & soon after sending it I came upon him by chance in Holborn. 'You write my sort of poetry,' he said and began to praise me and to promise to send his praise to 'The Commonwealth,' the League organ, and he would have said more of a certainty had he not caught sight of a new ornamental cast-iron lamp-post and got very heated upon that subject.

I did not read economics, having turned socialist because of Morris's lectures and pamphlets, and I think it unlikely that Morris himself could read economics. That old dogma of mine seemed germane to the matter. If the men and women imagined by the poets were the norm, and if Morris had, in, let us say, 'News from Nowhere,' then running through 'The Commonwealth,' described such men and women living under their natural conditions or as they would desire to live, then those conditions themselves must be the norm, and could we but get rid of certain institutions the world would turn from eccentricity. Perhaps Morris himself justified himself in his own heart by as simple an argument, and was, as the socialist D . . . said to me one night walking home after some lecture, 'an anarchist without knowing it.' Certainly I and all about me, including D . . . himself, were for chopping up the old king for Medea's pot. Morris had told us to have nothing to do with the parliamentary socialists, represented for men in general by the Fabian Society and Hyndman's Socialist Democratic Federation and for us in particular by D . . . During the period of transition mistakes must be made, and the discredit of these mistakes must be left to 'the bourgeoisie;' and besides, when you begin to talk of this measure or that other you lose sight of the goal and see, to reverse Swinburne's description of Tiresias, 'light on the way but darkness on the goal.' By mistakes Morris meant vexatious restrictions and compromises—'If any man puts me into a labour squad, I will lie on my back and kick.' That phrase very much expresses our idea of revolutionary tactics: we all intended to lie upon our back and kick. D . . ., pale and sedentary, did not dislike labour squads and we all hated him with the left side of our heads, while admiring him immensely with the right. He alone was invited to entertain Mrs. Morris, having many tales of his Irish uncles, more especially of one particular uncle who had tried to commit suicide by shutting his head into a carpet bag. At that time he was an obscure man, known only for a witty speaker at street corners and in Park demonstrations. He had, with an assumed truculence and fury, cold logic, an universal gentleness, an unruffled courtesy, and yet could never close a speech without being denounced by a journeyman hatter with an Italian name. Converted to socialism by D . . ., and to anarchism by himself, with swinging arm and uplifted voice this man perhaps exaggerated our scruple about parliament. 'I lack,' said D . . ., 'the bump of reverence;' whereon the wild man shouted 'You 'ave a 'ole.' There are moments when looking back I somewhat confuse my own figure with that of the hatter, image of our hysteria, for I too became violent with the violent solemnity of a religious devotee. I can even remember sitting behind D . . . and saying some rude thing or other over his shoulder. I don't remember why I gave it up but I did quite suddenly; and I think the push may have come from a young workman who was educating himself between Morris and Karl Marx. He had planned a history of the navy and when I had spoken of the battleship of Nelson's day, had said: 'Oh, that was the decadence of the battleship,' but if his naval interests were mediaeval, his ideas about religion were pure Karl Marx, and we were soon in perpetual argument. Then gradually the attitude towards religion of almost everybody but Morris, who avoided the subject altogether, got upon my nerves, for I broke out after some lecture or other with all the arrogance of raging youth. They attacked religion, I said, or some such words, and yet there must be a change of heart and only religion could make it. What was the use of talking about some near revolution putting all things right, when the change must come, if come it did, with astronomical slowness, like the cooling of the sun or, it may have been,

40

like the drying of the moon? Morris rang his chairman's bell, but I was too angry to listen, and he had to ring it a second time before I sat down. He said that night at supper: 'Of course I know there must be a change of heart, but it will not come as slowly as all that. I rang my bell because you were not being understood.' He did not show any vexation, but I never returned after that night; and yet I did not always believe what I had said and only gradually gave up thinking of and planning for some near sudden change for the better.

XI

I spent my days at the British Museum and must, I think, have been delicate, for I remember often putting off hour after hour consulting some necessary book because I shrank from lifting the heavy volumes of the catalogue; and yet to save money for my afternoon coffee and roll I often walked the whole way home to Bedford Park. I was compiling, for a series of shilling books, an anthology of Irish fairy stories and, for an American publisher, a two volume selection from the Irish novelists that would be somewhat dearer. I was not well paid, for each book cost me more than three months' reading; and I was paid for the first some twelve pounds, ('O Mr. E . . . ' said publisher to editor, 'you must never again pay so much') and for the second, twenty; but I did not think myself badly paid, for I had chosen the work for my own purposes.

Though I went to Sligo every summer, I was compelled to live out of Ireland the greater part of every year and was but keeping my mind upon what I knew must be the subject matter of my poetry. I believed that if Morris had set his stories amid the scenery of his own Wales (for I knew him to be of Welsh extraction and supposed wrongly that he had spent his childhood there) that if Shelley had nailed his Prometheus or some equal symbol upon some Welsh or Scottish rock, their art had entered more intimately, more microscopically, as it were, into our thought, and had given perhaps to modern poetry a breadth and stability like that of ancient poetry. The statues of Mausolus and Artemisia at the British Museum, private, half animal, half divine figures, all unlike the Grecian athletes and Egyptian kings in their near neighbourhood, that stand in the middle of the crowd's applause or sit above measuring it out unpersuadable justice, became to me, now or later, images of an unpremeditated joyous energy, that neither I nor any other man, racked by doubt and enquiry, can achieve; and that yet, if once achieved, might seem to men and women of Connemara or of Galway their very soul. In our study of that ruined tomb, raised by a queen to her dead lover, and finished by the unpaid labour of great sculptors after her death from grief, or so runs the tale, we cannot distinguish the handiworks of Scopas and Praxiteles; and I wanted to create once more an art, where the artist's handiwork would hide as under those half anonymous chisels, or as we find it in some old Scots ballads or in some twelfth or thirteenth century Arthurian romance. That handiwork assured, I had martyred no man for modelling his own image upon Pallas Athena's buckler; for I took great pleasure in certain allusions to the singer's life one finds in old romances and ballads, and thought his presence there all the more poignant because we discover it half lost, like portly Chaucer riding behind his Maunciple and his Pardoner. Wolfram von Eschenbach, singing his German Parsival, broke off some description of a famished city to remember that in his own house at home the very mice lacked food, and what old ballad singer was it who claimed to have fought by day in the very battle he sang by night? So masterful indeed was that instinct that when the minstrel knew not who his poet was he must needs make up a man: 'When any stranger asks who is the sweetest of singers, answer with one voice: "A blind man; he dwells upon rocky Chios; his songs shall be the most beautiful for ever."' Elaborate modern psychology sounds egotistical, I thought, when it speaks in the first person, but not those simple emotions which resemble the more, the more powerful they are, everybody's emotion, and I was soon to write many poems where an always personal emotion was woven into a general pattern of myth and symbol. When the Fenian poet says that his heart has grown cold and callous, 'For thy hapless fate, dear Ireland, and sorrows of my own,' he but follows tradition, and if he does not move us deeply, it is because he has no sensuous musical vocabulary that comes at need, without compelling him to sedentary

43

toil and so driving him out from his fellows. I thought to create that sensuous, musical vocabulary, and not for myself only but that I might leave it to later Irish poets, much as a mediaeval Japanese painter left his style as an inheritance to his family, and was careful to use a traditional manner and matter; yet did something altogether different, changed by that toil, impelled by my share in Cain's curse, by all that sterile modern complication, by my 'originality' as the newspapers call it. Morris set out to make a revolution that the persons of his 'Well at the World's End' or his 'Waters of the Wondrous Isles,' always, to my mind, in the likeness of Artemisia and her man, might walk his native scenery; and I, that my native scenery might find imaginary inhabitants, half planned a new method and a new culture. My mind began drifting vaguely towards that doctrine of 'the mask' which has convinced me that every passionate man (I have nothing to do with mechanist, or philanthropist, or man whose eyes have no preference) is, as it were, linked with another age, historical or imaginary, where alone he finds images that rouse his energy. Napoleon was never of his own time, as the naturalistic writers and painters bid all men be, but had some Roman Emperor's image in his head and some condottiere's blood in his heart; and when he crowned that head at Rome with his own hands, he had covered, as may be seen from David's painting, his hesitation with that Emperor's old suit.

XII

I had various women friends on whom I would call towards five o'clock, mainly to discuss my thoughts that I could not bring to a man without meeting some competing thought, but partly because their tea & toast saved my pennies for the 'bus ride home; but with women, apart from their intimate exchanges of thought, I was timid and abashed. I was sitting on a seat in front of the British Museum feeding pigeons, when a couple of girls sat near and began enticing my pigeons away, laughing and whispering to one another, and I looked straight in front of me, very indignant, and presently went into the Museum without turning my head towards them. Since then I have often wondered if they were pretty or merely very young. Sometimes I told myself very adventurous love stories with myself for hero, and at other times I planned out a life of lonely austerity, and at other times mixed the ideals and planned a life of lonely austerity mitigated by periodical lapses. I had still the ambition, formed in Sligo in my teens, of living in imitation of Thoreau on Innisfree, a little island in Lough Gill, and when walking through Fleet Street very homesick I heard a little tinkle of water and saw a fountain in a shop window which balanced a little ball upon its jet and began to remember lake water. From the sudden remembrance came my poem 'Innisfree,' my first lyric with anything in its rhythm of my own music. I had begun to loosen rhythm as an escape from rhetoric, and from that emotion of the crowd that rhetoric brings, but I only understood vaguely and occasionally that I must, for my special purpose, use nothing but the common syntax. A couple of years later I would not have written that first line with its conventional archaism—'Arise and go'—nor the inversion in the last stanza. Passing another day by the new Law Courts, a building that I admired because it was Gothic,—'It is not very good,' Morris had said, 'but it is better than any thing else they have got and so they hate it.'—I grew suddenly oppressed by the great weight of stone, and thought, 'There are miles and miles of stone and brick all round me,' and presently added, 'If John the Baptist, or his like, were to come again and had his mind set upon it, he could make all these people go out into some wilderness leaving their buildings empty,' and that thought, which does not seem very valuable now, so enlightened the day that it is still vivid in the memory. I spent a few days at Oxford copying out a seventeenth century translation of *Poggio's Liber Facetiarum* or the *Hypneroto-machia* of *Poliphili* for a publisher; I forget which, for I copied both; and returned very pale to my troubled family. I had lived upon bread and tea because I thought that if antiquity found locust and wild honey nutritive, my soul was strong enough to need no better. I was always planning some great gesture, putting the whole world into one scale of the balance and my soul into the other, and imagining that the whole world somehow kicked the beam. More than thirty years have passed and I have seen no forcible young man of letters brave the metropolis without some like stimulant; and all, after two or three, or twelve or fifteen years, according to obstinacy, have understood that we achieve, if we do achieve, in little diligent sedentary stitches as though we were making lace. I had one unmeasured advantage from my stimulant: I could ink my socks, that they might not show through my shoes, with a most haughty mind, imagining myself, and my torn tackle, somewhere else, in some far place 'under the canopy . . . i' the city of kites and crows.'

In London I saw nothing good, and constantly remembered that Ruskin had said to some friend of my father's—'As I go to my work at the British Museum I see the faces of the people become daily more corrupt.' I convinced myself for a time, that on the same journey I saw but what he saw. Certain old women's faces filled me with horror, faces that are no longer there, or if they are, pass before me unnoticed: the fat

46

blotched faces, rising above double chins, of women who have drunk too much beer and eaten too much meat. In Dublin I had often seen old women walking with erect heads and gaunt bodies, talking to themselves in loud voices, mad with drink and poverty, but they were different, they belonged to romance: Da Vinci has drawn women who looked so and so carried their bodies.

XIII

I attempted to restore one old friend of my father's to the practice of his youth, but failed though he, unlike my father, had not changed his belief. My father brought me to dine with Jack Nettleship at Wigmore Street, once inventor of imaginative designs and now a painter of melodramatic lions. At dinner I had talked a great deal—too much, I imagine, for so young a man, or may be for any man—and on the way home my father, who had been plainly anxious that I should make a good impression, was very angry. He said I had talked for effect and that talking for effect was precisely what one must never do; he had always hated rhetoric and emphasis and had made me hate it; and his anger plunged me into great dejection. I called at Nettleship's studio the next day to apologise and Nettleship opened the door himself and received me with enthusiasm. He had explained to some woman guest that I would probably talk well, being an Irishman, but the reality had surpassed, etc., etc. I was not flattered, though relieved at not having to apologise, for I soon discovered that what he really admired was my volubility, for he himself was very silent. He seemed about sixty, had a bald head, a grey beard, and a nose, as one of my father's friends used to say, like an opera glass, and sipped cocoa all the afternoon and evening from an enormous tea cup that must have been designed for him alone, not caring how cold the cocoa grew. Years before he had been thrown from his horse while hunting and broken his arm and, because it had been badly set, suffered great pain for along time. A little whiskey would always stop the pain, and soon a little became a great deal and he found himself a drunkard, but having signed his liberty away for certain months he was completely cured. He had acquired, however, the need of some liquid which he could sip constantly. I brought him an admiration settled in early boyhood, for my father had always said, 'George Wilson was our born painter but Nettleship our genius,' and even had he shown me nothing I could care for, I had admired him still because my admiration was in my bones. He showed me his early designs and they, though often badly drawn, fulfilled my hopes. Something of Blake they certainly did show, but had in place of Blake's joyous intellectual energy a Saturnian passion and melancholy. 'God creating evil' the death-like head with a woman and a tiger coming from the forehead, which Rossetti—or was it Browning?—had described 'as the most sublime design of ancient or modern art' had been lost, but there was another version of the same thought and other designs never published or exhibited. They rise before me even now in meditation, especially a blind Titan-like ghost floating with groping hands above the treetops. I wrote a criticism, and arranged for reproductions with the editor of an art magazine, but after it was written and accepted the proprietor, lifting what I considered an obsequious caw in the Huxley, Tyndall, Carolus Duran, Bastien-Lepage rookery, insisted upon its rejection. Nettleship did not mind its rejection, saying, 'Who cares for such things now? Not ten people,' but he did mind my refusal to show him what I had written. Though what I had written was all eulogy, I dreaded his judgment for it was my first art criticism. I hated his big lion pictures, where he attempted an art too much concerned with the sense of touch, with the softness or roughness, the minutely observed irregularity of surfaces, for his genius; and I think he knew it. 'Rossetti used to call my pictures 'pot-boilers,' he said, 'but they are all—all,' and he waved his arms to the canvases, 'symbols.' When I wanted him to design gods and angels and lost spirits once more, he always came back to the point, 'Nobody would be pleased.' 'Everybody should have a *raison d'etre*' was one of his phrases. 'Mrs—'s articles are not good but they are her *raison d'etre*.' I had but little knowledge of art, for there was little scholarship in the Dublin Art School, so I overrated the quality of anything that could be connected with my general beliefs about the world. If I had been able to give angelical, or diabolical names to his lions I might have liked them also and I think that Nettleship himself would have liked them better, and liking them better have become a better painter. We had the same kind of religious feeling, but I could give a crude philosophical expression to mine while he could only express his in action or with brush and pencil. He often told me of certain ascetic ambitions, very much like my own, for he had kept all the moral ambition of youth with a moral courage peculiar to himself, as for instance—'Yeats, the other night I was arrested by a policeman—was walking round Regent's Park barefooted to keep the flesh under—good sort of thing to do—I was carrying my boots in my hand and he thought I was a burglar; and even when I explained and gave him half a crown, he would not let me go till I had promised to put on my boots before I met the next policeman.'

He was very proud and shy, and I could not imagine anybody asking him questions, and so I was content to take these stories as they came, confirmations of stories I had heard in boyhood. One story in particular had stirred my imagination, for, ashamed all my boyhood of my lack of physical courage, I admired what was beyond my imitation. He thought that any weakness, even a weakness of body, had the character of sin, and while at breakfast with his brother, with whom he shared a room on the third floor of a corner house, he said that his nerves were out of order. Presently he left the table, and got out through the window and on to a stone ledge that ran along the wall under the windowsills. He sidled along the ledge, and turning the corner with it, got in at a different window and returned to the table. 'My nerves,' he said, 'are better than I thought.'

XIV

Nettleship said to me: 'Has Edwin Ellis ever said anything about the effect of drink upon my genius?' 'No,' I answered. 'I ask,' he said, 'because I have always thought that Ellis has some strange medical insight.' Though I had answered 'no,' Ellis had only a few days before used these words: 'Nettleship drank his genius away.' Ellis, but lately returned from Perugia, where he had lived many years, was another old friend of my father's but some years younger than Nettleship or my father. Nettleship had found his simplifying image, but in his painting had turned away from it, while Ellis, the son of Alexander Ellis, a once famous man of science, who was perhaps the last man in England to run the circle of the sciences without superficiality, had never found that image at all. He was a painter and poet, but his painting, which did not interest me, showed no influence but that of Leighton. He had started perhaps a couple of years too late for Pre-Raphaelite influence, for no great Pre-Raphaelite picture was painted after 1870, and left England too soon for that of the French painters. He was, however, sometimes moving as a poet and still more often an astonishment. I have known him cast something just said into a dozen lines of musical verse, without apparently ceasing to talk; but the work once done he could not or would not amend it, and my father thought he lacked all ambition. Yet he had at times nobility of rhythm—an instinct for grandeur—and after thirty years I still repeat to myself his address to Mother Earth:

O mother of the hills, forgive our towers;
O mother of the clouds, forgive our dreams

and there are certain whole poems that I read from time to time or try to make others read. There is that poem where the manner is unworthy of the matter, being loose and facile, describing Adam and Eve fleeing from Paradise. Adam asks Eve what she carries so carefully and Eve replies that it is a little of the apple core kept for their children. There is that vision of 'Christ the Less,' a too hurriedly written ballad, where the half of Christ, sacrificed to the divine half 'that fled to seek felicity,' wanders wailing through Golgotha; and there is 'The Saint and the Youth' in which I can discover no fault at all. He loved complexities—'seven silences like candles round her face' is a line of his—and whether he wrote well or ill had always a manner, which I would have known from that of any other poet. He would say to me, 'I am a mathematician with the mathematics left out'—his father was a great mathematician—or 'A woman once said to me, "Mr. Ellis why are your poems like sums?"' and certainly he loved symbols and abstractions. He said once, when I had asked him not to mention something or other, 'Surely you have discovered by this time that I know of no means whereby I can mention a fact in conversation.'

He had a passion for Blake, picked up in Pre-Raphaelite studios, and early in our acquaintance put into my hands a scrap of note paper on which he had written some years before an interpretation of the poem that begins

> The fields from Islington to Marylebone
> To Primrose Hill and St. John's Wood
> Were builded over with pillars of gold
> And there Jerusalem's pillars stood.

The four quarters of London represented Blake's four great mythological personages, the Zoas, and also the four elements. These few sentences were the foundation of all study of the philosophy of William Blake, that requires an exact knowledge for its pursuit and that traces the connection between his system and that of Swedenborg or of Boehme. I recognised certain attributions, from what is sometimes called the Christian Cabala, of which Ellis had never heard, and with this proof that his interpretation was more than phantasy, he and I began our four years' work upon the Prophetic Books of William Blake. We took it as almost a sign of Blake's personal help when we discovered that the spring of 1889, when we first joined our knowledge, was one hundred years from the publication of 'The Book of Thel,' the first published of the Prophetic Books, as though it were firmly established that the dead delight in anniversaries. After months of discussion and reading, we made a concordance of all Blake's mystical terms, and there was much copying to be done in the Museum & at Red Hill, where the descendants of Blake's friend and patron, the landscape painter, John Linnell, had many manuscripts. The Linnellswere narrow in their religious ideas & doubtful of Blake's orthodoxy, whom they held, however, in great honour, and I remember a timid old lady who had known Blake when a child saying: 'He had very wrong ideas, he did not believe in the historical Jesus.' One old man sat always beside us ostensibly to sharpen our pencils, but perhaps really to see that we did not steal the manuscripts, and they gave us very old port at lunch and I have upon my dining room walls their present of Blake's Dante engravings. Going thither and returning Ellis would entertain me by philosophical discussion, varied with improvised stories, at first folk tales which he professed to have picked up in Scotland; and though I had read and collected many folk tales, I did not see through the deceit. I have a partial memory of two more elaborate tales, one of an Italian conspirator flying barefoot from I forget what adventure through I forget what Italian city, in the early morning. Fearing to be recognised by his bare feet, he slipped past the sleepy porter at an hotel calling out 'number so and so' as if he were some belated guest. Then passing from bedroom door to door he tried on the boots, and just as he got a pair to fit a voice cried from the room 'Who is that?' 'Merely me, sir,' he called back, 'taking your boots.' The other was of a Martyr's Bible round which the cardinal virtues had taken personal form—this a fragment of Blake's

53

philosophy. It was in the possession of an old clergyman when a certain jockey called upon him, and the cardinal virtues, confused between jockey and clergyman, devoted themselves to the jockey. As whenever he sinned a cardinal virtue interfered and turned him back to virtue, he lived in great credit and made, but for one sentence, a very holy death. As his wife and family knelt round in admiration and grief, he suddenly said 'Damn.' 'O my dear,' said his wife, 'what a dreadful expression.' He answered, 'I am going to heaven' and straightway died. It was a long tale, for there were all the jockey's vain attempts to sin, as well as all the adventures of the clergyman, who became very sinful indeed, but it ended happily, for when the jockey died the cardinal virtues returned to the clergyman. I think he would talk to any audience that offered, one audience being the same as another in his eyes, and it may have been for this reason that my father called him unambitious. When he was a young man he had befriended a reformed thief and had asked the grateful thief to take him round the thieves' quarters of London. The thief, however, hurried him away from the worst saying, 'Another minute and they would have found you out. If they were not the stupidest men in London, they had done so already.' Ellis had gone through a no doubt romantic and witty account of all the houses he had robbed, and all the throats he had cut in one short life.

His conversation would often pass out of my comprehension, or indeed I think of any man's, into a labyrinth of abstraction and subtilty, and then suddenly return with some verbal conceit or turn of wit. The mind is known to attain, in certain conditions of trance, a quickness so extraordinary that we are compelled at times to imagine a condition of unendurable intellectual intensity, from which we are saved by the merciful stupidity of the body; & I think that the mind of Edwin Ellis was constantly upon the edge of trance. Once we were discussing the symbolism of sex, in the philosophy of Blake, and had been in disagreement all the afternoon. I began talking with a new sense of conviction, and after a moment Ellis, who was at his easel, threw down his brush and said that he had just seen the same explanation in a series of symbolic visions.

'In another moment,' he said, 'I should have been off.' We went into the open air and walked up and down to get rid of that feeling, but presently we came in again and I began again my explanation, Ellis lying upon the sofa. I had been talking some time when Mrs. Ellis came into the room and said: 'Why are you sitting in the dark?' Ellis answered, 'But we are not,' and then added in a voice of wonder, 'I thought the lamp was lit and that I was sitting up, and I find I am in the dark and lying down.' I had seen a flicker of light over the ceiling, but had thought it a reflection from some light outside the house, which may have been the case.

XV

I had already met most of the poets of my generation. I had said, soon after the publication of 'The Wanderings of Usheen,' to the editor of a series of shilling reprints, who had set me to compile tales of the Irish fairies, 'I am growing jealous of other poets, and we will all grow jealous of each other unless we know each other and so feel a share in each other's triumph.' He was a Welshman, lately a mining engineer, Ernest Rhys, a writer of Welsh translations and original poems that have often moved me greatly though I can think of no one else who has read them. He was seven or eight years older than myself and through his work as editor knew everybody who would compile a book for seven or eight pounds. Between us we founded 'The Rhymers' Club' which for some years was to meet every night in an upper room with a sanded floor in an ancient eating house in the Strand called 'The Cheshire Cheese.' Lionel Johnson, Ernest Dowson, Victor Plarr, Ernest Radford, John Davidson, Richard le Gallienne, T. W. Rolleston, Selwyn Image and two men of an older generation, Edwin Ellis and John Todhunter, came constantly for a time, Arthur Symons and Herbert Home less constantly, while William Watson joined but never came and Francis Thompson came once but never joined; and sometimes, if we met in a private house, which we did occasionally, Oscar Wilde came. It had been useless to invite him to the 'Cheshire Cheese' for he hated Bohemia. 'Olive Schreiner,' he said once to me, 'is staying in the East End because that is the only place where people do not wear masks upon their faces, but I have told her that I live in the West End because nothing in life interests me but the mask.'

56

We read our poems to one another and talked criticism and drank a little wine. I sometimes say when I speak of the club, 'We had such and such ideas, such and such a quarrel with the great Victorians, we set before us such and such aims,' as though we had many philosophical ideas. I say this because I am ashamed to admit that I had these ideas and that whenever I began to talk of them a gloomy silence fell upon the room. A young Irish poet, who wrote excellently but had the worst manners, was to say a few years later, 'You do not talk like a poet, you talk like a man of letters;' and if all the rhymers had not been polite, if most of them had not been to Oxford or Cambridge, they would have said the same thing. I was full of thought, often very abstract thought, longing all the while to be full of images, because I had gone to the art school instead of a university. Yet even if I had gone to a university, and learned all the classical foundations of English literature and English culture, all that great erudition which, once accepted, frees the mind from restlessness, I should have had to give up my Irish subject matter, or attempt to found a new tradition. Lacking sufficient recognised precedent I must needs find out some reason for all I did. I knew almost from the start that to overflow with reasons was to be not quite well-born, and when I could I hid them, as men hide a disagreeable ancestry; and that there was no help for it, seeing that my country was not born at all. I was of those doomed to imperfect achievement, and under a curse, as it were, like some race of birds compelled to spend the time, needed for the making of the nest, in argument as to the convenience of moss and twig and lichen. Le Gallienne and Davidson, and even Symons, were provincial at their setting out, but their provincialism was curable, mine incurable; while the one conviction shared by all the younger men, but principally by Johnson and Horne, who imposed their personalities upon us, was an opposition to all ideas, all generalisations that can be explained and debated. E . . . fresh from Paris would sometimes say—'We are concerned with nothing but impressions,' but that itself was a generalisation and met but stony silence. Conversation constantly dwindled into 'Do you like so and so's last book?' 'No, I prefer the book before it,' and I think that but for its Irish members, who said whatever came into their heads, the club would not have survived its first difficult months. I knew—now ashamed that I thought 'like a man of letters,' now exasperated at their indifference to the fashion of their own river bed—that Swinburne in one way, Browning in another, and Tennyson in a third, had filled their work with what I called 'impurities,' curiosities about politics, about science, about history, about religion; and that we must create once more the pure work.

Our clothes were for the most part unadventurous like our conversation, though I indeed wore a brown velveteen coat, a loose tie and a very old Inverness cape, discarded by my father twenty years before and preserved by my Sligo-born mother whose actions were unreasoning and habitual like the seasons. But no other member of the club, except Le Gallienne, who wore a loose tie, and Symons, who had an Inverness cape that was quite new & almost fashionable, would have shown himself for the world in any costume but 'that of an English gentleman.' 'One should be quite unnoticeable,' Johnson explained to me. Those who conformed most carefully to the fashion in their clothes generally departed furthest from it in their hand-writing, which was small, neat and studied, one poet—which I forget—having founded his upon the handwriting of George Herbert. Dowson and Symons I was to know better in later years when Symons became a very dear friend, and I never got behind John Davidson's Scottish roughness and exasperation, though I saw much of him, but from the first I devoted myself to Lionel Johnson. He and Horne and Image and one or two others shared a man-servant and an old house in Charlotte Street, Fitzroy Square, typical figures of transition, doing as an achievement of learning and of exquisite taste what their predecessors did in careless abundance. All were Pre-Raphaelite, and sometimes one might meet in the rooms of one or other a ragged figure, as of some fallen dynasty, Simeon Solomon, the Pre-Raphaelite painter, once the friend of Rossetti and of Swinburne, but fresh now from some low public house. Condemned to a long term of imprisonment for a criminal offence, he had sunk into drunkenness and misery. Introduced one night, however, to some man who mistook him, in the dim candle light, for another Solomon, a successful academic painter and R. A., he started to his feet in a rage with 'Sir, do you dare to mistake me for that mountebank?' Though not one had harkened to the feeblest caw, or been spattered by the smallest dropping from any Huxley, Tyndall, Carolus Duran, Bastien-Lepage bundle of old twigs, I began by suspecting them of lukewarmness, and even backsliding, and I owe it to that suspicion that I never became intimate with Horne, who lived to become the greatest English authority upon Italian life in the fourteenth century and to write the one standard work on Botticelli. Connoisseur in several arts, he had designed a little church in the manner of Inigo Jones for a burial ground near the Marble Arch. Though I now think his little church a masterpiece, its style was more than a century too late to hit my fancy at two or three and twenty; and I accused him of leaning towards that eighteenth century

> That taught a school
> Of dolts to smooth, inlay, and clip, and fit
> Till, like the certain wands of Jacob's wit,
> Their verses tallied.

Another fanaticism delayed my friendship with two men, who are now my friends and in certain matters my chief instructors. Somebody, probably Lionel Johnson, brought me to the studio of Charles Ricketts and Charles Shannon, certainly heirs of the great generation, and the first thing I saw was a Shannon picture of a lady and child arrayed in lace, silk and satin, suggesting that hated century. My eyes were full of some more mythological mother and child and I would have none of it, and I told Shannon that he had not painted a mother and child but elegant people expecting visitors and I thought that a great reproach. Somebody writing in 'The Germ' had said that a picture of a pheasant and an apple was merely a picture of something to eat, and I was so angry with the indifference to subject, which was the commonplace of

59

all art criticism since Bastien-Lepage, that I could at times see nothing else but subject. I thought that, though it might not matter to the man himself whether he loved a white woman or a black, a female pickpocket or a regular communicant of the Church of England, if only he loved strongly, it certainly did matter to his relations and even under some circumstances to his whole neighbourhood. Sometimes indeed, like some father in Moliere, I ignored the lover's feelings altogether and even refused to admit that a trace of the devil, perhaps a trace of colour, may lend piquancy, especially if the connection be not permanent.

Among these men, of whom so many of the greatest talents were to live such passionate lives and die such tragic deaths, one serene man, T. W. Rolleston, seemed always out of place. It was I brought him there, intending to set him to some work in Ireland later on. I have known young Dublin working men slip out of their workshop to see 'the second Thomas Davis' passing by, and even remember a conspiracy, by some three or four, to make him 'the leader of the Irish race at home & abroad,' and all because he had regular features; and when all is said, Alexander the Great & Alcibiades were personable men, and the Founder of the Christian religion was the only man who was neither a little too tall nor a little too short but exactly six feet high. We in Ireland thought as do the plays and ballads, not understanding that, from the first moment wherein nature foresaw the birth of Bastien-Lepage, she has only granted great creative power to men whose faces are contorted with extravagance or curiosity or dulled with some protecting stupidity.

I had now met all those who were to make the nineties of the last century tragic in the history of literature, but as yet we were all seemingly equal, whether in talent or in luck, and scarce even personalities to one another. I remember saying one night at the Cheshire Cheese, when more poets than usual had come, 'None of us can say who will succeed, or even who has or has not talent. The only thing certain about us is that we are too many.'

XVI

I have described what image—always opposite to the natural self or the natural world—Wilde, Henley, Morris copied or tried to copy, but I have not said if I found an image for myself. I know very little about myself and much less of that anti-self: probably the woman who cooks my dinner or the woman who sweeps out my study knows more than I. It is perhaps because nature made me a gregarious man, going hither and thither looking for conversation, and ready to deny from fear or favour his dearest conviction, that I love proud and lonely images. When I was a child and went daily to the sexton's daughter for writing lessons, I found one poem in her School Reader that delighted me beyond all others: a fragment of some metrical translation from Aristophanes wherein the birds sing scorn upon mankind. In later years my mind gave itself to gregarious Shelley's dream of a young man, his hair blanched with sorrow studying philosophy in some lonely tower, or of his old man, master of all human knowledge, hidden from human sight in some shell-strewn cavern on the Mediterranean shore. One passage above all ran perpetually in my ears—

> Some feign that he is Enoch: others dream
> He was pre-Adamite, and has survived
> Cycles of generation and of ruin.
> The sage, in truth, by dreadful abstinence,
> And conquering penance of the mutinous flesh,
> Deep contemplation and unwearied study,
> In years outstretched beyond the date of man,

May have attained to sovereignty and science
Over those strong and secret things and thoughts
Which others fear and know not.

MAHMUD
I would talk
With this old Jew.

HASSAN
Thy will is even now
Made known to him where he dwells in a sea-cavern
'Mid the Demonesi, less accessible
Than thou or God! He who would question him
Must sail alone at sunset where the stream
Of ocean sleeps around those foamless isles,
When the young moon is westering as now,
And evening airs wander upon the wave;
And, when the pines of that bee-pasturing isle,
Green Erebinthus, quench the fiery shadow
Of his gilt prow within the sapphire water,
Then must the lonely helmsman cry aloud
'Ahasuerus!' and the caverns round
Will answer 'Ahasuerus!' If his prayer
Be granted, a faint meteor will arise,
Lighting him over Marmora; and a wind
Will rush out of the sighing pine-forest,
And with the wind a storm of harmony
Unutterably sweet, and pilot him
Through the soft twilight to the Bosphorus:
Thence, at the hour and place and circumstance
Fit for the matter of their conference,

The Jew appears. Few dare, and few who dare
Win the desired communion.

Already in Dublin, I had been attracted to the Theosophists because
they had affirmed the real existence of the Jew, or of his like; and, apart
from whatever might have been imagined by Huxley, Tyndall, Carolus
Duran and Bastien-Lepage, I saw nothing against his reality. Presently
having heard that Madame Blavatsky had arrived from France, or from
India, I thought it time to look the matter up. Certainly if wisdom existed
anywhere in the world it must be in some such lonely mind admitting no
duty to us, communing with God only, conceding nothing from fear or
favour. Have not all peoples, while bound together in a single mind and
taste, believed that such men existed and paid them that honour, or paid
it to their mere shadow, which they have refused to philanthropists and
to men of learning?

I found Madame Blavatsky in a little house at Norwood, with but, as
she said, three followers left—the Society of Psychical Research had just
reported on her Indian phenomena—and as one of the three followers sat
in an outer room to keep out undesirable visitors, I was kept a long time
kicking my heels. Presently I was admitted and found an old woman in a
plain loose dark dress: a sort of old Irish peasant woman with an air of
humour and audacious power. I was still kept waiting, for she was deep in
conversation with a woman visitor. I strayed through folding doors into
the next room and stood, in sheer idleness of mind, looking at a cuckoo
clock. It was certainly stopped, for the weights were off and lying upon
the ground, and yet as I stood there the cuckoo came out and cuckooed
at me. I interrupted Madame Blavatsky to say. 'Your clock has hooted
me.' 'It often hoots at a stranger,' she replied. 'Is there a spirit in it?' I said.
'I do not know,' she said, 'I should have to be alone to know what is in it.'
I went back to the clock and began examining it and heard her say 'Do
not break my clock.' I wondered if there was some hidden mechanism,
and I should have been put out, I suppose, had I found any, though

63

Henley had said to me, 'Of course she gets up fraudulent miracles, but a person of genius has to do something; Sarah Bernhardt sleeps in her coffin.' Presently the visitor went away and Madame Blavatsky explained that she was a propagandist for women's rights who had called to find out 'why men were so bad.' 'What explanation did you give her?' I said. 'That men were born bad but women made themselves so,' and then she explained that I had been kept waiting because she had mistaken me for some man whose name resembled mine and who wanted to persuade her of the flatness of the earth.

When I next saw her she had moved into a house at Holland Park, and some time must have passed—probably I had been in Sligo where I returned constantly for long visits—for she was surrounded by followers. She sat nightly before a little table covered with green baize and on this green baize she scribbled constantly with a piece of white chalk. She would scribble symbols, sometimes humorously applied, and sometimes unintelligible figures, but the chalk was intended to mark down her score when she played patience. One saw in the next room a large table where every night her followers and guests, often a great number, sat down to their vegetarian meal, while she encouraged or mocked through the folding doors. A great passionate nature, a sort of female Dr. Johnson, impressive, I think, to every man or woman who had themselves any richness, she seemed impatient of the formalism, of the shrill abstract idealism of those about her, and this impatience broke out inrailing & many nicknames: 'O you are a flapdoodle, but then you are a theosophist and a brother. 'The most devout and learned of all her followers said to me, 'H.P.B. has just told me that there is another globe stuck on to this at the north pole, so that the earth has really a shape something like a dumb-bell.' I said, for I knew that her imagination contained all the folklore of the world, 'That must be some piece of Eastern mythology.' 'O no it is not,' he said, 'of that I am certain, and there must be something in it or she would not have said it.' Her mockery was not kept for her followers alone, and her voice would become harsh, and her mockery lose phantasy and humour, when she spoke of what seemed to her scientific materialism. Once I saw this antagonism, guided by some kind of telepathic divination, take a form of brutal phantasy. I brought a very able Dublin woman to see her and this woman had a brother, a physiologist whose reputation, though known to specialists alone, was European; and, because of this brother, a family pride in everything scientific and modern. The Dublin woman scarcely opened her mouth the whole evening and her name was certainly unknown to Madame Blavatsky, yet I saw at once in that wrinkled old face bent over the cards, and the only time I ever saw it there, a personal hostility, the dislike of one woman for another. Madame Blavatsky seemed to bundle herself up, becoming all primeval peasant, and began complaining of her ailments, more especially of her bad leg. But of late her master—her 'old Jew,' her 'Ahasuerus,' cured it, or set it on the way to be cured. 'I was sitting here in my chair,' she said, 'when the master came in and brought something with him which he put over my knee, something warm which enclosed my knee—it was a live dog which he had cut open.' I recognised a cure used sometimes in mediaeval medicine. She had two masters, and their portraits, ideal Indian heads, painted by some most incompetent artist, stood upon either side of the folding doors. One night, when talk was impersonal and general, I sat gazing through the folding doors into the dimly lighted dining-room beyond. I noticed a curious red light shining upon a picture and got up to see where the red light came from. It was the picture of an Indian and as I came near it slowly vanished. When I returned to my seat, Madame Blavatsky said, 'What did you see?' 'A picture,' I said. 'Tell it to go away.' 'It is already gone.' 'So much the better,' she said, 'I was afraid it was medium ship but it is only clairvoyance.' 'What is the difference?' 'If it had been medium ship, it would have stayed in spite of you. Beware of medium ship; it is a kind of madness; I know, for I have been through it.'

I found her almost always full of gaiety that, unlike the occasional joking of those about her, was illogical and incalculable and yet always kindly and tolerant. I had called one evening to find her absent, but expected every moment. She had been somewhere at the seaside for her health and arrived with a little suite of followers. She sat down at once in her big chair, and began unfolding a brown paper parcel, while all looked on full of curiosity. It contained a large family Bible. 'This is a present for my maid,' she said. 'What! A Bible and not even anointed!' said some shocked voice. 'Well my children,' was the answer, 'what is the good of giving lemons to those who want oranges?' When I first began to frequent her house, as I soon did very constantly, I noticed a handsome clever woman of the world there, who seemed certainly very much out of place, penitent though she thought herself. Presently there was much scandal and gossip, for the penitent was plainly entangled with two young men, who were expected to grow into ascetic sages. The scandal was so great that Madame Blavatsky had to call the penitent before her and to speak after this fashion, 'We think that it is necessary to crush the animal nature; you should live in chastity in act and thought. Initiation is granted only to those who are entirely chaste,' and so to run on for some time. However, after some minutes in that vehement style, the penitent standing crushed and shamed before her, she had wound up, 'I cannot permit you more than one.' She was quite sincere, but thought that nothing mattered but what happened in the mind, and that if we could not master the mind, our actions were of little importance. One young man filled her with exasperation; for she thought that his settled gloom came from his chastity. I had known him in Dublin, where he had been accustomed to interrupt long periods of asceticism, in which he would eat vegetables and drink water, with brief outbreaks of what he considered the devil. After an outbreak he would for a few hours dazzle the imagination of the members of the local theosophical society with poetical rhapsodies about harlots and street lamps, and then sink into weeks of melancholy. A fellow theosophist once found him hanging from the window pole, but cut him down in the nick of time. I said to the man who cut him down, 'What did you say to one another?' He said, 'We spent the night telling comic stories and laughing a great deal.' This man, torn between sensuality and visionary ambition, was now the most devout of all, and told me that in the middle of the night he could often hear the ringing of the little 'astral bell' whereby Madame Blavatsky's master called her attention, and that, although it was a low silvery sound it made the whole house shake. Another night I found him waiting in the hall to show in those who had the right of entrance on some night when the discussion was private, and as I passed he whispered into my ear, 'Madame Blavatsky is perhaps not a real woman at all. They say that her dead body was found many years ago upon some Russian battlefield.' She had two dominant moods, both of extreme activity, but one calm and philosophic, and this was the mood always on that night in the week, when she answered questions upon her system; and as I look back after thirty years I often ask myself 'Was her speech automatic? Was she for one night, in every week, a trance medium, or in some similar state?' In the other mood she was full of phantasy and inconsequent raillery. 'That is the Greek church, a triangle like all true religion,' I recall her saying, as she chalked out a triangle on the green baize, and then, as she made it disappear in meaningless scribbles 'it spread out and became a bramble-bush like the Church of Rome.' Then rubbing it all out except one straight line, 'Now they have lopped off the branches and turned it into a broomstick arid that is Protestantism.' And so it was, night after night, always varied and unforseen. I have observed a like sudden extreme change in others, half whose thought was supernatural, and Laurence Oliphant records some where or other like observations. I can remember only once finding her in a mood of reverie; something had happened to damp her spirits, some attack upon her movement, or upon herself. She spoke of Balzac, whom she had seen but once, of Alfred de Musset, whom she had known well enough to dislike for his morbidity, and of George Sand whom she had known so well that they had dabbled in magic together of which 'neither knew anything at all' in those days; and she ran on, as if there was nobody there to overhear her, 'I used to wonder at and pity the people who sell their souls to the devil, but now I only pity them. They do it to have somebody on their sides,' and added to that, after some words I have forgotten, 'I write, write, write as the Wandering Jew walks, walks, walks.' Besides the devotees, who came to listen and to turn every doctrine into a new sanction for the puritanical convictions of their Victorian childhood, cranks came from half Europe and from all America, and they came that they might talk. One American said to me, 'She has become the most famous woman in the world by sitting in a big chair and permitting us to talk.' They talked and she played patience, and totted up her score on the green baize, and generally seemed to listen, but sometimes she would listen no more. There was a woman who talked perpetually of 'the divine spark' within her, until Madame Blavatsky stopped her with—'Yes, my dear, you have a divine spark within you, and if you are not very careful you will hear it snore.' A certain Salvation Army captain probably pleased her, for, if vociferous and loud of voice, he had much animation. He had known hardship and spoke of his visions while starving in the streets and he was still perhaps a little light in the head. I wondered what he could preach to ignorant men, his head ablaze with wild mysticism, till I met a man who had heard him talking near Covent Garden to some crowd in the street. 'My friends,' he was saying, 'you have the kingdom of heaven within you and it would take a pretty big pill to get that out.'

XVII

Meanwhile I had not got any nearer to proving that 'Ahasuerus dwells in a sea-cavern 'mid the Demonesi,' but one conclusion I certainly did come to, which I find written out in an old diary and dated 1887. Madame Blavatsky's 'masters' were 'trance' personalities, but by 'trance personalities' I meant something almost as exciting as 'Ahasuerus' himself. Years before I had found, on a table in the Royal Irish Academy, a pamphlet on Japanese art, and read there of an animal painter so remarkable that horses he had painted upon a temple wall had stepped down after and trampled the neighbouring fields of rice. Somebody had come to the temple in the early morning, been startled by a shower of water drops, looked up and seen a painted horse, still wet from the dew-covered fields, but now 'trembling into stillness.' I thought that her masters were imaginary forms created by suggestion, but whether that suggestion came from Madame Blavatsky's own mind or from some mind, perhaps at a great distance, I did not know; and I believed that these forms could pass from Madame Blavatsky's mind to the minds of others, and even acquire external reality, and that it was even possible that they talked and wrote. They were born in the imagination, where Blake had declared that all men live after death, and where 'every man is king or priest in his own house.' Certainly the house at Holland Park was a romantic place, where one heard of constant apparitions and exchanged speculations like those of the middle ages, and I did not separate myself from it by my own will. The Secretary, an intelligent and friendly man, asked me to come and see him, and when I did, complained that I was causing discussion and disturbance, a certain fanatical hungry face had been noticed red and tearful, & it was quite plain that I was not in full agreement with their method or their philosophy. 'I know,' he said, 'that all these people become dogmatic and fanatical because they believe what they can never prove; that their withdrawal from family life is to them a great misfortune; but what are we to do? We have been told that all spiritual influx into the society will come to an end in 1897 for exactly one hundred years. Before that date our fundamental ideas must be spread through the world.' I knew the doctrine and it had made me wonder why that old woman, or rather 'the trance personalities' who directed her and were her genius, insisted upon it, for influx of some kind there must always be. Did they dread heresy after the death of Madame Blavatsky, or had they no purpose but the greatest possible immediate effort?

XVIII

At the British Museum reading-room I often saw a man of thirty-six or thirty-seven, in a brown velveteen coat, with a gaunt resolute face, and an athletic body, who seemed before I heard his name, or knew the nature of his studies, a figure of romance. Presently I was introduced, where or by what man or woman I do not remember. He was Macgregor Mathers, the author of the 'Kabbalas Unveiled,' & his studies were two only—magic and the theory of war, for he believed himself a born commander and all but equal in wisdom and in power to that old Jew. He had copied many manuscripts on magic ceremonial and doctrine in the British Museum, and was to copy many more in continental libraries, and it was through him mainly that I began certain studies and experiences that were to convince me that images well up before the mind's eye from a deeper source than conscious or subconscious memory. I believe that his mind in those early days did not belie his face and body, though in later years it became unhinged, for he kept a proud head amid great poverty. One that boxed with him nightly has told me that for many weeks he could knock him down, though Macgregor was the stronger man, and only knew long after that during those weeks Macgregor starved. With him I met an old white-haired Oxfordshire clergyman, the most panic-stricken person I have ever known, though Macgregor's introduction had been 'He unites us to the great adepts of antiquity.' This old man took me aside that he might say—'I hope you never invoke spirits—that is a very dangerous thing to do. I am told that even the planetary spirits turn upon us in the end.' I said, 'Have you ever seen an apparition?' 'O yes, once,' he said. 'I have my alchemical laboratory in a cellar under my house where the Bishop cannot see it. One day I was walking up & down there when I heard another footstep walking up and down beside me. I turned and saw a girl I had been in love with when I was a young man, but she died long ago. She wanted me to kiss her. Oh no, I would not do that.' 'Why not?' I said. 'Oh, she might have got power over me.' 'Has your alchemical research had any success?' I said. 'Yes, I once made the elixir of life. A French alchemist said it had the right smell and the right colour,' (The alchemist may have been Elephas Levi, who visited England in the sixties, & would have said anything) 'but the first effect of the elixir is that your nails fall out and your hair falls off. I was afraid that I might have made a mistake and that nothing else might happen, so I put it away on a shelf. I meant to drink it when I was an old man, but when I got it down the other day it had all dried up.'

XIX

I generalized a great deal and was ashamed of it. I thought that it was my business in life to bean artist and a poet, and that there could be no business comparable to that. I refused to read books, and even to meet people who excited me to generalization, but all to no purpose. I said my prayers much as in childhood, though without the old regularity of hour and place, and I began to pray that my imagination might somehow be rescued from abstraction, and become as pre-occupied with life as had been the imagination of Chaucer. For ten or twelve years more I suffered continual remorse, and only became content when my abstractions had composed themselves into picture and dramatization. My very remorse helped to spoil my early poetry, giving it an element of sentimentality through my refusal to permit it any share of an intellect which I considered impure. Even in practical life I only very gradually began to use generalizations, that have since become the foundation of all I have done, or shall do, in Ireland. For all I know, all men may have been as timid; for I am persuaded that our intellects at twenty contain all the truths we shall ever find, but as yet we do not know truths that belong to us from opinions caught up in casual irritation or momentary phantasy. As life goes on we discover that certain thoughts sustain us in defeat, or give us victory, whether over ourselves or others, & it is these thoughts, tested by passion, that we call convictions. Among subjective men (in all those, that is, who must spin a web out of their own bowels) the victory is an intellectual daily recreation of all that exterior fate snatches away, and so that fate's antithesis; while what I have called 'The mask' is an emotional antithesis to all that comes out of their internal nature. We begin to live when we have conceived life as a tragedy.

XX

A conviction that the world was now but a bundle of fragments possessed me without ceasing. I had tried this conviction on 'The Rhymers,' thereby plunging into greater silence an already too silent evening. 'Johnson,' I was accustomed to say, 'you are the only man I know whose silence has beak & claw.' I had lectured on it to some London Irish society, and I was to lecture upon it later on in Dublin, but I never found but one interested man, an official of the Primrose League, who was also an active member of the Fenian Brotherhood. 'I am an extreme conservative apart from Ireland,' I have heard him explain; and I have no doubt that personal experience made him share the sight of any eye that saw the world in fragments. I had been put into a rage by the followers of Huxley, Tyndall, Carolus Duran and Bastien-Lepage, who not only asserted the unimportance of subject, whether in art or literature, but the independence of the arts from one another. Upon the other hand I delighted in every age where poet and artist confined themselves gladly to some inherited subject matter known to the whole people, for I thought that in man and race alike there is something called 'unity of being,' using that term as Dante used it when he compared beauty in the *Convito* to a perfectly proportioned human body. My father, from whom I had learned the term, preferred a comparison to a musical instrument so strong that if we touch a string all the strings murmur faintly. There is not more desire, he had said, in lust than in true love; but in true love desire awakens pity, hope, affection, admiration, and, given appropriate circumstance, every emotion possible to man. When I began, however, to apply this thought to the State and to argue for a law-made balance among trades and occupations, my father displayed at once the violent free-trader and propagandist of liberty. I thought that the enemy of this unity was abstraction, meaning by abstraction not the distinction but the isolation of occupation, or class or faculty—

> 'Call down the hawk from the air
> Let him be hooded, or caged,
> Till the yellow eye has grown mild,
> For larder and spit are bare,
> The old cook enraged,
> The scullion gone wild.'

I knew no mediaeval cathedral, and Westminster, being a part of abhorred London, did not interest me; but I thought constantly of Homer and Dante and the tombs of Mausolus and Artemisa, the great figures of King and Queen and the lesser figures of Greek and Amazon, Centaur and Greek. I thought that all art should be a Centaur finding in the popular lore its back and its strong legs. I got great pleasure too from remembering that Homer was sung, and from that tale of Dante hearing a common man sing some stanza from 'The Divine Comedy,' and from Don Quixote's meeting with some common man that sang Ariosto. Morris had never seemed to care for any poet later than Chaucer; and though I preferred Shakespeare to Chaucer I begrudged my own preference. Had not Europe shared one mind and heart, until both mind and heart began to break into fragments a little before Shakespeare's birth? Music and verse began to fall apart when Chaucer robbed verse of its speed that he might give it greater meditation, though for another generation or so minstrels were to sing his long elaborated 'Troilus and Cressida;' painting parted from religion in the later Renaissance that it might study effects of tangibility undisturbed; while, that it might characterise, where it had once personified, it renounced, in our own age, all that inherited subject matter which we have named poetry. Presently I was indeed to number

75

character itself among the abstractions, encouraged by Congreve's saying that 'passions are too powerful in the fair sex to let humour,' or as we say character, 'have its course.' Nor have we fared better under the common daylight, for pure reason has notoriously made but light of practical reason, and has been made but light of in its turn, from that morning when Descartes discovered that he could think better in his bed than out of it; nor needed I original thought to discover, being so late of the school of Morris, that machinery had not separated from handicraft wholly for the world's good; nor to notice that the distinction of classes had become their isolation. If the London merchants of our day competed together in writing lyrics they would not, like the Tudor merchants, dance in the open street before the house of the victor; nor do the great ladies of London finish their balls on the pavement before their doors as did the great Venetian ladies even in the eighteenth century, conscious of an all enfolding sympathy. Doubtless because fragments broke into even smaller fragments we saw one another in a light of bitter comedy, and in the arts, where now one technical element reigned and now another, generation hated generation, and accomplished beauty was snatched away when it had most engaged our affections. One thing I did not foresee, not having the courage of my own thought—the growing murderousness of the world.

> Turning and turning in the widening gyre
> The falcon cannot hear the falconer;
> Things fall apart; the centre cannot hold;
> Mere anarchy is loosed upon the world,
> The blood-dimmed tide is loosed, and everywhere
> The ceremony of innocence is drowned;
> The best lack all conviction, while the worst
> Are full of passionate intensity.

XXI

The Huxley, Tyndall, Carolus Duran, Bastien-Lepage coven asserted that an artist or a poet must paint or write in the style of his own day, and this with 'The Fairy Queen,' and 'Lyrical Ballads,' and Blake's early poems in its ears, and plain to the eyes, in book or gallery, those great masterpieces of later Egypt, founded upon that work of the Ancient Kingdom already further in time from later Egypt than later Egypt is from us. I knew that I could choose my style where I pleased, that no man can deny to the human mind any power, that power once achieved; and yet I did not wish to recover the first simplicity. If I must be but a shepherd building his hut among the ruins of some fallen city, I might take porphyry or shaped marble, if it lay ready to my hand, instead of the baked clay of the first builders. If Chaucer's personages had disengaged themselves from Chaucer's crowd, forgotten their common goal and shrine, and after sundry magnifications become, each in his turn, the centre of some Elizabethan play, and a few years later split into their elements, and so given birth to romantic poetry, I need not reverse the cinematograph. I could take those separated elements, all that abstract love and melancholy, and give them a symbolical or mythological coherence. Not Chaucer's rough-tongued riders, but some procession of the Gods! a pilgrimage no more but perhaps a shrine! Might I not, with health and good luck to aid me, create some new 'Prometheus Unbound,' Patrick or Columbcille, Oisin or Fion, in Prometheus's stead, and, instead of Caucasus, Croagh-Patrick or Ben Bulben? Have not all races had their first unity from a polytheism that marries them to rock and hill? We had in Ireland imaginative stories, which the uneducated classes knew and even sang, and might we not make those stories current among the educated classes, re-discovering for the work's sake what I have called 'the applied arts of literature,' the association of literature, that is, with music, speech and dance; and at last, it might be, so deepen the political passion of the nation that all, artist and poet, craftsman and day labourer would accept a common design? Perhaps even these images, once created and associated with river and mountain, might move of themselves, and with some powerful even turbulent life, like those painted horses that trampled the rice fields of Japan.

XXII

I used to tell the few friends to whom I could speak these secret
thoughts that I would make the attempt in Ireland but fail, for our
civilisation, its elements multiplying by divisions like certain low forms
of life, was all powerful; but in reality I had the wildest hopes. To-day
I add to that first conviction, to that first desire for unity, this other
conviction, long a mere opinion vaguely or intermittently apprehended:
Nations, races and individual men are unified by an image, or bundle of
related images, symbolical or evocative of the state of mind, which is
of all states of mind not impossible, the most difficult to that man, race
or nation; because only the greatest obstacle that can be contemplated
without despair rouses the will to full intensity. A powerful class by terror,
rhetoric, and organised sentimentality, may drive their people to war, but
the day draws near when they cannot keep them there; and how shall they
face the pure nations of the East when the day comes to do it with but
equal arms? I had seen Ireland in my own time turn from the bragging
rhetoric and gregarious humour of O'Connell's generation and school,
and offer herself to the solitary and proud Parnell as to her anti-self,
buskin following hard on sock; and I had begun to hope, or to half-hope,
that we might be the first in Europe to seek unity as deliberately as it had
been sought by theologian, poet, sculptor, architect from the eleventh to
the thirteenth century. Doubtless we must seek it differently, no longer
considering it convenient to epitomise all human knowledge, but find it
we well might, could we first find philosophy and a little passion.

XXIII

It was the death of Parnell that convinced me that the moment had come for work in Ireland, for I knew that for a time the imagination of young men would turn from politics. There was a little Irish patriotic society of young people, clerks, shop-boys, shop-girls, and the like, called the Southwark Irish Literary Society. It had ceased to meet because each member of the committee had lectured so many times that the girls got the giggles whenever he stood up. I invited the committee to my father's house at Bedford Park and there proposed a new organisation. After a few months spent in founding, with the help of T. W. Rolleston, who came to that first meeting and had a knowledge of committee work I lacked, the Irish Literary Society, which soon included every London Irish author and journalist, I went to Dublin and founded there a similar society.

W. B. Yeats.

STORIES OF RED HANRAHAN

I owe thanks to Lady Gregory, who helped me to rewrite The Stories of Red Hanrahan in the beautiful country speech of Kiltartan, and nearer to the tradition of the people among whom he, or some likeness of him, drifted and is remembered.

RED HANRAHAN.

Hanrahan, the hedge schoolmaster, a tall, strong, red-haired young man, came into the barn where some of the men of the village were sitting on Samhain Eve. It had been a dwelling-house, and when the man that owned it had built a better one, he had put the two rooms together, and kept it for a place to store one thing or another. There was a fire on the old hearth, and there were dip candles stuck in bottles, and there was a black quart bottle upon some boards that had been put across two barrels to make a table. Most of the men were sitting beside the fire, and one of them was singing a long wandering song, about a Munster man and a Connaught man that were quarrelling about their two provinces.

Hanrahan went to the man of the house and said, 'I got your message'; but when he had said that, he stopped, for an old mountainy man that had a shirt and trousers of unbleached flannel, and that was sitting by himself near the door, was looking at him, and moving an old pack of cards about in his hands and muttering. 'Don't mind him,' said the man of the house; 'he is only some stranger came in awhile ago, and we bade him welcome, it being Samhain night, but I think he is not in his right wits. Listen to him now and you will hear what he is saying.'

They listened then, and they could hear the old man muttering to himself as he turned the cards, 'Spades and Diamonds, Courage and Power; Clubs and Hearts, Knowledge and Pleasure.'

'That is the kind of talk he has been going on with for the last hour,' said the man of the house, and Hanrahan turned his eyes from the old man as if he did not like to be looking at him.

'I got your message,' Hanrahan said then; '"he is in the barn with his three first cousins from Kilchriest," the messenger said, "and there are some of the neighbours with them."'

'It is my cousin over there is wanting to see you,' said the man of the house, and he called over a young frieze-coated man, who was listening to the song, and said, 'This is Red Hanrahan you have the message for.'

'It is a kind message, indeed,' said the young man, 'for it comes from your sweetheart, Mary Lavelle.'

'How would you get a message from her, and what do you know of her?'

'I don't know her, indeed, but I was in Loughrea yesterday, and a neighbour of hers that had some dealings with me was saying that she bade him send you word, if he met any one from this side in the market, that her mother has died from her, and if you have a mind yet to join with herself, she is willing to keep her word to you.'

'I will go to her indeed,' said Hanrahan.

'And she bade you make no delay, for if she has not a man in the house before the month is out, it is likely the little bit of land will be given to another.'

When Hanrahan heard that, he rose up from the bench he had sat down on. 'I will make no delay indeed,' he said, 'there is a full moon, and if I get as far as Gilchreist to-night, I will reach to her before the setting of the sun to-morrow.'

When the others heard that, they began to laugh at him for being in such haste to go to his sweetheart, and one asked him if he would leave his school in the old lime-kiln, where he was giving the children such good learning. But he said the children would be glad enough in the morning to find the place empty, and no one to keep them at their task; and as for his school he could set it up again in any place, having as he had his little inkpot hanging from his neck by a chain, and his big Virgil and his primer in the skirt of his coat.

Some of them asked him to drink a glass before he went, and a young man caught hold of his coat, and said he must not leave them without singing the song he had made in praise of Venus and of Mary Lavelle. He drank a glass of whiskey, but he said he would not stop but would set out on his journey.

'There's time enough, Red Hanrahan,' said the man of the house. 'It will be time enough for you to give up sport when you are after your marriage, and it might be a long time before we will see you again.'

'I will not stop,' said Hanrahan; 'my mind would be on the roads all the time, bringing me to the woman that sent for me, and she lonesome and watching till I come.'

Some of the others came about him, pressing him that had been such a pleasant comrade, so full of songs and every kind of trick and fun, not to leave them till the night would be over, but he refused them all, and shook them off, and went to the door. But as he put his foot over the threshold, the strange old man stood up and put his hand that was thin and withered like a bird's claw on Hanrahan's hand, and said: 'It is not Hanrahan, the learned man and the great songmaker, that should go out from a gathering like this, on a Samhain night. And stop here, now,' he said, 'and play a hand with me; and here is an old pack of cards has done its work many a night before this, and old as it is, there has been much of the riches of the world lost and won over it.'

One of the young men said, 'It isn't much of the riches of the world has stopped with yourself, old man,' and he looked at the old man's bare feet, and they all laughed. But Hanrahan did not laugh, but he sat down very quietly, without a word. Then one of them said, 'So you will stop with us after all, Hanrahan'; and the old man said: 'He will stop indeed, did you not hear me asking him?'

They all looked at the old man then as if wondering where he came from. 'It is far I am come,' he said, 'through France I have come, and through Spain, and by Lough Greine of the hidden mouth, and none has refused me anything.' And then he was silent and nobody liked to question him, and they began to play. There were six men at the boards playing, and the others were looking on behind. They played two or three games for nothing, and then the old man took a fourpenny bit, worn very thin and smooth, out from his pocket, and he called to the rest to put something on the game. Then they all put down something on the boards, and little as it was it looked much, from the way it was shoved from one to another, first one man winning it and then his neighbour. And some-times the luck would go against a man and he would have nothing left, and then one or another would lend him something, and he would pay it again out of his winnings, for neither good nor bad luck stopped long with anyone.

And once Hanrahan said as a man would say in a dream, 'It is time for me to be going the road'; but just then a good card came to him, and he played it out, and all the money began to come to him. And once he thought of Mary Lavelle, and he sighed; and that time his luck went from him, and he forgot her again.

But at last the luck went to the old man and it stayed with him, and all they had flowed into him, and he began to laugh little laughs to himself, and to sing over and over to himself, 'Spades and Diamonds, Courage and Power,' and so on, as if it was a verse of a song.

And after a while anyone looking at the men, and seeing the way their bodies were rocking to and fro, and the way they kept their eyes on the old man's hands, would think they had drink taken, or that the whole store they had in the world was put on the cards; but that was not so, for the quart bottle had not been disturbed since the game began, and was nearly full yet, and all that was on the game was a few sixpenny bits and shillings, and maybe a handful of coppers.

'You are good men to win and good men to lose,' said the old man, 'you have play in your hearts.' He began then to shuffle the cards and to mix them, very quick and fast, till at last they could not see them to be cards at all, but you would think him to be making rings of fire in the air, as little lads would make them with whirling a lighted stick; and after that it seemed to them that all the room was dark, and they could see nothing but his hands and the cards.

And all in a minute a hare made a leap out from between his hands, and whether it was one of the cards that took that shape, or whether it was made out of nothing in the palms of his hands, nobody knew, but there it was running on the floor of the barn, as quick as any hare that ever lived.

Some looked at the hare, but more kept their eyes on the old man, and while they were looking at him a hound made a leap out between his hands, the same way as the hare did, and after that another hound and another, till there was a whole pack of them following the hare round and round the barn.

The players were all standing up now, with their backs to the boards, shrinking from the hounds, and nearly deafened with the noise of their yelping, but as quick as the hounds were they could not overtake the hare, but it went round, till at the last it seemed as if a blast of wind burst open the barn door, and the hare doubled and made a leap over the boards where the men had been playing, and went out of the door and away through the night, and the hounds over the boards and through the door after it.

Then the old man called out, 'Follow the hounds, follow the hounds, and it is a great hunt you will see to-night,' and he went out after them. But used as the men were to go hunting after hares, and ready as they were for any sport, they were in dread to go out into the night, and it was only Hanrahan that rose up and that said, 'I will follow, I will follow on.'

'You had best stop here, Hanrahan,' the young man that was nearest him said, 'for you might be going into some great danger.' But Hanrahan said, 'I will see fair play, I will see fair play,' and he went stumbling out of the door like a man in a dream, and the door shut after him as he went.

He thought he saw the old man in front of him, but it was only his own shadow that the full moon cast on the road before him, but he could hear the hounds crying after the hare over the wide green fields of

Granagh, and he followed them very fast for there was nothing to stop him; and after a while he came to smaller fields that had little walls of loose stones around them, and he threw the stones down as he crossed them, and did not wait to put them up again; and he passed by the place where the river goes under ground at Ballylee, and he could hear the hounds going before him up towards the head of the river. Soon he found it harder to run, for it was uphill he was going, and clouds came over the moon, and it was hard for him to see his way, and once he left the path to take a short cut, but his foot slipped into a boghole and he had to come back to it. And how long he was going he did not know, or what way he went, but at last he was up on the bare mountain, with nothing but the rough heather about him, and he could neither hear the hounds nor any other thing. But their cry began to come to him again, at first far off and then very near, and when it came quite close to him, it went up all of a sudden into the air, and there was the sound of hunting over his head; then it went away northward till he could hear nothing more at all. 'That's not fair,' he said, 'that's not fair.' And he could walk no longer, but sat down on the heather where he was, in the heart of Slieve Echtge, for all the strength had gone from him, with the dint of the long journey he had made.

And after a while he took notice that there was a door close to him, and a light coming from it, and he wondered that being so close to him he had not seen it before. And he rose up, and tired as he was he went in at the door, of and although it was night time outside, it was daylight he found within. And presently he met with an old man that had been gathering summer thyme and yellow flag-flowers, and it seemed as if all the sweet smells of the summer were with them. And the old man said: 'It is a long time you have been coming to us, Hanrahan the learned man and the great songmaker.'

And with that he brought him into a very big shining house, and every grand thing Hanrahan had ever heard of, and every colour he had ever seen, were in it. There was a high place at the end of the house, and on it there was sitting in a high chair a woman, the most beautiful the world ever saw, having a long pale face and flowers about it, but she had the tired look of one that had been long waiting. And there was sitting on the step below her chair four grey old women, and the one of them was holding a great cauldron in her lap; and another a great stone on her knees, and heavy as it was it seemed light to her; and another of them had a very long spear that was made of pointed wood; and the last of them had a sword that was without a scabbard. Red Hanrahan stood looking at them for a long Hanrahan-time, but none of them spoke any word to him or looked at him at all. And he had it in his mind to ask who that woman in the chair was, that was like a queen, and what she was waiting for; but ready as he was with his tongue and afraid of no person, he was in dread now to speak to so beautiful a woman, and in so grand a place. And then he thought to ask what were the four things the four grey old women were holding like great treasures, but he could not think of the right words to bring out.

Then the first of the old women rose up, holding the cauldron between her two hands, and she said 'Pleasure,' and Hanrahan said no word. Then the second old woman rose up with the stone in her hands, and she said 'Power'; and the third old woman rose up with the spear in her hand, and she said 'Courage'; and the last of the old women rose up having the sword in her hands, and she said 'Knowledge.' And everyone, after she had spoken, waited as if for Hanrahan to question her, but he said nothing at all. And then the four old women went out of the door, bringing their tour treasures with them, and as they went out one of them said, 'He has no wish for us'; and another said, 'He is weak, he is weak'; and another said, 'He is afraid'; and the last said, 'His wits are gone from him.' And then they all said 'Echtge, daughter of the Silver Hand, must stay in her sleep. It is a pity, it is a great pity.'

And then the woman that was like a queen gave a very sad sigh, and it seemed to Hanrahan as if the sigh had the sound in it of hidden streams; and if the place he was in had been ten times grander and more shining than it was, he could not have hindered sleep from coming on him; and he staggered like a drunken man and lay down there and then.

When Hanrahan awoke, the sun was shining on his face, but there was white frost on the grass around him, and there was ice on the edge of the stream he was lying by, and that goes running on through Daire-caol and Druim-da-rod. He knew by the shape of the hills and by the shining of Lough Greine in the distance that he was upon one of the hills of Slieve Echtge, but he was not sure how he came there; for all that had happened in the barn had gone from him, and all of his journey but the soreness of his feet and the stiffness in his bones.

It was a year after that, there were men of the village of Cappaghtagle sitting by the fire in a house on the roadside, and Red Hanrahan that was now very thin and worn and his hair very long and wild, came to the half-door and asked leave to come in and rest himself; and they bid him welcome because it was Samhain night. He sat down with them, and they gave him a glass of whiskey out of a quart bottle; and they saw the little inkpot hanging about his neck, and knew he was a scholar, and asked for stories about the Greeks.

He took the Virgil out of the big pocket of his coat, but the cover was very black and swollen with the wet, and the page when he opened it was very yellow, but that was no great matter, for he looked at it like a man that had never learned to read. Some young man that was there began to laugh at him then, and to ask why did he carry so heavy a book with him when he was not able to read it.

It vexed Hanrahan to hear that, and he put the Virgil back in his pocket and asked if they had a pack of cards among them, for cards were better than books. When they brought out the cards he took them and began to shuffle them, and while he was shuffling them something seemed to come into his mind, and he put his hand to his face like one that is trying to remember, and he said: 'Was I ever here before, or where was I on a night like this?' and then of a sudden he stood up and let the cards fall to the floor, and he said, 'Who was it brought me a message from Mary Lavelle?'

'We never saw you before now, and we never heard of Mary Lavelle,' said the man of the house. 'And who is she,' he said, 'and what is it you are talking about?'

'It was this night a year ago, I was in a barn, and there were men playing cards, and there was money on the table, they were pushing it from one to another here and there—and I got a message, and I was going out of the door to look for my sweetheart that wanted me, Mary Lavelle.' And then Hanrahan called out very loud: 'Where have I been since then? Where was I for the whole year?'

'It is hard to say where you might have been in that time,' said the oldest of the men, 'or what part of the world you may have travelled; and it is like enough you have the dust of many roads on your feet; for there are many go wandering and forgetting like that,' he said, 'when once they have been given the touch.'

'That is true,' said another of the men. 'I knew a woman went wandering like that through the length of seven years; she came back after, and she told her friends she had often been glad enough to eat the food that was put in the pig's trough. And it is best for you to go to the priest now,' he said, 'and let him take off you whatever may have been put upon you.'

'It is to my sweetheart I will go, to Mary Lavelle,' said Hanrahan; 'it is too long I have delayed, how do I know what might have happened her in the length of a year?'

He was going out of the door then, but they all told him it was best for him to stop the night, and to get strength for the journey; and indeed he wanted that, for he was very weak, and when they gave him food he eat it like a man that had never seen food before, and one of them said, 'He is eating as if he had trodden on the hungry grass.' It was in the white light of the morning he set out, and the time seemed long to him till he could get to Mary Lavelle's house. But when he came to it, he found the door broken, and the thatch dropping from the roof, and no living person to be seen. And when he asked the neighbours what had happened her, all they could say was that she had been put out of the house, and had married some labouring man, and they had gone looking for work to London or Liverpool or some big place. And whether she found a worse place or a better he never knew, but anyway he never met with her or with news of her again.

THE TWISTING OF THE ROPE.

Hanrahan was walking the roads one time near Kinvara at the fall of day, and he heard the sound of a fiddle from a house a little way off the roadside. He turned up the path to it, for he never had the habit of passing by any place where there was music or dancing or good company, without going in. The man of the house was standing at the door, and when Hanrahan came near he knew him and he said: 'A welcome before you, Hanrahan, you have been lost to us this long time.' But the woman of the house came to the door and she said to her husband: 'I would be as well pleased for Hanrahan not to come in to-night, for he has no good name now among the priests, or with women that mind themselves, and I wouldn't wonder from his walk if he has a drop of drink taken.' But the man said, 'I will never turn away Hanrahan of the poets from my door,' and with that he bade him enter.

There were a good many neighbours gathered in the house, and some of them remembered Hanrahan; but some of the little lads that were in the corners had only heard of him, and they stood up to have a view of him, and one of them said: 'Is not that Hanrahan that had the school, and that was brought away by Them?' But his mother put her hand over his mouth and bade him be quiet, and not be saying things like that. 'For Hanrahan is apt to grow wicked,' she said, 'if he hears talk of that story, or if anyone goes questioning him.' One or another called out then, asking him for a song, but the man of the house said it was no time to ask him for a song, before he had rested himself; and he gave him whiskey in a glass, and Hanrahan thanked him and wished him good health and drank it off.

The fiddler was tuning his fiddle for another dance, and the man of the house said to the young men, they would all know what dancing was like when they saw Hanrahan dance, for the like of it had never been seen since he was there before. Hanrahan said he would not dance, he had better use for his feet now, travelling as he was through the five provinces of Ireland. Just as he said that, there came in at the half-door Oona, the daughter of the house, having a few bits of bog deal from Connemara in her arms for the fire. She threw them on the hearth and the flame rose up, and showed her to be very comely and smiling, and two or three of the young men rose up and asked for a dance. But Hanrahan crossed the floor and brushed the others away, and said it was with him she must dance, after the long road he had travelled before he came to her. And it is likely he said some soft word in her ear, for she said nothing against it, and stood out with him, and there were little blushes in her cheeks. Then other couples stood up, but when the dance was going to begin, Hanrahan chanced to look down, and he took notice of his boots that were worn and broken, and the ragged grey socks showing through them; and he said angrily it was a bad floor, and the music no great things, and he sat down in the dark place beside the hearth. But if he did, the girl sat down there with him.

The dancing went on, and when that dance was over another was called for, and no one took much notice of Oona and Red Hanrahan for a while, in the corner where they were. But the mother grew to be uneasy, and she called to Oona to come and help her to set the table in the inner room. But Oona that had never refused her before, said she would come soon, but not yet, for she was listening to whatever he was saying in her ear. The mother grew yet more uneasy then, and she would come nearer them, and let on to be stirring the fire or sweeping the hearth, and she would listen for a minute to hear what the poet was saying to her child. And one time she heard him telling about white-handed Deirdre, and how she brought the sons of Usnach to their death; and how the blush in her cheeks was not so red as the blood of kings' sons that was shed for her, and her sorrows had never gone out of mind; and he said it was maybe the memory of her that made the cry of the plover on the bog as sorrowful in the ear of the poets as the keening of young men for a comrade. And there would never have been that memory of her, he said, if it was not for the poets that had put her beauty in their songs. And the next time she did not well understand what he was saying, but as far as she could hear, it had the sound of poetry though it was not rhymed, and this is what she heard him say: 'The sun and the moon are the man and the girl, they are my life and your life, they are travelling and ever travelling through the skies as if under the one hood. It was God made them for one another. He made your life and my life before the beginning of the world, he made them that they might go through the world, up and down, like the two best dancers that go on with the dance up and down the long floor of the barn, fresh and laughing, when all the rest are tired out and leaning against the wall.'

The old woman went then to where her husband was playing cards, but he would take no notice of her, and then she went to a woman of the neighbours and said: 'Is there no way we can get them from one another?' and without waiting for an answer she said to some young men that were talking together: 'What good are you when you cannot make the best girl in the house come out and dance with you? And go now the whole of you,' she said, 'and see can you bring her away from the poet's talk.' But Oona would not listen to any of them, but only moved her hand as if to send them away. Then they called to Hanrahan and said he had best dance with the girl himself, or let her dance with one of them. When Hanrahan heard what they were saying he said: 'That is so, I will dance with her; there is no man in the house must dance with her but myself.'

He stood up with her then, and led her out by the hand, and some of the young men were vexed, and some began mocking at his ragged coat and his broken boots. But he took no notice, and Oona took no notice, but they looked at one another as if all the world belonged to themselves alone. But another couple that had been sitting together like lovers stood out on the floor at the same time, holding one another's hands and moving their feet to keep time with the music. But Hanrahan turned his back on them as if angry, and in place of dancing he began to sing, and as he sang he held her hand, and his voice grew louder, and the mocking of the young men stopped, and the fiddle stopped, and there was nothing heard but his voice that had in it the sound of the wind. And what he sang was a song he had heard or had made one time in his wanderings on Slieve Echtge, and the words of it as they can be put into English were like this:

> O Death's old bony finger
> Will never find us there
> In the high hollow townland
> Where love's to give and to spare;
> Where boughs have fruit and blossom
> At all times of the year;
> Where rivers are running over
> With red beer and brown beer.
> An old man plays the bagpipes
> In a gold and silver wood;
> Queens, their eyes blue like the ice,
> Are dancing in a crowd.

And while he was singing it Oona moved nearer to him, and the colour had gone from her cheek, and her eyes were not blue now, but grey with the tears that were in them, and anyone that saw her would have thought she was ready to follow him there and then from the west to the east of the world.

But one of the young men called out: 'Where is that country he is singing about? Mind yourself, Oona, it is a long way off, you might be a long time on the road before you would reach to it.' And another said: 'It is not to the Country of the Young you will be going if you go with him, but to Mayo of the bogs.' Oona looked at him then as if she would question him, but he raised her hand in his hand, and called out between singing and shouting: 'It is very near us that country is, it is on every side; it may be on the bare hill behind it is, or it may be in the heart of the wood.' And he said out very loud and clear: 'In the heart of the wood; oh, death will never find us in the heart of the wood. And will you come with me there, Oona?' he said.

But while he was saying this the two old women had gone outside the door, and Oona's mother was crying, and she said: 'He has put an enchantment on Oona. Can we not get the men to put him out of the house?'

'That is a thing you cannot do, said the other woman,' for he is a poet of the Gael, and you know well if you would put a poet of the Gael out of the house, he would put a curse on you that would wither the corn in the fields and dry up the milk of the cows, if it had to hang in the air seven years.'

'God help us,' said the mother, 'and why did I ever let him into the house at all, and the wild name he has!'

'It would have been no harm at all to have kept him outside, but there would great harm come upon you if you put him out by force. But listen to the plan I have to get him out of the house by his own doing, without anyone putting him from it at all.'

It was not long after that the two women came in again, each of them having a bundle of hay in her apron. Hanrahan was not singing now, but he was talking to Oona very fast and soft, and he was saying: 'The house is narrow but the world is wide, and there is no true lover that need be afraid of night or morning or sun or stars or shadows of evening, or any earthly thing.' 'Hanrahan,' said the mother then, striking him on the shoulder, 'will you give me a hand here for a minute?' 'Do that, Hanrahan,' said the woman of the neighbours, 'and help us to make this hay into a rope, for you are ready with your hands, and a blast of wind has loosened the thatch on the haystack.'

'I will do that for you,' said he, and he took the little stick in his hands, and the mother began giving out the hay, and he twisting it, but he was hurrying to have done with it, and to be free again. The women went on talking and giving out the hay, and encouraging him, and saying what a good twister of a rope he was, better than their own neighbours or than anyone they had ever seen. And Hanrahan saw that Oona was watching him, and he began to twist very quick and with his head high, and to boast of the readiness of his hands, and the learning he had in his head, and the strength in his arms. And as he was boasting, he went backward, twisting the rope always till he came to the door that was open behind him, and without thinking he passed the threshold and was out on the road. And no sooner was he there than the mother made a sudden rush, and threw out the rope after him, and she shut the door and the half-door and put a bolt upon them.

She was well pleased when she had done that, and laughed out loud, and the neighbours laughed and praised her. But they heard him beating at the door, and saying words of cursing outside it, and the mother had but time to stop Oona that had her hand upon the bolt to open it. She made a sign to the fiddler then, and he began a reel, and one of the young men asked no leave but caught hold of Oona and brought her into the thick of the dance. And when it was over and the fiddle had stopped, there was no sound at all of anything outside, but the road was as quiet as before.

As to Hanrahan, when he knew he was shut out and that there was neither shelter nor drink nor a girl's ear for him that night, the anger and the courage went out of him, and he went on to where the waves were beating on the strand.

He sat down on a big stone, and he began swinging his right arm and singing slowly to himself, the way he did always to hearten himself when every other thing failed him. And whether it was that time or another time he made the song that is called to this day 'The Twisting of the

Rope,' and that begins, 'What was the dead cat that put me in this place,' is not known.

But after he had been singing awhile, mist and shadows seemed to gather about him, sometimes coming out of the sea, and sometimes moving upon it. It seemed to him that one of the shadows was the queen-woman he had seen in her sleep at Slieve Echtge; not in her sleep now, but mocking, and calling out to them that were behind her: 'He was weak, he was weak, he had no courage.' And he felt the strands of the rope in his hand yet, and went on twisting it, but it seemed to him as he twisted, that it had all the sorrows of the world in it. And then it seemed to him as if the rope had changed in his dream into a great water-worm that came out of the sea, and that twisted itself about him, and held him closer and closer, and grew from big to bigger till the whole of the earth and skies were wound up in it, and the stars themselves were but the shining of the ridges of its skin. And then he got free of it, and went on, shaking and unsteady, along the edge of the strand, and the grey shapes were flying here and there around him. And this is what they were saying, 'It is a pity for him that refuses the call of the daughters of the Sidhe, for he will find no comfort in the love of the women of the earth to the end of life and time, and the cold of the grave is in his heart for ever. It is death he has chosen; let him die, let him die, let him die.'

HANRAHAN AND CATHLEEN THE DAUGHTER OF HOOLIHAN.

It was travelling northward Hanrahan was one time, giving a hand to a farmer now and again in the hurried time of the year, and telling his stories and making his share of songs at wakes and at weddings.

He chanced one day to overtake on the road to Collooney one Margaret Rooney, a woman he used to know in Munster when he was a young man. She had no good name at that time, and it was the priest routed her out of the place at last. He knew her by her walk and by the colour of her eyes, and by a way she had of putting back the hair off her face with her left hand. She had been wandering about, she said, selling herrings and the like, and now she was going back to Sligo, to the place in the Burrough where she was living with another woman, Mary Gillis, who had much the same story as herself. She would be well pleased, she said, if he would come and stop in the house with them, and be singing his songs to the bacachs and blind men and fiddlers of the Burrough. She remembered him well, she said, and had a wish for him; and as to Mary Gillis, she had some of his songs off by heart, so he need not be afraid of not getting good treatment, and all the bacachs and poor men that heard him would give him a share of their own earnings for his stories and his songs while he was with them, and would carry his name into all the parishes of Ireland.

He was glad enough to go with her, and to find a woman to be listening to the story of his troubles and to be comforting him. It was at the moment of the fall of day when every man may pass as handsome and every woman as comely. She put her arm about him when he told her of the misfortune of the Twisting of the Rope, and in the half light she looked as well as another.

They kept in talk all the way to the Burrough, and as for Mary Gillis, when she saw him and heard who he was, she went near crying to think of having a man with so great a name in the house.

Hanrahan was well pleased to settle down with them for a while, for he was tired with wandering; and since the day he found the little cabin fallen in, and Mary Lavelle gone from it, and the thatch scattered, he had never asked to have any place of his own; and he had never stopped long enough in any place to see the green leaves come where he had seen the old leaves wither, or to see the wheat harvested where he had seen it sown. It was a good change to him to have shelter from the wet, and a fire in the evening time, and his share of food put on the table without the asking.

He made a good many of his songs while he was living there, so well cared for and so quiet, The most of them were love songs, but some were songs of repentance, and some were songs about Ireland and her griefs, under one name or another.

Every evening the bacachs and beggars and blind men and fiddlers would gather into the house and listen to his songs and his poems, and his stories about the old time of the Fianna, and they kept them in their memories that were never spoiled with books; and so they brought his name to every wake and wedding and pattern in the whole of Connaught. He was never so well off or made so much of as he was at that time.

One evening of December he was singing a little song that he said he had heard from the green plover of the mountain, about the fair-haired boys that had left Limerick, and that were wandering and going astray in all parts of the world. There were a good many people in the room that night, and two or three little lads that had crept in, and sat on the floor near the fire, and were too busy with the roasting of a potato in the ashes or some such thing to take much notice of him; but they remembered long afterwards when his name had gone up, the sound of his voice, and what way he had moved his hand, and the look of him as he sat on the edge of the bed, with his shadow falling on the whitewashed wall behind him, and as he moved going up as high as the thatch. And they knew then that they had looked upon a king of the poets of the Gael, and a maker of the dreams of men.

Of a sudden his singing stopped, and his eyes grew misty as if he was looking at some far thing.

Mary Gillis was pouring whiskey into a mug that stood on a table beside him, and she left off pouring and said, 'Is it of leaving us you are thinking?'

Margaret Rooney heard what she said, and did not know why she said it, and she took the words too much in earnest and came over to him, and there was dread in her heart that she was going to lose so wonderful a poet and so good a comrade, and a man that was thought so much of, and that brought so many to her house.

'You would not go away from us, my heart?' she said, catching him by the hand.

'It is not of that I am thinking,' he said, 'but of Ireland and the weight of grief that is on her.' And he leaned his head against his hand, and began to sing these words, and the sound of his voice was like the wind in a lonely place.

The old brown thorn trees break in two high over Cummen
    Strand
Under a bitter black wind that blows from the left hand;
Our courage breaks like an old tree in a black wind and dies,
But we have hidden in our hearts the flame out of the eyes
Of Cathleen the daughter of Hoolihan.
The winds was bundled up the clouds high over Knocknarea
And thrown the thunder on the stones for all that Maeve can say;
Angers that are like noisy clouds have set our hearts abeat,
But we have all bent low and low and kissed the quiet feet

Of Cathleen the daughter of Hoolihan.
The yellow pool has overflowed high upon Clooth-na-Bare,
For the wet winds are blowing out of the clinging air;
Like heavy flooded waters our bodies and our blood,
But purer than a tall candle before the Holy Rood
Is Cathleen the daughter of Hoolihan.

While he was singing, his voice began to break, and tears came rolling down his cheeks, and Margaret Rooney put down her face into her hands and began to cry along with him. Then a blind beggar by the fire shook his rags with a sob, and after that there was no one of them all but cried tears down.

RED HANRAHAN'S CURSE.

One fine May morning a long time after Hanrahan had left Margaret Rooney's house, he was walking the road near Collooney, and the sound of the birds singing in the bushes that were white with blossom set him singing as he went. It was to his own little place he was going, that was no more than a cabin, but that pleased him well. For he was tired of so many years of wandering from shelter to shelter at all times of the year, and although he was seldom refused a welcome and a share of what was in the house, it seemed to him sometimes that his mind was getting stiff like his joints, and it was not so easy to him as it used to be to make fun and sport through the night, and to set all the boys laughing with his pleasant talk, and to coax the women with his songs. And a while ago, he had turned into a cabin that some poor man had left to go harvesting and had never come to again. And when he had mended the thatch and made a bed in the corner with a few sacks and bushes, and had swept out the floor, he was well content to have a little place for himself, where he could go in and out as he liked, and put his head in his hands through the length of an evening if the fret was on him, and loneliness after the old times. One by one the neighbours began to send their children in to get some learning from him, and with what they brought, a few eggs or an oaten cake or a couple of sods of turf, he made out a way of living. And if he went for a wild day and night now and again to the Burrough, no one would say a word, knowing him to be a poet, with wandering in his heart.

It was from the Burrough he was coming that May morning, light-hearted enough, and singing some new song that had come to him. But it was not long till a hare ran across his path, and made away into the fields, through the loose stones of the wall. And he knew it was no good sign a hare to have crossed his path, and he remembered the hare that had led him away to Slieve Echtge the time Mary Lavelle was waiting for him, and how he had never known content for any length of time since then. 'And it is likely enough they are putting some bad thing before me now,' he said.

And after he said that he heard the sound of crying in the field beside him, and he looked over the wall. And there he saw a young girl sitting under a bush of white hawthorn, and crying as if her heart would break. Her face was hidden in her hands, but her soft hair and her white neck and the young look of her, put him in mind of Bridget Purcell and Margaret Gillane and Maeve Connelan and Oona Curry and Celia Driscoll, and the rest of the girls he had made songs for and had coaxed the heart from with his flattering tongue.

She looked up, and he saw her to be a girl of the neighbours, a farmer's daughter. 'What is on you, Nora?' he said. 'Nothing you could take from me, Red Hanrahan.' 'If there is any sorrow on you it is I myself should be well able to serve you,' he said then, 'for it is I know the history of the Greeks, and I know well what sorrow is and parting, and the hardship of the world. And if I am not able to save you from trouble,' he said, 'there is many a one I have saved from it with the power that is in my songs, as it was in the songs of the poets that were before me from the beginning of the world. And it is with the rest of the poets I myself will be sitting and talking in some far place beyond the world, to the end of life and time,' he said. The girl stopped her crying, and she said, 'Owen Hanrahan, I often heard you have had sorrow and persecution, and that you know all the troubles of the world since the time you refused your love to the queen-woman in Slieve Echtge; and that she never left you in quiet since. But when it is people of this earth that have harmed you, it is yourself knows well the way to put harm on them again. And will you do now what I ask you, Owen Hanrahan?' she said. 'I will do that indeed,' said he.

'It is my father and my mother and my brothers,' she said, 'that are marrying me to old Paddy Doe, because he has a farm of a hundred acres under the mountain. And it is what you can do, Hanrahan,' she said, 'put him into a rhyme the same way you put old Peter Kilmartin in one the time you were young, that sorrow may be over him rising up and lying down, that will put him thinking of Collooney churchyard and not of marriage. And let you make no delay about it, for it is for to-morrow they have the marriage settled, and I would sooner see the sun rise on the day of my death than on that day.'

'I will put him into a song that will bring shame and sorrow over him; but tell me how many years has he, for I would put them in the song?'

'O, he has years upon years. He is as old as you yourself, Red Hanrahan.' 'As old as myself,' said Hanrahan, and his voice was as if broken; 'as old as myself; there are twenty years and more between us! It is a bad day indeed for Owen Hanrahan when a young girl with the blossom of May in her cheeks thinks him to be an old man. And my grief!' he said, 'you have put a thorn in my heart.'

He turned from her then and went down the road till he came to a stone, and he sat down on it, for it seemed as if all the weight of the years had come on him in the minute. And he remembered it was not many days ago that a woman in some house had said: 'It is not Red Hanrahan you are now but yellow Hanrahan, for your hair is turned to the colour of a wisp of tow.' And another woman he had asked for a drink had not given him new milk but sour; and sometimes the girls would be whispering and laughing with young ignorant men while he himself was in the middle of giving out his poems or his talk. And he thought of the stiffness of his joints when he first rose of a morning, and the pain of his knees after making a journey, and it seemed to him as if he was come to be a very old man, with cold in the shoulders and speckled shins and his wind breaking and he himself withering away. And with those thoughts there came on him a great anger against old age and all it brought with it. And just then he looked up and saw a great spotted eagle sailing slowly towards Ballygawley, and he cried out: 'You, too, eagle of Ballygawley, are old, and your wings are full of gaps, and I will put you and your ancient comrades, the Pike of Dargan Lake and the Yew of the Steep Place of the Strangers into my rhyme, that there may be a curse on you for ever.'

There was a bush beside him to the left, flowering like the rest, and a little gust of wind blew the white blossoms over his coat. 'May blossoms,' he said, gathering them up in the hollow of his hand, 'you never know age because you die away in your beauty, and I will put you into my rhyme and give you my blessing.'

He rose up then and plucked a little branch from the bush, and carried it in his hand. But it is old and broken he looked going home that day with the stoop in his shoulders and the darkness in his face.

When he got to his cabin there was no one there, and he went and lay down on the bed for a while as he was used to do when he wanted to make a poem or a praise or a curse. And it was not long he was in making it this time, for the power of the curse-making bards was upon him. And when he had made it he searched his mind how he could send it out over the whole countryside.

Some of the scholars began coming in then, to see if there would be any school that day, and Hanrahan rose up and sat on the bench by the hearth, and they all stood around him.

They thought he would bring out the Virgil or the Mass book or the primer, but instead of that he held up the little branch of hawthorn he had in his hand yet. 'Children,' he said, 'this is a new lesson I have for you to-day.

'You yourselves and the beautiful people of the world are like this blossom, and old age is the wind that comes and blows the blossom away. And I have made a curse upon old age and upon the old men, and listen now while I give it out to you.' And this is what he said—

107

The poet, Owen Hanrahan, under a bush of may
Calls down a curse on his own head because it withers grey;
Then on the speckled eagle cock of Ballygawley Hill,
Because it is the oldest thing that knows of cark and ill;
And on the yew that has been green from the times out of mind
By the Steep Place of the Strangers and the Gap of the Wind;
And on the great grey pike that broods in Castle Dargan Lake
Having in his long body a many a hook and ache;
Then curses he old Paddy Bruen of the Well of Bride
Because no hair is on his head and drowsiness inside.
Then Paddy's neighbour, Peter Hart, and Michael Gill, his friend,
Because their wandering histories are never at an end.
And then old Shemus Cullinan, shepherd of the Green Lands
Because he holds two crutches between his crooked hands;
Then calls a curse from the dark North upon old Paddy Doe,
Who plans to lay his withering head upon a breast of snow,
Who plans to wreck a singing voice and break a merry heart,
He bids a curse hang over him till breath and body part;
But he calls down a blessing on the blossom of the may,
Because it comes in beauty, and in beauty blows away.

He said it over to the children verse by verse till all of them could say
a part of it, and some that were the quickest could say the whole of it.

'That will do for to-day,' he said then. 'And what you have to do now is
to go out and sing that song for a while, to the tune of the Green Bunch
of Rushes, to everyone you meet, and to the old men themselves.'

'I will do that,' said one of the little lads; 'I know old Paddy Doe well.
Last Saint John's Eve we dropped a mouse down his chimney, but this is
better than a mouse.'

'I will go into the town of Sligo and sing it in the street,' said another
of the boys. 'Do that,' said Hanrahan, 'and go into the Burrough and tell
it to Margaret Rooney and Mary Gillis, and bid them sing to it, and to

make the beggars and the bacachs sing it wherever they go.' The children ran out then, full of pride and of mischief, calling out the song as they ran, and Hanrahan knew there was no danger it would not be heard.

He was sitting outside the door the next morning, looking at his scholars as they came by in twos and threes. They were nearly all come, and he was considering the place of the sun in the heavens to know whether it was time to begin, when he heard a sound that was like the buzzing of a swarm of bees in the air, or the rushing of a hidden river in time of flood. Then he saw a crowd coming up to the cabin from the road, and he took notice that all the crowd was made up of old men, and that the leaders of it were Paddy Bruen, Michael Gill and Paddy Doe, and there was not one in the crowd but had in his hand an ash stick or a blackthorn. As soon as they caught sight of him, the sticks began to wave hither and thither like branches in a storm, and the old feet to run.

He waited no longer, but made off up the hill behind the cabin till he was out of their sight.

After a while he came back round the hill, where he was hidden by the furze growing along a ditch. And when he came in sight of his cabin he saw that all the old men had gathered around it, and one of them was just at that time thrusting a rake with a wisp of lighted straw on it into the thatch.

'My grief,' he said, 'I have set Old Age and Time and Weariness and Sickness against me, and I must go wandering again. And, O Blessed Queen of Heaven,' he said, 'protect me from the Eagle of Ballygawley, the Yew Tree of the Steep Place of the Strangers, the Pike of Castle Dargan Lake, and from the lighted wisps of their kindred, the Old Men!'

HANRAHAN'S VISION.

It was in the month of June Hanrahan was on the road near Sligo, but he did not go into the town, but turned towards Beinn Bulben; for there were thoughts of the old times coming upon him, and he had no mind to meet with common men. And as he walked he was singing to himself a song that had come to him one time in his dreams:

O Death's old bony finger
Will never find us there
In the high hollow townland
Where love's to give and to spare;
Where boughs have fruit and blossom
At all times of the year;
Where rivers are running over
With red beer and brown beer.
An old man plays the bagpipes
In a gold and silver wood;
Queens, their eyes blue like the ice,
Are dancing in a crowd.

The little fox he murmured,
'O what of the world's bane?'
The sun was laughing sweetly,
The moon plucked at my rein;
But the little red fox murmured,
'O do not pluck at his rein,

He is riding to the townland
That is the world's bane.'

When their hearts are so high
That they would come to blows,
They unhook their heavy swords
From golden and silver boughs:
But all that are killed in battle
Awaken to life again:
It is lucky that their story
Is not known among men.
For O, the strong farmers
That would let the spade lie,
Their hearts would be like a cup
That somebody had drunk dry.

Michael will unhook his trumpet
From a bough overhead,
And blow a little noise
When the supper has been spread.
Gabriel will come from the water
With a fish tail, and talk
Of wonders that have happened
On wet roads where men walk,
And lift up an old horn
Of hammered silver, and drink
Till he has fallen asleep
Upon the starry brink.

Hanrahan had begun to climb the mountain then, and he gave over singing, for it was a long climb for him, and every now and again he had to sit down and to rest for a while. And one time he was resting he took notice of a wild briar bush, with blossoms on it, that was growing beside a rath, and it brought to mind the wild roses he used to bring to Mary Lavelle, and to no woman after her. And he tore off a little branch of the bush, that had buds on it and open blossoms, and he went on with his song:

> The little fox he murmured,
> 'O what of the world's bane?'
> The sun was laughing sweetly,
> The moon plucked at my rein;
> But the little red fox murmured,
> 'O do not pluck at his rein,
> He is riding to the townland
> That is the world's bane.'

And he went on climbing the hill, and left the rath, and there came to his mind some of the old poems that told of lovers, good and bad, and of some that were awakened from the sleep of the grave itself by the strength of one another's love, and brought away to a life in some shadowy place, where they are waiting for the judgment and banished from the face of God.

And at last, at the fall of day, he came to the Steep Gap of the Strangers, and there he laid himself down along a ridge of rock, and looked into the valley, that was full of grey mist spreading from mountain to mountain.

And it seemed to him as he looked that the mist changed to shapes of shadowy men and women, and his heart began to beat with the fear and the joy of the sight. And his hands, that were always restless, began to pluck off the leaves of the roses on the little branch, and he watched them as they went floating down into the valley in a little fluttering troop.

Suddenly he heard a faint music, a music that had more laughter in it and more crying than all the music of this world. And his heart rose when he heard that, and he began to laugh out loud, for he knew that music was made by some who had a beauty and a greatness beyond the people of this world. And it seemed to him that the little soft rose leaves as they went fluttering down into the valley began to change their shape till they looked like a troop of men and women far off in the mist, with the colour of the roses on them. And then that colour changed to many colours, and what he saw was a long line of tall beautiful young men, and of queen-women, that were not going from him but coming towards him and past him, and their faces were full of tenderness for all their proud looks, and were very pale and worn, as if they were seeking and ever seeking for high sorrowful things. And shadowy arms were stretched out of the mist as if to take hold of them, but could not touch them, for the quiet that was about them could not be broken. And before them and beyond them, but at a distance as if in reverence, there were other shapes, sinking and rising and coming and going, and Hanrahan knew them by their whirling flight to be the Sidhe, the ancient defeated gods; and the shadowy arms did not rise to take hold of them, for they were of those that can neither sin nor obey. And they all lessened then in the distance, and they seemed to be going towards the white door that is in the side of the mountain.

The mist spread out before him now like a deserted sea washing the mountains with long grey waves, but while he was looking at it, it began to fill again with a flowing broken witless life that was a part of itself, and arms and pale heads covered with tossing hair appeared in the greyness. It rose higher and higher till it was level with the edge of the steep rock, and then the shapes grew to be solid, and a new procession half lost in mist passed very slowly with uneven steps, and in the midst of each shadow there was something shining in the starlight. They came nearer and nearer, and Hanrahan saw that they also were lovers, and that they had heart-shaped mirrors instead of hearts, and they were looking and ever looking on their own faces in one another's mirrors. They passed on, sinking downward as they passed, and other shapes rose in their place, and these did not keep side by side, but followed after one another, holding out wild beckoning arms, and he saw that those who were followed were women, and as to their heads they were beyond all beauty, but as to their bodies they were but shadows without life, and their long hair was moving and trembling about them, as if it lived with some terrible life of its own. And then the mist rose of a sudden and hid them, and then a light gust of wind blew them away towards the north-east, and covered Hanrahan at the same time with a white wing of cloud.

He stood up trembling and was going to turn away from the valley, when he saw two dark and half-hidden forms standing as if in the air just beyond the rock, and one of them that had the sorrowful eyes of a beggar said to him in a woman's voice, 'Speak to me, for no one in this world or any other world has spoken to me for seven hundred years.'

'Tell me who are those that have passed by,' said Hanrahan.

'Those that passed first,' the woman said, 'are the lovers that had the greatest name in the old times, Blanad and Deirdre and Grania and their dear comrades, and a great many that are not so well known but are as well loved. And because it was not only the blossom of youth they were looking for in one another, but the beauty that is as lasting as the night and the stars, the night and the stars hold them for ever from the warring and the perishing, in spite of the wars and the bitterness their love brought into the world. And those that came next,' she said, 'and that still breathe the sweet air and have the mirrors in their hearts, are not put in songs by the poets, because they sought only to triumph one over the other, and so to prove their strength and beauty, and out of this they made a kind of love. And as to the women with shadow-bodies, they desired neither to triumph nor to love but only to be loved, and there is no blood in their hearts or in their bodies until it flows through them from a kiss, and their life is but for a moment. All these are unhappy, but I am the unhappiest of all, for I am Dervadilla, and this is Dermot, and it was our sin brought the Norman into Ireland. And the curses of all the generations are upon us, and none are punished as we are punished. It was but the blossom of the man and of the woman we loved in one another, the dying beauty of the dust and not the everlasting beauty. When we died there was no lasting unbreakable quiet about us, and the bitterness of the battles we brought into Ireland turned to our own punishment. We go wandering together for ever, but Dermot that was my lover sees me always as a body that has been a long time in the ground, and I know that is the way he sees me. Ask me more, ask me more, for all the years have left their wisdom in my heart, and no one has listened to me for seven hundred years.'

A great terror had fallen upon Hanrahan, and lifting his arms above his head he screamed out loud three times, and the cattle in the valley lifted their heads and lowed, and the birds in the wood at the edge of the mountain awaked out of their sleep and fluttered through the trembling leaves. But a little below the edge of the rock, the troop of rose leaves still fluttered in the air, for the gateway of Eternity had opened and shut again in one beat of the heart.

THE DEATH OF HANRAHAN.

Hanrahan, that was never long in one place, was back again among the villages that are at the foot of Slieve Echtge, Illeton and Scalp and Ballylee, stopping sometimes in one house and sometimes in another, and finding a welcome in every place for the sake of the old times and of his poetry and his learning. There was some silver and some copper money in the little leather bag under his coat, but it was seldom he needed to take anything from it, for it was little he used, and there was not one of the people that would have taken payment from him. His hand had grown heavy on the blackthorn he leaned on, and his cheeks were hollow and worn, but so far as food went, potatoes and milk and a bit of oaten cake, he had what he wanted of it; and it is not on the edge of so wild and boggy a place as Echtge a mug of spirits would be wanting, with the taste of the turf smoke on it. He would wander about the big wood at Kinadife, or he would sit through many hours of the day among the rushes about Lake Belshragh, listening to the streams from the hills, or watching the shadows in the brown bog pools; sitting so quiet as not to startle the deer that came down from the heather to the grass and the tilled fields at the fall of night. As the days went by it seemed as if he was beginning to belong to some world out of sight and misty, that has for its mearing the colours that are beyond all other colours and the silences that are beyond all silences of this world. And sometimes he would hear coming and going in the wood music that when it stopped went from his memory like a dream; and once in the stillness of midday he heard a sound like the clashing of many swords, that went on for long time without any break. And at the fall of night and at moonrise the lake would grow to be like a gateway of silver and shining stones, and there would come from its silence the faint sound of keening and of frightened laughter broken by the wind, and many pale beckoning hands.

He was sitting looking into the water one evening in harvest time, thinking of all the secrets that were shut into the lakes and the mountains, when he heard a cry coming from the south, very faint at first, but getting louder and clearer as the shadow of the rushes grew longer, till he could hear the words, 'I am beautiful, I am beautiful; the birds in the air, the moths under the leaves, the flies over the water look at me, for they never saw any one so beautiful as myself. I am young; I am young: look upon me, mountains; look upon me, perishing woods, for my body will shine like the white waters when you have been hurried away. You and the whole race of men, and the race of the beasts and the race of the fish and the winged race are dropping like a candle that is nearly burned out, but I laugh out because I am in my youth.' The voice would break off from time to time, as if tired, and then it would begin again, calling out always the same words, 'I am beautiful, I am beautiful.' Presently the bushes at the edge of the little lake trembled for a moment, and a very old woman forced her way among them, and passed by Hanrahan, walking with very slow steps. Her face was of the colour of earth, and more wrinkled than the face of any old hag that was ever seen, and her grey hair was hanging in wisps, and the rags she was wearing did not hide her dark skin that was roughened by all weathers. She passed by him with her eyes wide open, and her head high, and her arms hanging straight beside her, and she went into the shadow of the hills towards the west.

A sort of dread came over Hanrahan when he saw her, for he knew her to be one Winny Byrne, that went begging from place to place crying always the same cry, and he had often heard that she had once such wisdom that all the women of the neighbours used to go looking for advice from her, and that she had a voice so beautiful that men and women would come from every part to hear her sing at a wake or a wedding; and that the Others, the great Sidhe, had stolen her wits one

Samhain night many years ago, when she had fallen asleep on the edge of a rath, and had seen in her dreams the servants of Echtge of the hills.

And as she vanished away up the hillside, it seemed as if her cry, 'I am beautiful, I am beautiful,' was coming from among the stars in the heavens.

There was a cold wind creeping among the rushes, and Hanrahan began to shiver, and he rose up to go to some house where there would be a fire on the hearth. But instead of turning down the hill as he was used, he went on up the hill, along the little track that was maybe a road and maybe the dry bed of a stream. It was the same way Winny had gone, and it led to the little cabin where she stopped when she stopped in any place at all. He walked very slowly up the hill as if he had a great load on his back, and at last he saw a light a little to the left, and he thought it likely it was from Winny's house it was shining, and he turned from the path to go to it. But clouds had come over the sky, and he could not well see his way, and after he had gone a few steps his foot slipped and he fell into a bog drain, and though he dragged himself out of it, holding on to the roots of the heather, the fall had given him a great shake, and he felt better fit to lie down than to go travelling. But he had always great courage, and he made his way on, step by step, till at last he came to Winny's cabin, that had no window, but the light was shining from the door. He thought to go into it and to rest for a while, but when he came to the door he did not see Winny inside it, but what he saw was four old grey-haired women playing cards, but Winny herself was not among them. Hanrahan sat down on a heap of turf beside the door, for he was tired out and out, and had no wish for talking or for card-playing, and his bones and his joints aching the way they were. He could hear the four women talking as they played, and calling out their hands. And it seemed to him that they were saying, like the strange man in the barn long ago: 'Spades and Diamonds, Courage and Power. Clubs and Hearts, Knowledge and Pleasure.' And he went on saying those words over and over to himself; and whether or not he was in his dreams, the pain that was in his shoulder never left him. And after a while the four women in the cabin began to quarrel, and each one to say the other had not played fair, and their voices grew from loud to louder, and their screams and their curses, till at last the whole air was filled with the noise of them around and above the house, and Hanrahan, hearing it between sleep and waking, said: 'That is the sound of the fighting between the friends and the ill-wishers of a man that is near his death. And I wonder,' he said, 'who is the man in this lonely place that is near his death.'

It seemed as if he had been asleep a long time, and he opened his eyes, and the face he saw over him was the old wrinkled face of Winny of the Cross Road. She was looking hard at him, as if to make sure he was not dead, and she wiped away the blood that had grown dry on his face with a wet cloth, and after a while she partly helped him and partly lifted him into the cabin, and laid him down on what served her for a bed. She gave him a couple of potatoes from a pot on the fire, and, what served him better, a mug of spring water. He slept a little now and again, and sometimes he heard her singing to herself as she moved about the house, and so the night wore away. When the sky began to brighten with the dawn he felt for the bag; where his little store of money was, and held it out to her, and she took out a bit of copper and a bit of silver money, but she let it drop again as if it was nothing to her, maybe because it was not money she was used to beg for, but food and rags; or maybe because the rising of the dawn was filling her with pride and a new belief in her own great beauty. She went out and cut a few armfuls of heather, and brought it in and heaped it over Hanrahan, saying something about the cold of the morning, and while she did that he took notice of the wrinkles in her face, and the greyness of her hair, and the broken teeth that were black and full of gaps. And when he was well covered with the heather she went out of the door and away down the side of the mountain, and he could hear her cry, 'I am beautiful, I am beautiful,' getting less and less as she went, till at last it died away altogether.

Hanrahan lay there through the length of the day, in his pains and his weakness, and when the shadows of the evening were falling he heard her voice again coming up the hillside, and she came in and boiled the potatoes and shared them with him the same way as before. And one day after another passed like that, and the weight of his flesh was heavy about him. But little by little as he grew weaker he knew there were some greater than himself in the room with him, and that the house began to be filled with them; and it seemed to him they had all power in their hands, and that they might with one touch of the hand break down the wall the hardness of pain had built about him, and take him into their own world. And sometimes he could hear voices, very faint and joyful, crying from the rafters or out of the flame on the hearth, and other times the whole house was filled with music that went through it like a wind. And after a while his weakness left no place for pain, and there grew up about him a great silence like the silence in the heart of a lake, and there came through it like the flame of a rushlight the faint joyful voices ever and always.

One morning he heard music somewhere outside the door, and as the day passed it grew louder and louder until it drowned the faint joyful voices, and even Winny's cry upon the hillside at the fall of evening. About midnight and in a moment, the walls seemed to melt away and to leave his bed floating on a pale misty light that shone on every side as far as the eye could see; and after the first blinding of his eyes he saw that it was full of great shadowy figures rushing here and there.

At the same time the music came very clearly to him, and he knew that it was but the continual clashing of swords.

'I am after my death,' he said, 'and in the very heart of the music of Heaven. O Cheruhim and Seraphim, receive my soul!'

At his cry the light where it was nearest to him filled with sparks of yet brighter light, and he saw that these were the points of swords turned towards his heart; and then a sudden flame, bright and burning like God's love or God's hate, swept over the light and went out and he was in darkness. At first he could see nothing, for all was as dark as if there was black bog earth about him, but all of a sudden the fire blazed up as if a wisp of straw had been thrown upon it. And as he looked at it, the light was shining on the big pot that was hanging from a hook, and on the flat stone where Winny used to bake a cake now and again, and on the long rusty knife she used to be cutting the roots of the heather with, and on the long blackthorn stick he had brought into the house himself. And when he saw those four things, some memory came into Hanrahan's mind, and strength came back to him, and he rose sitting up in the bed, and he said very loud and clear: 'The Cauldron, the Stone, the Sword, the Spear. What are they? Who do they belong to? And I have asked the question this time,' he said.

And then he fell back again, weak, and the breath going from him.

Winny Byrne, that had been tending the fire, came over then, having her eyes fixed on the bed; and the faint laughing voices began crying out again, and a pale light, grey like a wave, came creeping over the room, and he did not know from what secret world it came. He saw Winny's withered face and her withered arms that were grey like crumbled earth, and weak as he was he shrank back farther towards the wall. And then there came out of the mud-stiffened rags arms as white and as shadowy as the foam on a river, and they were put about his body, and a voice that he could hear well but that seemed to come from a long way off said to him in a whisper: 'You will go looking for me no more upon the breasts of women.'

'Who are you?' he said then.

'I am one of the lasting people, of the lasting unwearied Voices, that make my dwelling in the broken and the dying, and those that have lost their wits; and I came looking for you, and you are mine until the whole world is burned out like a candle that is spent. And look up now,' she said, 'for the wisps that are for our wedding are lighted.'

He saw then that the house was crowded with pale shadowy hands, and that every hand was holding what was sometimes like a wisp lighted for a marriage, and sometimes like a tall white candle for the dead.

When the sun rose on the morning of the morrow Winny of the Cross Roads rose up from where she was sitting beside the body, and began her begging from townland to townland, singing the same song as she walked, 'I am beautiful, I am beautiful. The birds in the air, the moths under the leaves, the flies over the water look at me. Look at me, perishing woods, for my body will be shining like the lake water after you have been hurried away. You and the old race of men, and the race of the beasts, and the race of the fish, and the winged race, are wearing away like a candle that has been burned out. But I laugh out loud, because I am in my youth.'

She did not come back that night or any night to the cabin, and it was not till the end of two days that the turf cutters going to the bog found the body of Red Owen Hanrahan, and gathered men to wake him and women to keen him, and gave him a burying worthy of so great a poet.

THE HOUR-GLASS

A MORALITY

DRAMATIS PERSONAE

A WISE MAN
A FOOL
SOME PUPILS
AN ANGEL
THE WISE MAN'S WIFE AND TWO CHILDREN

SCENE: A large room with a door at the back and another at the side opening to an inner room. A desk and a chair in the middle. An hour-glass on a bracket near the door. A creepy stool near it. Some benches. The WISE MAN sitting at his desk.

WISE MAN [turning over the pages of a book]. Where is that passage I am to explain to my pupils to-day? Here it is, and the book says that it was written by a beggar on the walls of Babylon: "There are two living countries, the one visible and the one invisible; and when it is winter with us it is summer in that country; and when the November winds are up among us it is lambing-time there." I wish that my pupils had asked me to explain any other passage, for this is a hard passage. [The FOOL comes in and stands at the door, holding out his hat. He has a pair of shears in the other hand.] It sounds to me like foolishness; and yet that cannot be, for the writer of this book, where I have found so much knowledge, would not have set it by itself on this page, and surrounded it with so many images and so many deep colors and so much fine gilding, if it had been foolishness.

FOOL. Give me a penny.

WISE MAN. [Turns to another page.] Here he has written: "The learned in old times forgot the visible country." That I understand, but I have taught my learners better.

FOOL. Won't you give me a penny?

WISE MAN. What do you want? The words of the wise Saracen will not teach you much.

FOOL. Such a great wise teacher as you are will not refuse a penny to a Fool.

WISE MAN. What do you know about wisdom?

FOOL. Oh, I know! I know what I have seen.

WISE MAN. What is it you have seen?

FOOL. When I went by Kilcluan where the bells used to be ringing at the break of every day, I could hear nothing but the people snoring in their houses. When I went by Tubbervanach where the young men used to be climbing the hill to the blessed well, they were sitting at the crossroads playing cards. When I went by Carrigoras where the friars used to be fasting and serving the poor, I saw them drinking wine and obeying their wives. And when I asked what misfortune had brought all these changes, they said it was no misfortune, but it was the wisdom they had learned from your teaching.

WISE MAN. Run round to the kitchen, and my wife will give you something to eat.

FOOL. That is foolish advice for a wise man to give.

WISE MAN. Why, Fool?

FOOL. What is eaten is gone. I want pennies for my bag. I must buy bacon in the shops, and nuts in the market, and strong drink for the time when the sun is weak. And I want snares to catch the rabbits and the squirrels and the bares, and a pot to cook them in.

WISE MAN. Go away. I have other things to think of now than giving you pennies.

FOOL. Give me a penny and I will bring you luck. Bresal the Fisherman lets me sleep among the nets in his loft in the winter-time because he says I bring him luck; and in the summer-time the wild creatures let me sleep near their nests and their holes. It is lucky even to look at me or to touch me, but it is much more lucky to give me a penny. [Holds out his hand.] If I wasn't lucky, I'd starve.

WISE MAN. What have you got the shears for?

FOOL. I won't tell you. If I told you, you would drive them away.

WISE MAN. Whom would I drive away?

FOOL. I won't tell you.

WISE MAN. Not if I give you a penny?

FOOL. No.

WISE MAN. Not if I give you two pennies.

FOOL. You will be very lucky if you give me two pennies, but I won't tell you.

WISE MAN. Three pennies?

FOOL. Four, and I will tell you!

WISE MAN. Very well, four. But I will not call you Teigue the Fool any longer.

FOOL. Let me come close to you where nobody will hear me. But first you must promise you will not drive them away. [WISE MAN nods.] Every day men go out dressed in black and spread great black nets over the hill, great black nets.

WISE MAN. Why do they do that?

FOOL. That they may catch the feet of the angels. But every morning, just before the dawn, I go out and cut the nets with my shears, and the angels fly away.

WISE MAN. Ah, now I know that you are Teigue the Fool. You have told me that I am wise, and I have never seen an angel.

FOOL. I have seen plenty of angels.

WISE MAN. Do you bring luck to the angels too.

FOOL. Oh, no, no! No one could do that. But they are always there if one looks about one; they are like the blades of grass.

WISE MAN. When do you see them?

FOOL. When one gets quiet; then something wakes up inside one, something happy and quiet like the stars—not like the seven that move, but like the fixed stars.   [He points upward.]

WISE MAN. And what happens then?

FOOL. Then all in a minute one smells summer flowers, and tall people go by, happy and laughing, and their clothes are the color of burning sods.

WISE MAN. Is it long since you have seen them, Teigue the Fool?

FOOL. Not long, glory be to God! I saw one coming behind me just now. It was not laughing, but it had clothes the color of burning sods, and there was something shining about its head.

WISE MAN. Well, there are your four pennies. You, a fool, say "Glory be to God," but before I came the wise men said it. Run away now. I must ring the bell for my scholars.

FOOL. Four pennies! That means a great deal of luck. Great teacher, I have brought you plenty of luck! [He goes out shaking the bag.]

WISE MAN. Though they call him Teigue the Fool, he is not more foolish than everybody used to be, with their dreams and their preachings and their three worlds; but I have overthrown their three worlds with the seven sciences. [He touches the books with his hands.] With Philosophy that was made for the lonely star, I have taught them to forget Theology; with Architecture, I have hidden the ramparts of their cloudy heaven; with Music, the fierce planets' daughter whose hair is always on fire, and with Grammar that is the moon's daughter, I have shut their ears to the imaginary harpings and speech of the angels; and I have made formations of battle with Arithmetic that have put the hosts of heaven to the rout. But, Rhetoric and Dialectic, that have been born out of the light star and out of the amorous star, you have been my spearman and my catapult! Oh! my swift horseman! Oh! my keen darting arguments, it is because of you that I have overthrown the hosts of foolishness! [An ANGEL, in a dress the color of embers, and carrying a blossoming apple bough in his hand

and with a gilded halo about his head, stands upon the threshold.] Before I came, men's minds were stuffed with folly about a heaven where birds sang the hours, and about angels that came and stood upon men's thresholds. But I have locked the visions into heaven and turned the key upon them. Well, I must consider this passage about the two countries. My mother used to say something of the kind. She would say that when our bodies sleep our souls awake, and that whatever withers here ripens yonder, and that harvests are snatched from us that they may feed invisible people. But the meaning of the book must be different, for only fools and women have thoughts like that; their thoughts were never written upon the walls of Babylon. [He sees the ANGEL.] What are you? Who are you? I think I saw some that were like you in my dreams when I was a child—that bright thing, that dress that is the color of embers! But I have done with dreams, I have done with dreams.

ANGEL. I am the Angel of the Most High God.

WISE MAN. Why have you come to me?

ANGEL. I have brought you a message.

WISE MAN. What message have you got for me?

ANGEL. You will die within the hour. You will die when the last grains have fallen in this glass.   [He turns the hour-glass.]

WISE MAN. My time to die has not come. I have my pupils. I have a young wife and children that I cannot leave. Why must I die?

ANGEL. You must die because no souls have passed over the threshold of heaven since you came into this country. The threshold is grassy, and the gates are rusty, and the angels that keep watch there are lonely.

WISE MAN. Where will death bring me to?

ANGEL. The doors of heaven will not open to you, for you have denied the existence of heaven; and the doors of purgatory will not open to you, for you have denied the existence of purgatory.

WISE MAN. But I have also denied the existence of hell!

ANGEL. Hell is the place of those who deny.

WISE MAN [kneeling]. I have indeed denied everything and have taught others to deny. I have believed in nothing but what my senses told me. But, oh! beautiful Angel, forgive me, forgive me!

ANGEL. You should have asked forgiveness long ago.

WISE MAN. Had I seen your face as I see it now, oh! beautiful Angel, I would have believed, I would have asked forgiveness. Maybe you do not know how easy it is to doubt. Storm, death, the grass rotting, many sicknesses, those are the messengers that came to me. Oh! why are you silent? You carry the pardon of the Most High; give it to me! I would kiss your hands if I were not afraid—no, no, the hem of your dress!

ANGEL. You let go undying hands too long ago to take hold of them now.

WISE MAN. You cannot understand. You live in that country people only see in their dreams. You live in a country that we can only dream about. Maybe it is as hard for you to understand why we disbelieve as it is for us to believe. Oh! what have I said! You know everything! Give me time to undo what I have done. Give me a year—a month—a day—an hour! Give me this hour's end, that I may undo what I have done!

ANGEL. You cannot undo what you have done. Yet I have this power with my message. If you can find one that believes before the hour's end, you shall come to heaven after the years of purgatory. For, from one fiery seed, watched over by those that sent me, the harvest can come again to heap the golden threshing-floor. But now farewell, for I am weary of the weight of time.

WISE MAN. Blessed be the Father, blessed be the Son, blessed be the Spirit, blessed be the Messenger They have sent!

ANGEL [at the door and pointing at the hour-glass]. In a little while the uppermost glass will be empty.   [Goes out.]

WISE MAN. Everything will be well with me. I will call my pupils; they only say they doubt. [Pulls the bell.] They will be here in a moment. I hear their feet outside on the path. They want to please me; they pretend that they disbelieve. Belief is too old to be overcome all in a minute. Besides, I can prove what I once disproved. [Another pull at the bell.] They are coming now. I will go to my desk. I will speak quietly, as if nothing had happened.

[He stands at the desk with a fixed look in his eyes.]

[Enter PUPILS and the FOOL.]

FOOL. Leave me alone. Leave me alone. Who is that pulling at my bag? King's son, do not pull at my bag.

A YOUNG MAN. Did your friends the angels give you that bag? Why don't they fill your bag for you?

FOOL. Give me pennies! Give me some pennies!

A YOUNG MAN. Let go his cloak, it is coming to pieces. What do you want pennies for, with that great bag at your waist?

FOOL. I want to buy bacon in the shops, and nuts in the market, and strong drink for the time when the sun is weak, and snares to catch rabbits and the squirrels that steal the nuts, and hares, and a great pot to cook them in.

A YOUNG MAN. Why don't your friends tell you where buried treasures are?

ANOTHER. Why don't they make you dream about treasures? If one dreams three times, there is always treasure.

FOOL [holding out his hat]. Give me pennies! Give me pennies!

[They throw pennies into his hat. He is standing close to the door, that he may hold out his hat to each newcomer.]

A YOUNG MAN. Master, will you have Teigue the Fool for a scholar?

ANOTHER YOUNG MAN. Teigue, will you give us pennies if we teach you lessons? No, he goes to school for nothing on the mountains. Tell us what you learn on the mountains, Teigue?

WISE MAN. Be silent all. [He has been standing silent, looking away.] Stand still in your places, for there is something I would have you tell me.

[A moment's pause. They all stand round in their places. TEIGUE still stands at the door.]

WISE MAN. Is there any one amongst you who believes in God? In heaven? Or in purgatory? Or in hell?

ALL THE YOUNG MEN. No one; Master! No one!

WISE MAN. I knew you would all say that; but do not be afraid. I will not be angry. Tell me the truth. Do you not believe?

A YOUNG MAN. We once did, but you have taught us to know better.

WISE MAN. Oh! teaching, teaching does not go very deep! The heart remains unchanged under it all. You believe just as you always did, and you are afraid to tell me.

A YOUNG MAN. No, no, master.

WISE MAN. If you tell me that you believe I shall be glad and not angry.

A YOUNG MAN. [To his neighbor.] He wants somebody to dispute with.

HIS NEIGHBOR. I knew that from the beginning.

A YOUNG MAN. That is not the subject for to-day; you were going to talk about the words the beggar wrote upon the walls of Babylon.

WISE MAN. If there is one amongst you that believes, he will be my best friend. Surely there is one amongst you. [They are all silent.] Surely what you learned at your mother's knees has not been so soon forgotten.

A YOUNG MAN. Master, till you came, no teacher in this land was able to get rid of foolishness and ignorance. But every one has listened to you, every one has learned the truth. You have had your last disputation.

ANOTHER. What a fool you made of that monk in the market-place! He had not a word to say.

134

WISE MAN. [Comes from his desk and stands among them in the middle of the room.] Pupils, dear friends, I have deceived you all this time. It was I myself who was ignorant. There is a God. There is a heaven. There is fire that passes, and there is fire that lasts for ever.

[TEIGUE, through all this, is sitting on a stool by the door, reckoning on his fingers what he will buy with his money.]

A YOUNG MAN [to another]. He will not be satisfied till we dispute with him. [To the WISE MAN.] Prove it, master. Have you seen them?

WISE MAN [in a low, solemn voice]. Just now, before you came in, some one came to the door, and when I looked up I saw an angel standing there.

A YOUNG MAN. You were in a dream. Anybody can see an angel in his dreams.

WISE MAN. Oh, my God! it was not a dream. I was awake, waking as I am now. I tell you I was awake as I am now.

A YOUNG MAN. Some dream when they are awake, but they are the crazy, and who would believe what they say? Forgive me, master, but that is what you taught me to say. That is what you said to the monk when he spoke of the visions of the saints and the martyrs.

ANOTHER YOUNG MAN. You see how well we remember your teaching.

WISE MAN. Out, out from my sight! I want some one with belief. I must find that grain the Angel spoke of before I die. I tell you I must find it, and you answer me with arguments. Out with you, or I will beat you with my stick! [The young men laugh.]

A YOUNG MAN. How well he plays at faith! He is like the monk when he had nothing more to say.

WISE MAN. Out, out, or I will lay this stick about your shoulders! Out with you, though you are a king's son!

[They begin to hurry out.]

A YOUNG MAN. Come, come; he wants us to find some one who will dispute with him.   [All go out.]

WISE MAN [alone. He goes to the door at the side]. I will call my wife. She will believe; women always believe. [He opens the door and calls.] Bridget! Bridget! [BRIDGET comes in wearing her apron, her sleeves turned up from her floury arms.] Bridget, tell me the truth; do not say what you think will please me. Do you sometimes say your prayers?

BRIDGET. Prayers! No, you taught me to leave them off long ago. At first I was sorry, but I am glad now, for I am sleepy in the evenings.

WISE MAN. But do you not believe in God?

BRIDGET. Oh, a good wife only believes what her husband tells her!

WISE MAN. But sometimes when you are alone, when I am in the school and the children asleep, do you not think about the saints, about the things you used to believe in? What do you think of when you are alone?

BRIDGET [considering]. I think about nothing. Sometimes I wonder if the pig is fattening well, or I go out to see if the crows are picking up the chickens' food.

WISE MAN. Oh, what can I do! Is there nobody who believes? I must go and find somebody! [He goes toward the door but with his eyes fixed on the hour-glass.] I cannot go out; I cannot leave that!

BRIDGET. You want somebody to get up argument with.

WISE MAN. Oh, look out of the door and tell me if there is anybody there in the street. I cannot leave this glass; somebody might shake it! Then the sand would fall quickly.

BRIDGET. I don't understand what you are saying. [Looks out.] There is a crowd of people talking to your pupils.

WISE MAN. Oh, run out, Bridget, and see if they have found somebody that believes!

BRIDGET [wiping her arms in her apron and pulling down her sleeves]. It's a hard thing to be married to a man of learning that must be always having arguments. [Goes out and shouts through the kitchen door.] Don't be meddling with the bread, children, while I'm out.

WISE MAN. [Kneels down.] "Salvum me fac, Deus—salvum—salvum. . . ." I have forgotten it all. It is thirty years since I said a prayer. I must pray in the common tongue, like a clown begging in the market like Teigue the Fool! [He prays.] Help me, Father, Son, and Spirit!

   [BRIDGET enters, followed by the FOOL, who is holding out his hat to her.]

FOOL. Give me something; give me a penny to buy bacon in the shops, and nuts in the market, and strong drink for the time when the sun grows weak.

BRIDGET. I have no pennies. [To the WISE MAN.] Your pupils cannot find anybody to argue with you. There is nobody in the whole country who had enough belief to fill a pipe with since you put down the monk. Can't you be quiet now and not always be wanting to have arguments? It must be terrible to have a mind like that.

WISE MAN. I am lost! I am lost!

BRIDGET. Leave me alone now; I have to make the bread for you and the children.

WISE MAN. Out of this, woman, out of this, I say! [BRIDGET goes through the kitchen door.] Will nobody find a way to help me! But she spoke of my children. I had forgotten them. They will believe. It is only those who have reason that doubt; the young are full of faith. Bridget, Bridget, send my children to me!

BRIDGET [inside]. Your father wants you, run to him now.

[The two children came in. They stand together a little way from the threshold of the kitchen door, looking timidly at their father.]

WISE MAN. Children, what do you believe? Is there a heaven? Is there a hell? Is there a purgatory?

FIRST CHILD. We haven't forgotten, father.

THE OTHER CHILD. Oh, no, father. [They both speak together as if in school.] There is no heaven; there is no hell; there is nothing we cannot see.

FIRST CHILD. Foolish people used to think that there were, but you are very learned and you have taught us better.

138

WISE MAN. You are just as bad as the others, just as bad as the others! Out of the room with you, out of the room! [The children begin to cry and run away.] Go away, go away! I will teach you better—no, I will never teach you again. Go to your mother—no, she will not be able to teach them. . . . Help them, O God! [Alone.] The grains are going very quickly. There is very little sand in the uppermost glass. Somebody will come for me in a moment; perhaps he is at the door now! All creatures that have reason doubt. O that the grass and the planets could speak! Somebody has said that they would wither if they doubted. O speak to me, O grass blades! O fingers of God's certainty, speak to me. You are millions and you will not speak. I dare not know the moment the messenger will come for me. I will cover the glass. [He covers it and brings it to the desk, and the FOOL, is sitting by the door fiddling with some flowers which he has stuck in his hat. He has begun to blow a dandelion head.] What are you doing?

FOOL. Wait a moment. [He blows.] Four, five, six.

WISE MAN. What are you doing that for?

FOOL. I am blowing at the dandelion to find out what time it is.

WISE MAN. You have heard everything! That is why you want to find out what hour it is! You are waiting to see them coming through the door to carry me away. [FOOL goes on blowing.] Out through the door with you! I will have no one here when they come. [He seizes the FOOL by the shoulders, and begins to force him out through the door, then suddenly changes his mind.] No, I have something to ask you. [He drags him back into the room.] Is there a heaven? Is there a hell? Is there a purgatory?

FOOL. So you ask me now. I thought when you were asking your pupils, I said to myself, if he would ask Teigue the Fool, Teigue could tell him all about it, for Teigue has learned all about it when he has been cutting the nets.

WISE MAN. Tell me; tell me!

FOOL. I said, Teigue knows everything. Not even the owls and the hares that milk the cows have Teigue's wisdom. But Teigue will not speak; he says nothing.

WISE MAN. Tell me, tell me! For under the cover the grains are falling, and when they are all fallen I shall die; and my soul will be lost if I have not found somebody that believes! Speak, speak!

FOOL [looking wise]. No, no, I won't tell you what is in my mind, and I won't tell you what is in my bag. You might steal away my thoughts. I met a bodach on the road yesterday, and he said, "Teigue, tell me how many pennies are in your bag. I will wager three pennies that there are not twenty pennies in your bag; let me put in my hand and count them." But I pulled the strings tighter, like this; and when I go to sleep every night I hide the bag where no one knows.

WISE MAN. [Goes toward the hour-glass as if to uncover it.] No, no, I have not the courage! [He kneels.] Have pity upon me, Fool, and tell me!

FOOL. Ah! Now, that is different. I am not afraid of you now. But I must come near you; somebody in there might hear what the Angel said.

WISE MAN. Oh, what did the Angel tell you?

FOOL. Once I was alone on the hills, and an Angel came by and he said, "Teigue the Fool, do not forget the Three Fires: the Fire that punishes, the Fire that purifies, and the Fire wherein the soul rejoices for ever!"

WISE MAN. He believes! I am saved! Help me. The sand has run out. I am dying. ... [FOOL helps him to his chair.] I am going from the country of the seven wandering stars, and I am going to the country of the fixed stars! Ring the bell. [FOOL rings the bell.] Are they coming ? Ah! now I hear their feet. ... I will speak to them. I understand it all now. One sinks in on God: we do not see the truth; God sees the truth in us. I cannot speak, I am too weak. Tell them, Fool, that when the life and the mind are broken, the truth comes through them like peas through a broken peascod. But no, I will pray—yet I cannot pray. Pray Fool, that they may be given a sign and save their souls alive. Your prayers are better than mine.

[FOOL bows his head. WISE MAN'S head sinks on his arm on the books. PUPILS enter.]

A YOUNG MAN. Look at the Fool turned bell-ringer!

ANOTHER. What have you called us in for, Teigue? What are you going to tell us?

ANOTHER. No wonder he has had dreams! See, he is fast asleep now. [Goes over and touches the WISE MAN.] Oh, he is dead!

FOOL. Do not stir! He asked for a sign that you might be saved. [All are silent for a moment.] Look what has come from his mouth. . . . a little winged thing . . . a little shining thing. It has gone to the door. [The ANGEL appears in the doorway, stretches out her hands and closes them again.] The Angel has taken it in her hands . . . she will open her hands in the Garden of Paradise.

[They all kneel.]

SYNGE AND THE IRELAND OF HIS TIME

WITH A NOTE CONCERNING A WALK THROUGH CONNEMARA WITH HIM

PREFACE

At times during Synge's last illness, Lady Gregory and I would speak of his work and always find some pleasure in the thought that unlike ourselves, who had made our experiments in public, he would leave to the world nothing to be wished away—nothing that was not beautiful or powerful in itself, or necessary as an expression of his life and thought. When he died we were in much anxiety, for a letter written before his last illness, and printed in the selection of his poems published at the Cuala Press, had shown that he was anxious about the fate of his manuscripts and scattered writings. On the evening of the night he died he had asked that I might come to him the next day; and my diary of the days following his death shows how great was our anxiety. Presently however, all seemed to have come right, for the Executors sent me the following letter that had been found among his papers, and promised to carry out his wishes.

'May 4th, 1908

'Dear Yeats,
    'This is only to go to you if anything should go wrong with me under the operation or after it. I am a little bothered about my 'papers.' I have a certain amount of verse that I think would be worth preserving, possibly also the 1st and 3rd acts of 'Deirdre,' and then I have a lot of Kerry and Wicklow articles that would go together into a book. The other early stuff I wrote I have kept as a sort of curiosity, but I am anxious that it should not get into print. I wonder could you get someone—say . . .

who is now in Dublin to go through them for you and do whatever you and Lady Gregory think desirable. It is rather a hard thing to ask you but I do not want my good things destroyed or my bad things printed rashly—especially a morbid thing about a mad fiddler in Paris which I hate. Do what you can—Good luck.

'J.M. Synge'

In the summer of 1909, the Executors sent me a large bundle of papers, cuttings from newspapers and magazines, manuscript and typewritten prose and verse, put together and annotated by Synge himself before his last illness. I spent a portion of each day for weeks reading and re-reading early dramatic writing, poems, essays, and so forth, and with the exception of ninety pages which have been published without my consent, made consulting Lady Gregory from time to time the Selection of his work published by Messrs. Maunsel. It is because of these ninety pages, that neither Lady Gregory's name nor mine appears in any of the books, and that the Introduction which I now publish, was withdrawn by me after it had been advertised by the publishers. Before the publication of the books the Executors discovered a scrap of paper with a sentence by J.M. Synge saying that Selections might be taken from his Essays on the Congested Districts. I do not know if this was written before his letter to me, which made no mention of them, or contained his final directions. The matter is unimportant, for the publishers decided to ignore my offer to select as well as my original decision to reject, and for this act of theirs they have given me no reasons except reasons of convenience, which neither Lady Gregory nor I could accept.

W.B. Yeats.

* * * * *

I

On Saturday, January 26th, 1907, I was lecturing in Aberdeen, and when my lecture was over I was given a telegram which said, 'Play great success.' It had been sent from Dublin after the second Act of 'The Playboy of the Western World,' then being performed for the first time. After one in the morning, my host brought to my bedroom this second telegram, 'Audience broke up in disorder at the word shift.' I knew no more until I got the Dublin papers on my way from Belfast to Dublin on Tuesday morning. On the Monday night no word of the play had been heard. About forty young men had sat on the front seats of the pit, and stamped and shouted and blown trumpets from the rise to the fall of the curtain. On the Tuesday night also the forty young men were there. They wished to silence what they considered a slander upon Ireland's womanhood. Irish women would never sleep under the same roof with a young man without a chaperon, nor admire a murderer, nor use a word like 'shift;' nor could anyone recognise the country men and women of Davis and Kickham in these poetical, violent, grotesque persons, who used the name of God so freely, and spoke of all things that hit their fancy.

A patriotic journalism which had seen in Synge's capricious imagination the enemy of all it would have young men believe, had for years prepared for this hour, by that which is at once the greatest and most ignoble power of journalism, the art of repeating a name again and again with some ridiculous or evil association. The preparation had begun after the first performance of 'The Shadow of the Glen,' Synge's first play, with an assertion made in ignorance but repeated in dishonesty, that he had taken his fable and his characters, not from his own mind nor that profound knowledge of cot and curragh he was admitted to possess, but 'from a writer of the Roman decadence.' Some spontaneous dislike had been but natural, for genius like his can but slowly, amid what it has of harsh and strange, set forth the nobility of its beauty, and the depth of its compassion; but the frenzy that would have silenced his master-work was, like most violent things artificial, the defence of virtue by those that have but little, which is the pomp and gallantry of journalism and its right to govern the world.

As I stood there watching, knowing well that I saw the dissolution of a school of patriotism that held sway over my youth, Synge came and stood beside me, and said, 'A young doctor has just told me that he can hardly keep himself from jumping on to a seat, and pointing out in that howling mob those whom he is treating for venereal disease.'

II

Thomas Davis, whose life had the moral simplicity which can give to actions the lasting influence that style alone can give to words, had understood that a country which has no national institutions must show its young men images for the affections, although they be but diagrams of what it should be or may be. He and his school imagined the Soldier, the Orator, the Patriot, the Poet, the Chieftain, and above all the Peasant; and these, as celebrated in essay and songs and stories, possessed so many virtues that no matter how England, who as Mitchell said 'had the ear of the world,' might slander us, Ireland, even though she could not come at the world's other ear, might go her way unabashed. But ideas and images which have to be understood and loved by large numbers of people, must appeal to no rich personal experience, no patience of study, no delicacy of sense; and if at rare moments some 'Memory of the Dead' can take its strength from one; at all other moments manner and matter will be rhetorical, conventional, sentimental; and language, because it is carried beyond life perpetually, will be as wasted as the thought, with unmeaning pedantries and silences, and a dread of all that has salt and savour. After a while, in a land that has given itself to agitation over-much, abstract thoughts are raised up between men's minds and Nature, who never does the same thing twice, or makes one man like another, till minds, whose patriotism is perhaps great enough to carry them to the scaffold, cry down natural impulse with the morbid persistence of minds unsettled by some fixed idea. They are preoccupied with the nation's future, with heroes, poets, soldiers, painters, armies, fleets, but only as these things are understood by a child in a national school, while a secret feeling that what is so unreal needs continual defence makes them bitter and restless. They are like some state which has only paper money, and seeks by punishments to make it buy whatever gold can buy. They no longer love, for only life is loved, and at last, a generation is like an hysterical woman who will make unmeasured accusations and believe impossible things, because of some logical deduction from a solitary thought which has turned a portion of her mind to stone.

III

Even if what one defends be true, an attitude of defence, a continual apology, whatever the cause, makes the mind barren because it kills intellectual innocence; that delight in what is unforeseen, and in the mere spectacle of the world, the mere drifting hither and thither that must come before all true thought and emotion. A zealous Irishman, especially if he lives much out of Ireland, spends his time in a never-ending argument about Oliver Cromwell, the Danes, the penal laws, the rebellion of 1798, the famine, the Irish peasant, and ends by substituting a traditional casuistry for a country; and if he be a Catholic, yet another casuistry that has professors, schoolmasters, letter-writing priests, and the authors of manuals to make the meshes fine, comes between him and English literature, substituting arguments and hesitations for the excitement at the first reading of the great poets which should be a sort of violent imaginative puberty. His hesitations and arguments may have been right, the Catholic philosophy may be more profound than Milton's morality, or Shelley's vehement vision; but none the less do we lose life by losing that recklessness Castiglione thought necessary even in good manners, and offend our Lady Truth, who would never, had she desired an anxious courtship, have digged a well to be her parlour.

I admired though we were always quarrelling on some matter, J.F. Taylor, the orator, who died just before the first controversy over these plays. It often seemed to me that when he spoke Ireland herself had spoken, one got that sense of surprise that comes when a man has said what is unforeseen because it is far from the common thought, and yet obvious because when it has been spoken, the gate of the mind seems suddenly to roll back and reveal forgotten sights and let loose lost passions. I have never heard him speak except in some Irish literary or political society, but there at any rate, as in conversation, I found a man whose life was a ceaseless reverie over the religious and political history of Ireland. He saw himself pleading for his country before an invisible jury, perhaps of the great dead, against traitors at home and enemies abroad, and a sort of frenzy in his voice and the moral elevation of his thoughts gave him for the moment style and music. One asked oneself again and again, 'Why is not this man an artist, a man of genius, a creator of some kind?' The other day under the influence of memory, I read through his one book, a life of Owen Roe O'Neill, and found there no sentence detachable from its context because of wisdom or beauty. Everything was argued from a premise; and wisdom, and style, whether in life or letters come from the presence of what is self-evident, from that which requires but statement, from what Blake called 'naked beauty displayed.' The sense of what was unforeseen and obvious, the rolling backward of the gates had gone with the living voice, with the nobility of will that made one understand what he saw and felt in what was now but argument and logic. I found myself in the presence of a mind like some noisy and powerful machine, of thought that was no part of wisdom but the apologetic of a moment, a woven thing, no intricacy of leaf and twig, of words with no more of salt and of savour than those of a Jesuit professor of literature, or of any other who does not know that there is no lasting writing which does not define the quality, or carry the substance of some pleasure. How can one, if one's mind be full of abstractions and images created not for their own sake but for the sake of party, even if there were still the need, find words that delight the ear, make pictures to the mind's eye, discover thoughts that tighten the muscles, or quiver and tingle in the flesh, and stand like St. Michael with the trumpet that calls the body to resurrection?

IV

Young Ireland had taught a study of our history with the glory of Ireland for event, and this for lack, when less than Taylor studied, of comparison with that of other countries wrecked the historical instinct. An old man with an academic appointment, who was a leader in the attack upon Synge, sees in the 11th century romance of Deirdre a re-telling of the first five act tragedy outside the classic languages, and this tragedy from his description of it was certainly written on the Elizabethan model; while an allusion to a copper boat, a marvel of magic like Cinderella's slipper, persuades him that the ancient Irish had forestalled the modern dockyards in the making of metal ships. The man who doubted, let us say, our fabulous ancient kings running up to Adam, or found but mythology in some old tale, was as hated as if he had doubted the authority of Scripture. Above all no man was so ignorant, that he had not by rote familiar arguments and statistics to drive away amid familiar applause, all those had they but found strange truth in the world or in their mind, whose knowledge has passed out of memory and become an instinct of hand or eye. There was no literature, for literature is a child of experience always, of knowledge never; and the nation itself, instead of being a dumb struggling thought seeking a mouth to utter it or hand to show it, a teeming delight that would re-create the world, had become, at best, a subject of knowledge.

V

Taylor always spoke with confidence though he was no determined man, being easily flattered or jostled from his way; and this, putting as it were his fiery heart into his mouth made him formidable. And I have noticed that all those who speak the thoughts of many, speak confidently, while those who speak their own thoughts are hesitating and timid, as though they spoke out of a mind and body grown sensitive to the edge of bewilderment among many impressions. They speak to us that we may give them certainty, by seeing what they have seen; and so it is, that enlargement of experience does not come from those oratorical thinkers, or from those decisive rhythms that move large numbers of men, but from writers that seem by contrast as feminine as the soul when it explores in Blake's picture the recesses of the grave, carrying its faint lamp trembling and astonished; or as the Muses who are never pictured as one-breasted amazons, but as women needing protection. Indeed, all art which appeals to individual man and awaits the confirmation of his senses and his reveries, seems when arrayed against the moral zeal, the confident logic, the ordered proof of journalism, a trifling, impertinent, vexatious thing, a tumbler who has unrolled his carpet in the way of a marching army.

VI

I attack things that are as dear to many as some holy image carried hither and thither by some broken clan, and can but say that I have felt in my body the affections I disturb, and believed that if I could raise them into contemplation I would make possible a literature, that finding its subject-matter all ready in men's minds would be, not as ours is, an interest for scholars, but the possession of a people. I have founded societies with this aim, and was indeed founding one in Paris when I first met with J.M. Synge, and I have known what it is to be changed by that I would have changed, till I became argumentative and unmannerly, hating men even in daily life for their opinions. And though I was never convinced that the anatomies of last year's leaves are a living forest, or thought a continual apologetic could do other than make the soul a vapour and the body a stone; or believed that literature can be made by anything but by what is still blind and dumb within ourselves, I have had to learn how hard in one who lives where forms of expression and habits of thought have been born, not for the pleasure of begetting but for the public good, is that purification from insincerity, vanity, malignity, arrogance, which is the discovery of style. But it became possible to live when I had learnt all I had not learnt in shaping words, in defending Synge against his enemies, and knew that rich energies, fine, turbulent or gracious thoughts, whether in life or letters, are but love-children.

VII

Synge seemed by nature unfitted to think a political thought, and with the exception of one sentence, spoken when I first met him in Paris, that implied some sort of nationalist conviction, I cannot remember that he spoke of politics or showed any interest in men in the mass, or in any subject that is studied through abstractions and statistics. Often for months together he and I and Lady Gregory would see no one outside the Abbey Theatre, and that life, lived as it were in a ship at sea, suited him, for unlike those whose habit of mind fits them to judge of men in the mass, he was wise in judging individual men, and as wise in dealing with them as the faint energies of ill-health would permit; but of their political thoughts he long understood nothing. One night when we were still producing plays in a little hall, certain members of the Company told him that a play on the Rebellion of '98 would be a great success. After a fortnight he brought them a scenario which read like a chapter out of Rabelais. Two women, a Protestant and a Catholic, take refuge in a cave, and there quarrel about religion, abusing the Pope or Queen Elizabeth and Henry VIII, but in low voices, for the one fears to be ravished by the soldiers, the other by the rebels. At last one woman goes out because she would sooner any fate than such wicked company. Yet, I doubt if he would have written at all if he did not write of Ireland, and for it, and I know that he thought creative art could only come from such preoccupation. Once, when in later years, anxious about the educational effect of our movement, I proposed adding to the Abbey Company a second Company to play international drama, Synge, who had not hitherto opposed me, thought the matter so important that he did so in a formal letter.

I had spoken of a German municipal theatre as my model, and he said that the municipal theatres all over Europe gave fine performances of old classics but did not create (he disliked modern drama for its sterility of speech, and perhaps ignored it) and that we would create nothing if we did not give all our thoughts to Ireland. Yet in Ireland he loved only what was wild in its people, and in 'the grey and wintry sides of many glens.' All the rest, all that one reasoned over, fought for, read of in leading articles, all that came from education, all that came down from Young Ireland—though for this he had not lacked a little sympathy—first wakened in him perhaps that irony which runs through all he wrote, but once awakened, he made it turn its face upon the whole of life. The women quarrelling in the cave would not have amused him, if something in his nature had not looked out on most disputes, even those wherein he himself took sides, with a mischievous wisdom. He told me once that when he lived in some peasant's house, he tried to make those about him forget that he was there, and it is certain that he was silent in any crowded room. It is possible that low vitality helped him to be observant and contemplative, and made him dislike, even in solitude, those thoughts which unite us to others, much as we all dislike, when fatigue or illness has sharpened the nerves, hoardings covered with advertisements, the fronts of big theatres, big London hotels, and all architecture which has been made to impress the crowd. What blindness did for Homer, lameness for Hephaestus, asceticism for any saint you will, bad health did for him by making him ask no more of life than that it should keep him living, and above all perhaps by concentrating his imagination upon one thought, health itself. I think that all noble things are the result of warfare; great nations and classes, of warfare in the visible world, great poetry and philosophy, of invisible warfare, the division of a mind within itself, a victory, the sacrifice of a man to himself. I am certain that my friend's noble art, so full of passion and heroic beauty, is the victory of a man who in poverty and sickness created from the delight of expression, and in the contemplation that is born of the minute and delicate arrangement of images, happiness, and health of mind. Some early poems have a morbid melancholy, and he himself spoke of early work he had destroyed as morbid, for as yet the craftmanship was not fine enough to bring the artist's joy which is of one substance with that of sanctity. In one poem he waits at some street corner for a friend, a woman perhaps, and while he waits and gradually understands that nobody is coming, sees two funerals and shivers at the future; and in another written on his 25th birthday, he wonders if the 25 years to come shall be as evil as those gone by. Later on, he can see himself as but a part of the spectacle of the world and mix into all he sees that flavour of extravagance, or of humour, or of philosophy, that makes one understand that he contemplates even his own death as if it were another's, and finds in his own destiny but as it were a projection through a burning glass of that general to men. There is in the creative joy an acceptance of what life brings, because we have understood the beauty of what it brings, or a hatred of death for what it takes away, which arouses within us, through some sympathy perhaps with all other men, an energy so noble, so powerful, that we laugh aloud and mock, in the terror or the sweetness of our exaltation, at death and oblivion.

In no modern writer that has written of Irish life before him, except it may be Miss Edgeworth in 'Castle Rackrent,' was there anything to change a man's thought about the world or stir his moral nature, for they but play with pictures, persons, and events, that whether well or ill observed are but an amusement for the mind where it escapes from meditation, a child's show that makes the fables of his art as significant by contrast as some procession painted on an Egyptian wall; for in these fables, an intelligence, on which the tragedy of the world had been thrust in so few years, that Life had no time to brew her sleepy drug, has spoken of the moods that are the expression of its wisdom. All minds that have a wisdom come of tragic reality seem morbid to those that are accustomed to writers who have not faced reality at all; just as the saints, with that Obscure Night of the Soul, which fell so certainly that they numbered it among spiritual states, one among other ascending steps, seem morbid to the rationalist and the old-fashioned Protestant controversialist. The thought of journalists, like that of the Irish novelists, is neither healthy nor unhealthy, for it has not risen to that state where either is possible, nor should we call it happy; for who would have sought happiness, if happiness were not the supreme attainment of man, in heroic toils, in the cell of the ascetic, or imagined it above the cheerful newspapers, above the clouds?

VIII

Not that Synge brought out of the struggle with himself any definite philosophy, for philosophy in the common meaning of the word is created out of an anxiety for sympathy or obedience, and he was that rare, that distinguished, that most noble thing, which of all things still of the world is nearest to being sufficient to itself, the pure artist. Sir Philip Sidney complains of those who could hear 'sweet tunes' (by which he understands could look upon his lady) and not be stirred to 'ravishing delight.'

'Or if they do delight therein, yet are so closed with wit,
As with sententious lips to set a title vain on it;
Oh let them hear these sacred tunes, and learn in Wonder's schools
To be, in things past bonds of wit, fools if they be not fools!'

Ireland for three generations has been like those churlish logicians. Everything is argued over, everything has to take its trial before the dull sense and the hasty judgment, and the character of the nation has so changed that it hardly keeps but among country people, or where some family tradition is still stubborn, those lineaments that made Borrow cry out as he came from among the Irish monks, his friends and entertainers for all his Spanish Bible scattering, 'Oh, Ireland, mother of the bravest soldiers and of the most beautiful women!' It was as I believe, to seek that old Ireland which took its mould from the duellists and scholars of the 18th century and from generations older still, that Synge returned again and again to Aran, to Kerry, and to the wild Blaskets.

IX

'When I got up this morning' he writes, after he had been a long time in Innismaan, 'I found that the people had gone to Mass and latched the kitchen door from the outside, so that I could not open it to give myself light.

'I sat for nearly an hour beside the fire with a curious feeling that I should be quite alone in this little cottage. I am so used to sitting here with the people that I have never felt the room before as a place where any man might live and work by himself. After a while as I waited, with just light enough from the chimney to let me see the rafters and the greyness of the walls, I became indescribably mournful, for I felt that this little corner on the face of the world, and the people who live in it, have a peace and dignity from which we are shut for ever.' This life, which he describes elsewhere as the most primitive left in Europe, satisfied some necessity of his nature. Before I met him in Paris he had wandered over much of Europe, listening to stories in the Black Forest, making friends with servants and with poor people, and this from an aesthetic interest, for he had gathered no statistics, had no money to give, and cared nothing for the wrongs of the poor, being content to pay for the pleasure of eye and ear with a tune upon the fiddle. He did not love them the better because they were poor and miserable, and it was only when he found Innismaan and the Blaskets, where there is neither riches nor poverty, neither what he calls 'the nullity of the rich' nor 'the squalor of the poor' that his writing lost its old morbid brooding, that he found his genius and his peace. Here were men and women who under the weight of their necessity lived, as the artist lives, in the presence of death and childhood, and the great affections and the orgiastic moment when life outleaps its limits, and who, as it is always with those who have refused or escaped the trivial and the temporary, had dignity and good manners where manners mattered. Here above all was silence from all our great orator took delight in, from formidable men, from moral indignation, from the 'sciolist' who 'is never sad,' from all in modern life that would destroy the arts; and here, to take a thought from another playwright of our school, he could love Time as only women and great artists do and need never sell it.

X

As I read 'The Aran Islands' right through for the first time since he showed it me in manuscript, I come to understand how much knowledge of the real life of Ireland went to the creation of a world which is yet as fantastic as the Spain of Cervantes. Here is the story of 'The Playboy,' of 'The Shadow of the Glen;' here is the 'ghost on horseback' and the finding of the young man's body of 'Riders to the Sea,' numberless ways of speech and vehement pictures that had seemed to owe nothing to observation, and all to some overflowing of himself, or to some mere necessity of dramatic construction. I had thought the violent quarrels of 'The Well of the Saints' came from his love of bitter condiments, but here is a couple that quarrel all day long amid neighbours who gather as for a play. I had defended the burning of Christy Mahon's leg on the ground that an artist need but make his characters self-consistent, and yet, that too was observation, for 'although these people are kindly towards each other and their children, they have no sympathy for the suffering of animals, and little sympathy for pain when the person who feels it is not in danger.' I had thought it was in the wantonness of fancy Martin Dhoul accused the smith of plucking his living ducks, but a few lines further on, in this book where moral indignation is unknown, I read, 'Sometimes when I go into a cottage, I find all the women of the place down on their knees plucking the feathers from live ducks and geese.'

He loves all that has edge, all that is salt in the mouth, all that is rough to the hand, all that heightens the emotions by contest, all that stings into life the sense of tragedy; and in this book, unlike the plays where nearness to his audience moves him to mischief, he shows it without thought of

163

other taste than his. It is so constant, it is all set out so simply, so naturally, that it suggests a correspondence between a lasting mood of the soul and this life that shares the harshness of rocks and wind. The food of the spiritual-minded is sweet, an Indian scripture says, but passionate minds love bitter food. Yet he is no indifferent observer, but is certainly kind and sympathetic to all about him. When an old and ailing man, dreading the coming winter, cries at his leaving, not thinking to see him again; and he notices that the old man's mitten has a hole in it where the palm is accustomed to the stick, one knows that it is with eyes full of interested affection as befits a simple man and not in the curiosity of study. When he had left the Blaskets for the last time, he travelled with a lame pensioner who had drifted there, why heaven knows, and one morning having missed him from the inn where they were staying, he believed he had gone back to the island and searched everywhere and questioned everybody, till he understood of a sudden that he was jealous as though the island were a woman.

The book seems dull if you read much at a time, as the later Kerry essays do not, but nothing that he has written recalls so completely to my senses the man as he was in daily life; and as I read, there are moments when every line of his face, every inflection of his voice, grows so clear in memory that I cannot realize that he is dead. He was no nearer when we walked and talked than now while I read these unarranged, unspeculating pages, wherein the only life he loved with his whole heart reflects itself as in the still water of a pool. Thought comes to him slowly, and only after long seemingly unmeditative watching, and when it comes, (and he had the same character in matters of business) it is spoken without hesitation and never changed. His conversation was not an experimental thing, an instrument of research, and this made him silent; while his essays recall events, on which one feels that he pronounces no judgment even in the depth of his own mind, because the labour of Life itself had not yet brought the philosophic generalization, which was almost as much his object as the emotional generalization of beauty. A mind that generalizes rapidly, continually prevents the experience that would have made it feel and see deeply, just as a man whose character is too complete in

164

youth seldom grows into any energy of moral beauty. Synge had indeed no obvious ideals, as these are understood by young men, and even as I think disliked them, for he once complained to me that our modern poetry was but the poetry 'of the lyrical boy,' and this lack makes his art have a strange wildness and coldness, as of a man born in some far-off spacious land and time.

XI

There are artists like Byron, like Goethe, like Shelley, who have impressive personalities, active wills and all their faculties at the service of the will; but he belonged to those who like Wordsworth, like Coleridge, like Goldsmith, like Keats, have little personality, so far as the casual eye can see, little personal will, but fiery and brooding imagination. I cannot imagine him anxious to impress, or convince in any company, or saying more than was sufficient to keep the talk circling. Such men have the advantage that all they write is a part of knowledge, but they are powerless before events and have often but one visible strength, the strength to reject from life and thought all that would mar their work, or deafen them in the doing of it; and only this so long as it is a passive act. If Synge had married young or taken some profession, I doubt if he would have written books or been greatly interested in a movement like ours; but he refused various opportunities of making money in what must have been an almost unconscious preparation. He had no life outside his imagination, little interest in anything that was not its chosen subject. He hardly seemed aware of the existence of other writers. I never knew if he cared for work of mine, and do not remember that I had from him even a conventional compliment, and yet he had the most perfect modesty and simplicity in daily intercourse, self-assertion was impossible to him. On the other hand, he was useless amidst sudden events. He was much shaken by the Playboy riot; on the first night confused and excited, knowing not what to do, and ill before many days, but it made no difference in his work. He neither exaggerated out of defiance nor softened out of timidity. He wrote on as if nothing had happened, altering

'The Tinker's Wedding' to a more unpopular form, but writing a beautiful serene 'Deirdre,' with, for the first time since his 'Riders to the Sea,' no touch of sarcasm or defiance. Misfortune shook his physical nature while it left his intellect and his moral nature untroubled. The external self, the mask, the persona was a shadow, character was all.

XII

He was a drifting silent man full of hidden passion, and loved wild islands, because there, set out in the light of day, he saw what lay hidden in himself. There is passage after passage in which he dwells upon some moment of excitement. He describes the shipping of pigs at Kilronan on the North Island for the English market: 'when the steamer was getting near, the whole drove was moved down upon the slip and the curraghs were carried out close to the sea. Then each beast was caught in its turn and thrown on its side, while its legs were hitched together in a single knot, with a tag of rope remaining, by which it could be carried.

Probably the pain inflicted was not great, yet the animals shut their eyes and shrieked with almost human intonations, till the suggestion of the noise became so intense that the men and women who were merely looking on grew wild with excitement, and the pigs waiting their turn foamed at the mouth and tore each other with their teeth.

After a while there was a pause. The whole slip was covered with a mass of sobbing animals, with here and there a terrified woman crouching among the bodies and patting some special favourite, to keep it quiet while the curraghs were being launched. Then the screaming began again while the pigs were carried out and laid in their places, with a waistcoat tied round their feet to keep them from damaging the canvas. They seemed to know where they were going, and looked up at me over the gunnel with an ignoble desperation that made me shudder to think that I had eaten this whimpering flesh. When the last curragh went out, I was left on the slip with a band of women and children, and one old boar who sat looking out over the sea.

The women were over-excited, and when I tried to talk to them they crowded round me and began jeering and shrieking at me because I am not married. A dozen screamed at a time, and so rapidly that I could not understand all they were saying, yet I was able to make out that they were taking advantage of the absence of their husbands to give me the full volume of their contempt. Some little boys who were listening threw themselves down, writhing with laughter among the sea-weed, and the young girls grew red and embarrassed and stared down in the surf.' The book is full of such scenes. Now it is a crowd going by train to the Parnell celebration, now it is a woman cursing her son who made himself a spy for the police, now it is an old woman keening at a funeral. Kindred to his delight in the harsh grey stones, in the hardship of the life there, in the wind and in the mist, there is always delight in every moment of excitement, whether it is but the hysterical excitement of the women over the pigs, or some primary passion. Once indeed, the hidden passion instead of finding expression by its choice among the passions of others, shows itself in the most direct way of all, that of dream. 'Last night,' he writes, at Innismaan, 'after walking in a dream among buildings with strangely intense light on them, I heard a faint rhythm of music beginning far away on some stringed instrument.

It came closer to me, gradually increasing in quickness and volume with an irresistibly definite progression. When it was quite near the sound began to move in my nerves and blood, to urge me to dance with them.

I knew that if I yielded I would be carried away into some moment of terrible agony, so I struggled to remain quiet, holding my knees together with my hands.

The music increased continually, sounding like the strings of harps tuned to a forgotten scale, and having a resonance as searching as the strings of the 'cello.

Then the luring excitement became more powerful than my will, and my limbs moved in spite of me.

In a moment I was swept away in a whirlwind of notes. My breath and my thoughts and every impulse of my body became a form of the dance, till I could not distinguish between the instrument or the rhythm and my own person or consciousness. For a while it seemed an excitement that was filled with joy; then it grew into an ecstasy where all existence was lost in the vortex of movement. I could not think that there had been a life beyond the whirling of the dance.

Then with a shock, the ecstasy turned to agony and rage. I struggled to free myself but seemed only to increase the passion of the steps I moved to. When I shrieked I could only echo the notes of the rhythm. At last, with a movement of uncontrollable frenzy I broke back to consciousness and awoke.

I dragged myself trembling to the window of the cottage and looked out. The moon was glittering across the bay and there was no sound anywhere on the island.'

XIII

In all drama which would give direct expression to reverie, to the speech of the soul with itself, there is some device that checks the rapidity of dialogue. When Oedipus speaks out of the most vehement passions, he is conscious of the presence of the chorus, men before whom he must keep up appearances 'children latest born of Cadmus' line' who do not share his passion. Nobody is hurried or breathless. We listen to reports and discuss them, taking part as it were in a council of state. Nothing happens before our eyes. The dignity of Greek drama, and in a lesser degree of that of Corneille and Racine depends, as contrasted with the troubled life of Shakespearean drama, on an almost even speed of dialogue, and on a so continuous exclusion of the animation of common life, that thought remains lofty and language rich. Shakespeare, upon whose stage everything may happen, even the blinding of Gloster, and who has no formal check except what is implied in the slow, elaborate structure of blank verse, obtains time for reverie by an often encumbering Euphuism, and by such a loosening of his plot as will give his characters the leisure to look at life from without. Maeterlinck, to name the first modern of the old way who comes to mind—reaches the same end, by choosing instead of human beings persons who are as faint as a breath upon a looking-glass, symbols who can speak a language slow and heavy with dreams because their own life is but a dream. Modern drama, on the other hand, which accepts the tightness of the classic plot, while expressing life directly, has been driven to make indirect its expression of the mind, which it leaves to be inferred from some common-place sentence or gesture as we infer it in ordinary life; and this is, I believe, the cause of the perpetual disappointment of the hope imagined this hundred years that France or Spain or Germany or Scandinavia will at last produce the master we await.

The divisions in the arts are almost all in the first instance technical, and the great schools of drama have been divided from one another by the form or the metal of their mirror, by the check chosen for the rapidity of dialogue. Synge found the check that suited his temperament in an elaboration of the dialects of Kerry and Aran. The cadence is long and meditative, as befits the thought of men who are much alone, and who when they meet in one another's houses—as their way is at the day's end—listen patiently, each man speaking in turn and for some little time, and taking pleasure in the vaguer meaning of the words and in their sound. Their thought, when not merely practical, is as full of traditional wisdom and extravagant pictures as that of some Aeschylean chorus, and no matter what the topic is, it is as though the present were held at arms length. It is the reverse of rhetoric, for the speaker serves his own delight, though doubtless he would tell you that like Raftery's whiskey-drinking it was but for the company's sake. A medicinal manner of speech too, for it could not even express, so little abstract it is and so rammed with life, those worn generalizations of national propaganda. 'I'll be telling you the finest story you'd hear any place from Dundalk to Ballinacree with great queens in it, making themselves matches from the start to the end, and they with shiny silks on them . . . I've a grand story of the great queens of Ireland, with white necks on them the like of Sarah Casey, and fine arms would hit you a slap . . . What good am I this night, God help me? What good are the grand stories I have when it's few would listen to an old woman, few but a girl maybe would be in great fear the time her hour was come, or a little child wouldn't be sleeping with the hunger on a cold night.' That has the flavour of Homer, of the Bible, of Villon, while Cervantes would have thought it sweet in the mouth though not his food. This use of Irish dialect for noble purpose by Synge, and by Lady Gregory, who had it already in her Cuchulain of Muirthemne, and by Dr. Hyde in those first translations he has not equalled since, has done much for National dignity. When I was a boy I was often troubled and sorrowful because Scottish dialect was capable of noble use, but the Irish of obvious roystering humour only; and this error fixed on my imagination by so many novelists and rhymers made me listen badly. Synge wrote down words and phrases wherever he went, and with that knowledge of Irish which made all our country idioms easy to his hand, found it so rich a thing, that he had begun translating into it fragments of the great literatures of the world, and had planned a complete version of the Imitation of Christ. It gave him imaginative richness and yet left to him the sting and tang of reality. How vivid in his translation from Villon are those 'eyes with a big gay look out of them would bring folly from a great scholar.' More vivid surely than anything in Swinburne's version, and how noble those words which are yet simple country speech, in which his Petrarch mourns that death came upon Laura just as time was making chastity easy, and the day come when 'lovers may sit together and say out all things arc in their hearts,' and 'my sweet enemy was making a start, little by little, to give over her great wariness, the way she was wringing a sweet thing out of my sharp sorrow.'

XIV

Once when I had been saying that though it seemed to me that a conventional descriptive passage encumbered the action at the moment of crisis. I liked 'The Shadow of the Glen' better than 'Riders to the Sea' that is, for all the nobility of its end, its mood of Greek tragedy, too passive in suffering; and had quoted from Matthew Arnold's introduction to 'Empedocles on Etna,' Synge answered, 'It is a curious thing that "The Riders to the Sea" succeeds with an English but not with an Irish audience, and "The Shadow of the Glen" which is not liked by an English audience is always liked in Ireland, though it is disliked there in theory.' Since then 'The Riders to the Sea' has grown into great popularity in Dublin, partly because with the tactical instinct of an Irish mob, the demonstrators against 'The Playboy' both in the press and in the theatre, where it began the evening, selected it for applause. It is now what Shelley's 'Cloud' was for many years, a comfort to those who do not like to deny altogether the genius they cannot understand. Yet I am certain that, in the long run, his grotesque plays with their lyric beauty, their violent laughter, 'The Playboy of the Western World' most of all, will be loved for holding so much of the mind of Ireland. Synge has written of 'The Playboy' 'anyone who has lived in real intimacy with the Irish peasantry will know that the wildest sayings in this play are tame indeed compared with the fancies one may hear at any little hillside cottage of Geesala, or Carraroe, or Dingle Bay.' It is the strangest, the most beautiful expression in drama of that Irish fantasy, which overflowing through all Irish Literature that has come out of Ireland itself (compare the fantastic Irish account of the Battle of Clontarf with the sober Norse account) is the unbroken character of Irish genius. In modern days this genius has delighted in mischievous extravagance, like that of the Gaelic poet's curse upon his children, 'There are three things that I hate, the devil that is waiting for my soul, the worms that are waiting for my body, my children, who are waiting for my wealth and care neither for my body nor my soul: Oh, Christ hang all in the same noose!' I think those words were spoken with a delight in their vehemence that took out of anger half the bitterness with all the gloom. An old man on the Aran Islands told me the very tale on which 'The Playboy' is founded, beginning with the words, 'If any gentleman has done a crime we'll hide him. There was a gentleman that killed his father, & I had him in my own house six months till he got away to America.' Despite the solemnity of his slow speech his eyes shone as the eyes must have shone in that Trinity College branch of the Gaelic League, which began every meeting with prayers for the death of an old Fellow of College who disliked their movement, or as they certainly do when patriots are telling how short a time the prayers took to the killing of him. I have seen a crowd, when certain Dublin papers had wrought themselves into an imaginary loyalty, so possessed by what seemed the very genius of satiric fantasy, that one all but looked to find some feathered heel among the cobble stones. Part of the delight of crowd or individual is always that somebody will be angry, somebody take the sport for gloomy earnest. We are mocking at his solemnity, let us therefore so hide our malice that he may be more solemn still, and the laugh run higher yet. Why should we speak his language and so wake him from a dream of all those emotions which men feel because they should, and not because they must? Our minds, being sufficient to themselves, do not wish for victory but are content to elaborate our extravagance, if fortune aid, into wit or lyric beauty, and as for the rest 'There are nights when a king like Conchobar would spit upon his arm-ring and queens will stick out their tongues at the rising moon.' This habit of the mind has made Oscar Wilde and Mr. Bernard Shaw the most celebrated makers of comedy to our time, and if it has sounded plainer still in the conversation of the one, and in some few speeches of the other, that is but because they have not been able to turn out of their plays an alien trick of zeal picked up in struggling youth. Yet, in Synge's plays also, fantasy gives the form and not the thought, for the core is always as in all great art, an over-powering vision of certain virtues, and our capacity for sharing in that vision is the measure of our delight. Great art chills us at first by its coldness or its strangeness, by what seems capricious, and yet it is from these qualities it has authority, as though it had fed on locust and wild honey. The imaginative writer shows us the world as a painter does his picture, reversed in a looking-glass that we may see it, not as it seems to eyes habit has made dull, but as we were Adam and this the first morning; and when the new image becomes as little strange as the old we shall stay with him, because he has, beside the strangeness, not strange to him, that made us share his vision, sincerity that makes us share his feeling.

To speak of one's emotions without fear or moral ambition, to come out from under the shadow of other men's minds, to forget their needs, to be utterly oneself, that is all the Muses care for. Villon, pander, thief, and man-slayer, is as immortal in their eyes, and illustrates in the cry of his ruin as great a truth as Dante in abstract ecstasy, and touches our compassion more. All art is the disengaging of a soul from place and history, its suspension in a beautiful or terrible light, to await the Judgement, and yet, because all its days were a Last Day, judged already. It may show the crimes of Italy as Dante did, or Greek mythology like Keats, or Kerry and Galway villages, and so vividly that ever after I shall look at all with like eyes, and yet I know that Cino da Pistoia thought Dante unjust, that Keats knew no Greek, that those country men and women are neither so lovable nor so lawless as 'mine author sung it me;' that I have added to my being, not my knowledge.

XV

I wrote the most of these thoughts in my diary on the coast of Normandy, and as I finished came upon Mont Saint Michel, and thereupon doubted for a day the foundation of my school. Here I saw the places of assembly, those cloisters on the rock's summit, the church, the great halls where monks, or knights, or men at arms sat at meals, beautiful from ornament or proportion. I remembered ordinances of the Popes forbidding drinking-cups with stems of gold to these monks who had but a bare dormitory to sleep in. Even when imagining, the individual had taken more from his fellows and his fathers than he gave; one man finishing what another had begun; and all that majestic fantasy, seeming more of Egypt than of Christendom, spoke nothing to the solitary soul, but seemed to announce whether past or yet to come an heroic temper of social men, a bondage of adventure and of wisdom. Then I thought more patiently and I saw that what had made these but as one and given them for a thousand years the miracles of their shrine and temporal rule by land and sea, was not a condescension to knave or dolt, an impoverishment of the common thought to make it serviceable and easy, but a dead language and a communion in whatever, even to the greatest saint, is of incredible difficulty. Only by the substantiation of the soul I thought, whether in literature or in sanctity, can we come upon those agreements, those separations from all else that fasten men together lastingly; for while a popular and picturesque Burns and Scott can but create a province, and our Irish cries and grammars serve some passing need, Homer, Shakespeare, Dante, Goethe and all who travel in their road with however poor a stride, define races and create everlasting loyalties. Synge, like all of the great kin, sought for the race, not through the eyes or in history, or even in the future, but where those monks found God, in the depths of the mind, and in all art like his, although it does not command—indeed because it does not—may lie the roots of far-branching events. Only that which does not teach, which does not cry out, which does not persuade, which does not condescend, which does not explain is irresistible. It is made by men who expressed themselves to the full, and it works through the best minds; whereas the external and picturesque and declamatory writers, that they may create kilts and bagpipes and newspapers and guide-books, leave the best minds empty, and in Ireland and Scotland England runs into the hole. It has no array of arguments and maxims, because the great and the simple (and the Muses have never known which of the two most pleases them) need their deliberate thought for the day's work, and yet will do it worse if they have not grown into or found about them, most perhaps in the minds of women, the nobleness of emotion, associated with the scenery and events of their country, by those great poets, who have dreamed it in solitude, and who to this day in Europe are creating indestructible spiritual races, like those religion has created in the East.

W. B. Yeats.
September 14th. 1910.

* * * * *

WITH SYNGE IN CONNEMARA

I had often spent a day walking with John Synge, but a year or two ago I travelled for a month alone through the west of Ireland with him. He was the best companion for a roadway any one could have, always ready and always the same; a bold walker, up hill and down dale, in the hot sun and the pelting rain. I remember a deluge on the Erris Peninsula, where we lay among the sand hills and at his suggestion heaped sand upon ourselves to try and keep dry.

When we started on our journey, as the train steamed out of Dublin, Synge said: 'Now the elder of us two should be in command on this trip.' So we compared notes and I found that he was two months older than myself. So he was boss and whenever it was a question whether we should take the road to the west or the road to the south, it was Synge who finally decided.

Synge was fond of little children and animals. I remember how glad he was to stop and lean on a wall in Gorumna and watch a woman in afield shearing a sheep. It was an old sheep and must have often been sheared before by the same hand, for the woman hardly held it; she just knelt beside it and snipped away. I remember the sheep raised its lean old head to look at the stranger, and the woman just put her hand on its cheek and gently pressed its head down on the grass again.

Synge was delighted with the narrow paths made of sods of grass alongside the newly-metalled roads, because he thought they had been put there to make soft going for the bare feet of little children. Children knew, I think, that he wished them well. In Bellmullet on Saint John's eve, when we stood in the market square watching the fire-play, flaming sods of turf soaked in paraffine, hurled to the sky and caught and skied again, and burning snakes of hay-rope, I remember a little girl in the crowd, in an ecstasy of pleasure and dread, clutched Synge by the hand and stood close in his shadow until the fiery games were done.

His knowledge of Gaelic was a great assistance to him in talking to the people. I remember him holding a great conversation in Irish and English with an innkeeper's wife in a Mayo inn. She had lived in America in Lincoln's day. She told us what living cost in America then, and of her life there; her little old husband sitting by and putting in an odd word. By the way, the husband was a wonderful gentle-mannered man, for we had luncheon in his house of biscuits and porter, and rested there an hour, waiting for a heavy shower to blow away; and when we said good-bye and our feet were actually on the road, Synge said, 'Did we pay for what we had?' So I called back to the innkeeper, 'Did we pay you?' and he said quietly, 'Not yet sir.'

Synge was always delighted to hear and remember any good phrase. I remember his delight at the words of a local politician who told us how he became a Nationalist. 'I was,' he said plucking a book from the mantlepiece (I remember the book—it was 'Paul and Virginia') and clasping it to his breast—'I was but a little child with my little book going to school, and by the house there I saw the agent. He took the unfortunate tenant and thrun him in the road, and I saw the man's wife come out crying and the agent's wife thrun her in the channel, and when I saw that, though I was but a child, I swore I'd be a Nationalist. I swore by heaven, and I swore by hell and all the rivers that run through them.'

Synge must have read a great deal at one time, but he was not a man you would see often with a book in his hand; he would sooner talk, or rather listen to talk—almost anyone's talk.

Synge was always ready to go anywhere with one, and when there to enjoy what came. He went with me to see an ordinary melodrama at the Queen's Theatre, Dublin, and he delighted to see how the members of the company could by the vehemence of their movements and the resources of their voices hold your attention on a play where everything was commonplace. He enjoyed seeing the contrite villain of the piece come up from the bottom of the gulch, hurled there by the adventuress, and flash his sweating blood-stained face up against the footlights; and, though he told us he had but a few short moments to live, roar his contrition with the voice of a bull.

Synge had travelled a great deal in Italy in tracks he beat out for himself, and in Germany and in France, but he only occasionally spoke to me about these places. I think the Irish peasant had all his heart. He loved them in the east as well as he loved them in the west, but the western men on the Aran Islands and in the Blaskets fitted in with his humour more than any; the wild things they did and said were a joy to him.

Synge was by spirit well equipped for the roads. Though his health was often bad, he had beating under his ribs a brave heart that carried him over rough tracks. He gathered about him very little gear, and cared nothing for comfort except perhaps that of a good turf fire. He was, though young in years, 'an old dog for a hard road and not a young pup for a tow-path.'

He loved mad scenes. He told me how once at the fair of Tralee he saw an old tinker-woman taken by the police, and she was struggling with them in the centre of the fair; when suddenly, as if her garments were held together with one cord, she hurled every shred of clothing from her, ran down the street and screamed, 'let this be the barrack yard,' which was perfectly understood by the crowd as suggesting that the police strip and beat their prisoners when they get them shut in, in the barrack yard. The young men laughed, but the old men hurried after the naked fleeting figure trying to throw her clothes on her as she ran.

But all wild sights appealed to Synge, he did not care whether they were typical of anything else or had any symbolical meaning at all. If he had lived in the days of piracy he would have been the fiddler in a pirate-schooner, him they called 'the music—' 'The music' looked on at every thing with dancing eyes but drew no sword, and when the schooner was taken and the pirates hung at Cape Corso Castle or The Island of Saint Christopher's, 'the music' was spared because he *was* 'the music.'

Jack B. Yeats

THE CELTIC TWILIGHT

Time drops in decay
Like a candle burnt out.
And the mountains and woods
Have their day, have their day;
But, kindly old rout
Of the fire-born moods,
You pass not away.

THE HOSTING OF THE SIDHE

The host is riding from Knocknarea,
And over the grave of Clooth-na-bare;
Caolte tossing his burning hair,
And Niamh calling, "Away, come away;
Empty your heart of its mortal dream.
The winds awaken, the leaves whirl round,
Our cheeks are pale, our hair is unbound,
Our breasts are heaving, our eyes are a-gleam,
Our arms are waving, our lips are apart,
And if any gaze on our rushing band,
We come between him and the deed of his hand,
We come between him and the hope of his heart."
The host is rushing 'twixt night and day;
And where is there hope or deed as fair?
Caolte tossing his burning hair,
And Niamh calling, "Away, come away."

THIS BOOK

I

I have desired, like every artist, to create a little world out of the beautiful, pleasant, and significant things of this marred and clumsy world, and to show in a vision something of the face of Ireland to any of my own people who would look where I bid them. I have therefore written down accurately and candidly much that I have heard and seen, and, except by way of commentary, nothing that I have merely imagined. I have, however, been at no pains to separate my own beliefs from those of the peasantry, but have rather let my men and women, dhouls and faeries, go their way unoffended or defended by any argument of mine. The things a man has heard and seen are threads of life, and if he pull them carefully from the confused distaff of memory, any who will can weave them into whatever garments of belief please them best. I too have woven my garment like another, but I shall try to keep warm in it, and shall be well content if it do not unbecome me.

Hope and Memory have one daughter and her name is Art, and she has built her dwelling far from the desperate field where men hang out their garments upon forked boughs to be banners of battle. O beloved daughter of Hope and Memory, be with me for a little.

1893.

185

II

I have added a few more chapters in the manner of the old ones, and would have added others, but one loses, as one grows older, something of the lightness of one's dreams; one begins to take life up in both hands, and to care more for the fruit than the flower, and that is no great loss per haps. In these new chapters, as in the old ones, I have invented nothing but my comments and one or two deceitful sentences that may keep some poor story-teller's commerce with the devil and his angels, or the like, from being known among his neighbours. I shall publish in a little while a big book about the commonwealth of faery, and shall try to make it systematical and learned enough to buy pardon for this handful of dreams.

1902.
W. B. YEATS.

A TELLER OF TALES

Many of the tales in this book were told me by one Paddy Flynn, a little bright-eyed old man, who lived in a leaky and one-roomed cabin in the village of Ballisodare, which is, he was wont to say, "the most gentle"—whereby he meant faery—"place in the whole of County Sligo." Others hold it, however, but second to Drumcliff and Drumahair. The first time I saw him he was cooking mushrooms for himself; the next time he was asleep under a hedge, smiling in his sleep. He was indeed always cheerful, though I thought I could see in his eyes (swift as the eyes of a rabbit, when they peered out of their wrinkled holes) a melancholy which was well-nigh a portion of their joy; the visionary melancholy of purely instinctive natures and of all animals.

And yet there was much in his life to depress him, for in the triple solitude of age, eccentricity, and deafness, he went about much pestered by children. It was for this very reason perhaps that he ever recommended mirth and hopefulness. He was fond, for instance, of telling how Collumcille cheered up his mother. "How are you to-day, mother?" said the saint. "Worse," replied the mother. "May you be worse to-morrow," said the saint. The next day Collumcille came again, and exactly the same conversation took place, but the third day the mother said, "Better, thank God." And the saint replied, "May you be better to-morrow." He was fond too of telling how the Judge smiles at the last day alike when he rewards the good and condemns the lost to unceasing flames. He had many strange sights to keep him cheerful or to make him sad. I asked him had he ever seen the faeries, and got the reply, "Am I not annoyed with them?" I asked too if he had ever seen the banshee. "I have seen it," he said, "down there by the water, batting the river with its hands."

I have copied this account of Paddy Flynn, with a few verbal alterations, from a note-book which I almost filled with his tales and sayings, shortly after seeing him. I look now at the note-book regretfully, for the blank pages at the end will never be filled up. Paddy Flynn is dead; a friend of mine gave him a large bottle of whiskey, and though a sober man at most times, the sight of so much liquor filled him with a great enthusiasm, and he lived upon it for some days and then died. His body, worn out with old age and hard times, could not bear the drink as in his young days. He was a great teller of tales, and unlike our common romancers, knew how to empty heaven, hell, and purgatory, faeryland and earth, to people his stories. He did not live in a shrunken world, but knew of no less ample circumstance than did Homer himself. Perhaps the Gaelic people shall by his like bring back again the ancient simplicity and amplitude of imagination. What is literature but the expression of moods by the vehicle of symbol and incident? And are there not moods which need heaven, hell, purgatory, and faeryland for their expression, no less than this dilapidated earth? Nay, are there not moods which shall find no expression unless there be men who dare to mix heaven, hell, purgatory, and faeryland together, or even to set the heads of beasts to the bodies of men, or to thrust the souls of men into the heart of rocks? Let us go forth, the tellers of tales, and seize whatever prey the heart long for, and have no fear. Everything exists, everything is true, and the earth is only a little dust under our feet.

BELIEF AND UNBELIEF

There are some doubters even in the western villages. One woman told me last Christmas that she did not believe either in hell or in ghosts. Hell she thought was merely an invention got up by the priest to keep people good; and ghosts would not be permitted, she held, to go "trapsin about the earth" at their own free will; "but there are faeries," she added, "and little leprechauns, and water-horses, and fallen angels." I have met also a man with a mohawk Indian tattooed upon his arm, who held exactly similar beliefs and unbeliefs. No matter what one doubts one never doubts the faeries, for, as the man with the mohawk Indian on his arm said to me, "they stand to reason." Even the official mind does not escape this faith.

A little girl who was at service in the village of Grange, close under the seaward slopes of Ben Bulben, suddenly disappeared one night about three years ago. There was at once great excitement in the neighbourhood, because it was rumoured that the faeries had taken her. A villager was said to have long struggled to hold her from them, but at last they prevailed, and he found nothing in his hands but a broomstick. The local constable was applied to, and he at once instituted a house-to-house search, and at the same time advised the people to burn all the bucalauns (ragweed) on the field she vanished from, because bucalauns are sacred to the faeries. They spent the whole night burning them, the constable repeating spells the while. In the morning the little girl was found, the story goes, wandering in the field. She said the faeries had taken her away a great distance, riding on a faery horse. At last she saw a big river, and the man who had tried to keep her from being carried off was drifting down it—such are the topsy-turvydoms of faery glamour—in a cockleshell. On the way her companions had mentioned the names of several people who were about to die shortly in the village.

Perhaps the constable was right. It is better doubtless to believe much unreason and a little truth than to deny for denial's sake truth and unreason alike, for when we do this we have not even a rush candle to guide our steps, not even a poor sowlth to dance before us on the marsh, and must needs fumble our way into the great emptiness where dwell the mis-shapen dhouls. And after all, can we come to so great evil if we keep a little fire on our hearths and in our souls, and welcome with open hand whatever of excellent come to warm itself, whether it be man or phantom, and do not say too fiercely, even to the dhouls themselves, "Be ye gone"? When all is said and done, how do we not know but that our own unreason may be better than another's truth? for it has been warmed on our hearths and in our souls, and is ready for the wild bees of truth to hive in it, and make their sweet honey. Come into the world again, wild bees, wild bees!

MORTAL HELP

One hears in the old poems of men taken away to help the gods in a battle, and Cuchullan won the goddess Fand for a while, by helping her married sister and her sister's husband to overthrow another nation of the Land of Promise. I have been told, too, that the people of faery cannot even play at hurley unless they have on either side some mortal, whose body, or whatever has been put in its place, as the story-teller would say, is asleep at home. Without mortal help they are shadowy and cannot even strike the balls. One day I was walking over some marshy land in Galway with a friend when we found an old, hard-featured man digging a ditch. My friend had heard that this man had seen a wonderful sight of some kind, and at last we got the story out of him. When he was a boy he was working one day with about thirty men and women and boys. They were beyond Tuam and not far from Knock-na-gur. Presently they saw, all thirty of them, and at a distance of about half-a-mile, some hundred and fifty of the people of faery. There were two of them, he said, in dark clothes like people of our own time, who stood about a hundred yards from one another, but the others wore clothes of all colours, "bracket" or chequered, and some with red waistcoats.

He could not see what they were doing, but all might have been playing hurley, for "they looked as if it was that." Sometimes they would vanish, and then he would almost swear they came back out of the bodies of the two men in dark clothes. These two men were of the size of living men, but the others were small. He saw them for about half-an-hour, and then the old man he and those about him were working for took up a whip and said, "Get on, get on, or we will have no work done!" I asked if he saw the faeries too, "Oh, yes, but he did not want work he was paying wages for to be neglected." He made every body work so hard that nobody saw what happened to the faeries.

1902.

A VISIONARY

A young man came to see me at my lodgings the other night, and began to talk of the making of the earth and the heavens and much else. I questioned him about his life and his doings. He had written many poems and painted many mystical designs since we met last, but latterly had neither written nor painted, for his whole heart was set upon making his mind strong, vigorous, and calm, and the emotional life of the artist was bad for him, he feared. He recited his poems readily, however. He had them all in his memory. Some indeed had never been written down. They, with their wild music as of winds blowing in the reeds,[1] seemed to me the very inmost voice of Celtic sadness, and of Celtic longing for infinite things the world has never seen. Suddenly it seemed to me that he was peering about him a little eagerly. "Do you see anything, X——?" I said. "A shining, winged woman, covered by her long hair, is standing near the doorway," he answered, or some such words. "Is it the influence of some living person who thinks of us, and whose thoughts appear to us in that symbolic form?" I said; for I am well instructed in the ways of the visionaries and in the fashion of their speech. "No," he replied; "for if it were the thoughts of a person who is alive I should feel the living influence in my living body, and my heart would beat and my breath

---

1 I wrote this sentence long ago. This sadness now seems to me a part of all peoples who preserve the moods of the ancient peoples of the world. I am not so pre-occupied with the mystery of Race as I used to be, but leave this sentence and other sentences like it unchanged. We once believed them, and have, it may be, not grown wiser.

would fail. It is a spirit. It is some one who is dead or who has never lived."

I asked what he was doing, and found he was clerk in a large shop. His pleasure, however, was to wander about upon the hills, talking to half-mad and visionary peasants, or to persuade queer and conscience-stricken persons to deliver up the keeping of their troubles into his care. Another night, when I was with him in his own lodging, more than one turned up to talk over their beliefs and disbeliefs, and sun them as it were in the subtle light of his mind. Sometimes visions come to him as he talks with them, and he is rumoured to have told divers people true matters of their past days and distant friends, and left them hushed with dread of their strange teacher, who seems scarce more than a boy, and is so much more subtle than the oldest among them.

The poetry he recited me was full of his nature and his visions. Sometimes it told of other lives he believes himself to have lived in other centuries, sometimes of people he had talked to, revealing them to their own minds. I told him I would write an article upon him and it, and was told in turn that I might do so if I did not mention his name, for he wished to be always "unknown, obscure, impersonal." Next day a bundle of his poems arrived, and with them a note in these words: "Here are copies of verses you said you liked. I do not think I could ever write or paint any more. I prepare myself for a cycle of other activities in some other life. I will make rigid my roots and branches. It is not now my turn to burst into leaves and flowers."

The poems were all endeavours to capture some high, impalpable mood in a net of obscure images. There were fine passages in all, but these were often embedded in thoughts which have evidently a special value to his mind, but are to other men the counters of an unknown coinage. To them they seem merely so much brass or copper or tarnished silver at the best. At other times the beauty of the thought was obscured by careless writing as though he had suddenly doubted if writing was not a foolish labour. He had frequently illustrated his verses with drawings, in which an unperfect anatomy did not altogether hide extreme beauty of feeling. The faeries in whom he believes have given him many subjects, notably Thomas of Ercildoune sitting motionless in the twilight while a young and beautiful creature leans softly out of the shadow and whispers in his ear. He had delighted above all in strong effects of colour: spirits who have upon their heads instead of hair the feathers of peacocks; a phantom reaching from a swirl of flame towards a star; a spirit passing with a globe of iridescent crystal-symbol of the soul-half shut within his hand. But always under this largess of colour lay some tender homily addressed to man's fragile hopes. This spiritual eagerness draws to him all those who, like himself, seek for illumination or else mourn for a joy that has gone. One of these especially comes to mind. A winter or two ago he spent much of the night walking up and down upon the mountain talking to an old peasant who, dumb to most men, poured out his cares for him. Both were unhappy: X—because he had then first decided that art and poetry were not for him, and the old peasant because his life was ebbing out with no achievement remaining and no hope left him. Both how Celtic! how full of striving after a something never to be completely expressed in word or deed. The peasant was wandering in his mind with prolonged sorrow. Once he burst out with "God possesses the heavens—God possesses the heavens—but He covets the world"; and once he lamented that his old neighbours were gone, and that all had forgotten him: they used to draw a chair to the fire for him in every cabin, and now they said, "Who is that old fellow there?" "The fret [Irish for doom] is over me," he repeated, and then went on to talk once more of God and heaven. More than once also he said, waving his arm towards the mountain, "Only myself knows what happened under the thorn-tree forty years ago"; and as he said it the tears upon his face glistened in the moonlight.

This old man always rises before me when I think of X—. Both seek—one in wandering sentences, the other in symbolic pictures and subtle allegoric poetry-to express a something that lies beyond the range

195

of expression; and both, if X——will forgive me, have within them the vast and vague extravagance that lies at the bottom of the Celtic heart. The peasant visionaries that are, the landlord duelists that were, and the whole hurly-burly of legends—Cuchulain fighting the sea for two days until the waves pass over him and he dies, Caolte storming the palace of the gods, Oisin seeking in vain for three hundred years to appease his insatiable heart with all the pleasures of faeryland, these two mystics walking up and down upon the mountains uttering the central dreams of their souls in no less dream-laden sentences, and this mind that finds them so interesting—all are a portion of that great Celtic phantasmagoria whose meaning no man has discovered, nor any angel revealed.

VILLAGE GHOSTS

In the great cities we see so little of the world, we drift into our minority. In the little towns and villages there are no minorities; people are not numerous enough. You must see the world there, perforce. Every man is himself a class; every hour carries its new challenge. When you pass the inn at the end of the village you leave your favourite whimsy behind you; for you will meet no one who can share it. We listen to eloquent speaking, read books and write them, settle all the affairs of the universe. The dumb village multitudes pass on unchanging; the feel of the spade in the hand is no different for all our talk: good seasons and bad follow each other as of old. The dumb multitudes are no more concerned with us than is the old horse peering through the rusty gate of the village pound. The ancient map-makers wrote across unexplored regions, "Here are lions." Across the villages of fishermen and turners of the earth, so different are these from us, we can write but one line that is certain, "Here are ghosts."

My ghosts inhabit the village of H—, in Leinster. History has in no manner been burdened by this ancient village, with its crooked lanes, its old abbey churchyard full of long grass, its green background of small fir-trees, and its quay, where lie a few tarry fishing-luggers. In the annals of entomology it is well known. For a small bay lies westward a little, where he who watches night after night may see a certain rare moth fluttering along the edge of the tide, just at the end of evening or the beginning of dawn. A hundred years ago it was carried here from Italy by smugglers in a cargo of silks and laces. If the moth-hunter would throw down his

197

net, and go hunting for ghost tales or tales of the faeries and such-like children of Lillith, he would have need for far less patience.

To approach the village at night a timid man requires great strategy. A man was once heard complaining, "By the cross of Jesus! how shall I go? If I pass by the hill of Dunboy old Captain Burney may look out on me. If I go round by the water, and up by the steps, there is the headless one and another on the quays, and a new one under the old churchyard wall. If I go right round the other way, Mrs. Stewart is appearing at Hillside Gate, and the devil himself is in the Hospital Lane."

I never heard which spirit he braved, but feel sure it was not the one in the Hospital Lane. In cholera times a shed had been there set up to receive patients. When the need had gone by, it was pulled down, but ever since the ground where it stood has broken out in ghosts and demons and faeries. There is a farmer at H——, Paddy B——by name-a man of great strength, and a teetotaller. His wife and sister-in-law, musing on his great strength, often wonder what he would do if he drank. One night when passing through the Hospital Lane, he saw what he supposed at first to be a tame rabbit; after a little he found that it was a white cat. When he came near, the creature slowly began to swell larger and larger, and as it grew he felt his own strength ebbing away, as though it were sucked out of him. He turned and ran.

By the Hospital Lane goes the "Faeries Path." Every evening they travel from the hill to the sea, from the sea to the hill. At the sea end of their path stands a cottage. One night Mrs. Arbunathy, who lived there, left her door open, as she was expecting her son. Her husband was asleep by the fire; a tall man came in and sat beside him. After he had been sitting there for a while, the woman said, "In the name of God, who are you?" He got up and went out, saying, "Never leave the door open at this hour, or evil may come to you." She woke her husband and told him. "One of the good people has been with us," said he.

Probably the man braved Mrs. Stewart at Hillside Gate. When she lived she was the wife of the Protestant clergyman. "Her ghost was never known to harm any one," say the village people; "it is only doing a penance upon the earth." Not far from Hillside Gate, where she haunted, appeared for a short time a much more remarkable spirit. Its haunt was the bogeen, a green lane leading from the western end of the village. I quote its history at length: a typical village tragedy. In a cottage at the village end of the bogeen lived a house-painter, Jim Montgomery, and his wife. They had several children. He was a little dandy, and came of a higher class than his neighbours. His wife was a very big woman. Her husband, who had been expelled from the village choir for drink, gave her a beating one day. Her sister heard of it, and came and took down one of the window shutters—Montgomery was neat about everything, and had shutters on the outside of every window—and beat him with it, being big and strong like her sister. He threatened to prosecute her; she answered that she would break every bone in his body if he did. She never spoke to her sister again, because she had allowed herself to be beaten by so small a man. Jim Montgomery grew worse and worse: his wife soon began to have not enough to eat. She told no one, for she was very proud. Often, too, she would have no fire on a cold night. If any neighbours came in she would say she had let the fire out because she was just going to bed. The people about often heard her husband beating her, but she never told any one. She got very thin. At last one Saturday there was no food in the house for herself and the children. She could bear it no longer, and went to the priest and asked him for some money. He gave her thirty shillings. Her husband met her, and took the money, and beat her. On the following Monday she got very W, and sent for a Mrs. Kelly. Mrs. Kelly, as soon as she saw her, said, "My woman, you are dying," and sent for the priest and the doctor. She died in an hour. After her death, as Montgomery neglected the children, the landlord had them taken to the workhouse. A few nights after they had gone, Mrs. Kelly was going home through the bogeen when the ghost of Mrs. Montgomery appeared and followed her. It did not leave her until she reached her own house. She told the priest, Father R, a noted antiquarian, and could not get him to believe her. A few nights afterwards Mrs. Kelly again met the spirit in the same place. She was in too great terror to go the whole way, but stopped at a neighbour's cottage midway, and asked them to let her in. They answered they were going to bed. She cried out, "In the name of God let me in, or I will break open the door." They opened, and so she escaped from the ghost. Next day she told the priest again. This time he believed, and said it would follow her until she spoke to it.

She met the spirit a third time in the bogeen. She asked what kept it from its rest. The spirit said that its children must be taken from the workhouse, for none of its relations were ever there before, and that three masses were to be said for the repose of its soul. "If my husband does not believe you," she said, "show him that," and touched Mrs. Kelly's wrist with three fingers. The places where they touched swelled up and blackened. She then vanished. For a time Montgomery would not believe that his wife had appeared: "she would not show herself to Mrs. Kelly," he said—"she with respectable people to appear to." He was convinced by the three marks, and the children were taken from the workhouse. The priest said the masses, and the shade must have been at rest, for it has not since appeared. Some time afterwards Jim Montgomery died in the workhouse, having come to great poverty through drink.

I know some who believe they have seen the headless ghost upon the quay, and one who, when he passes the old cemetery wall at night, sees a woman with white borders to her cap[2] creep out and follow him. The apparition only leaves him at his own door. The villagers imagine that she follows him to avenge some wrong. "I will haunt you when I die" is a favourite threat. His wife was once half-scared to death by what she considers a demon in the shape of a dog.

---

2 I wonder why she had white borders to her cap. The old Mayo woman, who has told me so many tales, has told me that her brother-in-law saw "a woman with white borders to her cap going around the stacks in a field, and soon after he got a hurt, and he died in six months."

These are a few of the open-air spirits; the more domestic of their tribe gather within-doors, plentiful as swallows under southern eaves.

One night a Mrs. Nolan was watching by her dying child in Fluddy's Lane. Suddenly there was a sound of knocking heard at the door. She did not open, fearing it was some unhuman thing that knocked. The knocking ceased. After a little the front-door and then the back-door were burst open, and closed again. Her husband went to see what was wrong. He found both doors bolted. The child died. The doors were again opened and closed as before. Then Mrs. Nolan remembered that she had forgotten to leave window or door open, as the custom is, for the departure of the soul. These strange openings and closings and knockings were warnings and reminders from the spirits who attend the dying.

The house ghost is usually a harmless and well-meaning creature. It is put up with as long as possible. It brings good luck to those who live with it. I remember two children who slept with their mother and sisters and brothers in one small room. In the room was also a ghost. They sold herrings in the Dublin streets, and did not mind the ghost much, because they knew they would always sell their fish easily while they slept in the "ha'nted" room.

I have some acquaintance among the ghost-seers of western villages. The Connaught tales are very different from those of Leinster. These H—spirits have a gloomy, matter-of-fact way with them. They come to announce a death, to fulfil some obligation, to revenge a wrong, to pay their bills even—as did a fisherman's daughter the other day—and then hasten to their rest. All things they do decently and in order. It is demons, and not ghosts, that transform themselves into white cats or black dogs. The people who tell the tales are poor, serious-minded fishing people, who find in the doings of the ghosts the fascination of fear. In the western tales is a whimsical grace, a curious extravagance. The people who recount them live in the most wild and beautiful scenery, under a sky ever loaded and fantastic with flying clouds. They are farmers and labourers, who do a little fishing now and then. They do not fear the spirits too much to feel an artistic and humorous pleasure in their doings. The ghosts themselves share in their quaint hilarity. In one western town, on whose deserted wharf the grass grows, these spirits have so much vigour that, when a misbeliever ventured to sleep in a haunted house, I have been told they flung him through the window, and his bed after him. In the surrounding villages the creatures use the most strange disguises. A dead old gentleman robs the cabbages of his own garden in the shape of a large rabbit. A wicked sea-captain stayed for years inside the plaster of a cottage wall, in the shape of a snipe, making the most horrible noises. He was only dislodged when the wall was broken down; then out of the solid plaster the snipe rushed away whistling.

"DUST HATH CLOSED HELEN'S EYE"

I

I have been lately to a little group of houses, not many enough to be called a village, in the barony of Kiltartan in County Galway, whose name, Ballylee, is known through all the west of Ireland. There is the old square castle, Ballylee, inhabited by a farmer and his wife, and a cottage where their daughter and their son-in-law live, and a little mill with an old miller, and old ash-trees throwing green shadows upon a little river and great stepping-stones. I went there two or three times last year to talk to the miller about Biddy Early, a wise woman that lived in Clare some years ago, and about her saying, "There is a cure for all evil between the two mill-wheels of Ballylee," and to find out from him or another whether she meant the moss between the running waters or some other herb. I have been there this summer, and I shall be there again before it is autumn, because Mary Hynes, a beautiful woman whose name is still a wonder by turf fires, died there sixty years ago; for our feet would linger where beauty has lived its life of sorrow to make us understand that it is not of the world. An old man brought me a little way from the mill and the castle, and down a long, narrow boreen that was nearly lost in brambles and sloe bushes, and he said, "That is the little old foundation of the house, but the most of it is taken for building walls, and the goats have ate those bushes that are growing over it till they've got cranky, and they won't grow any more. They say she was the handsomest girl in Ireland, her skin was like dribbled snow"—he meant driven snow, perhaps,—

"and she had blushes in her cheeks. She had five handsome brothers, but all are gone now!" I talked to him about a poem in Irish, Raftery, a famous poet, made about her, and how it said, "there is a strong cellar in Ballylee." He said the strong cellar was the great hole where the river sank underground, and he brought me to a deep pool, where an otter hurried away under a grey boulder, and told me that many fish came up out of the dark water at early morning "to taste the fresh water coming down from the hills."

I first heard of the poem from an old woman who fives about two miles further up the river, and who remembers Raftery and Mary Hynes. She says, "I never saw anybody so handsome as she was, and I never will till I die," and that he was nearly blind, and had "no way of living but to go round and to mark some house to go to, and then all the neighbours would gather to hear. If you treated him well he'd praise you, but if you did not, he'd fault you in Irish. He was the greatest poet in Ireland, and he'd make a song about that bush if he chanced to stand under it. There was a bush he stood under from the rain, and he made verses praising it, and then when the water came through he made verses dispraising it." She sang the poem to a friend and to myself in Irish, and every word was audible and expressive, as the words in a song were always, as I think, before music grew too proud to be the garment of words, flowing and changing with the flowing and changing of their energies. The poem is not as natural as the best Irish poetry of the last century, for the thoughts are arranged in a too obviously traditional form, so the old poor half-blind man who made it has to speak as if he were a rich farmer offering the best of everything to the woman he loves, but it has naive and tender phrases. The friend that was with me has made some of the translation, but some of it has been made by the country people themselves. I think it has more of the simplicity of the Irish verses than one finds in most translations.

Going to Mass by the will of God,
The day came wet and the wind rose;

I met Mary Hynes at the cross of Kiltartan,
And I fell in love with her then and there.

I spoke to her kind and mannerly,
As by report was her own way;
And she said, "Raftery, my mind is easy,
You may come to-day to Ballylee."

When I heard her offer I did not linger,
When her talk went to my heart my heart rose.
We had only to go across the three fields,
We had daylight with us to Ballylee.

The table was laid with glasses and a quart measure,
She had fair hair, and she sitting beside me;
And she said, "Drink, Raftery, and a hundred welcomes,
There is a strong cellar in Ballylee."

O star of light and O sun in harvest,
O amber hair, O my share of the world,
Will you come with me upon Sunday
Till we agree together before all the people?

I would not grudge you a song every Sunday evening,
Punch on the table, or wine if you would drink it,
But, O King of Glory, dry the roads before me,
Till I find the way to Ballylee.

There is sweet air on the side of the hill
When you are looking down upon Ballylee;
When you are walking in the valley picking nuts and blackberries,
There is music of the birds in it and music of the Sidhe.

What is the worth of greatness till you have the light
Of the flower of the branch that is by your side?
There is no god to deny it or to try and hide it,
She is the sun in the heavens who wounded my heart.

There was no part of Ireland I did not travel,
From the rivers to the tops of the mountains,
To the edge of Lough Greine whose mouth is hidden,
And I saw no beauty but was behind hers.

Her hair was shining, and her brows were shining too;
Her face was like herself, her mouth pleasant and sweet.
She is the pride, and I give her the branch,
She is the shining flower of Ballylee.

It is Mary Hynes, this calm and easy woman,
Has beauty in her mind and in her face.
If a hundred clerks were gathered together,
They could not write down a half of her ways.

An old weaver, whose son is supposed to go away among the Sidhe
(the faeries) at night, says, "Mary Hynes was the most beautiful thing
ever made. My mother used to tell me about her, for she'd be at every
hurling, and wherever she was she was dressed in white. As many as
eleven men asked her in marriage in one day, but she wouldn't have any
of them. There was a lot of men up beyond Kilbecanty one night, sitting
together drinking, and talking of her, and one of them got up and set out
to go to Ballylee and see her; but Cloon Bog was open then, and when
he came to it he fell into the water, and they found him dead there in the
morning. She died of the fever that was before the famine." Another old
man says he was only a child when he saw her, but he remembered that
"the strongest man that was among us, one John Madden, got his death

of the head of her, cold he got crossing rivers in the night-time to get to Ballylee." This is perhaps the man the other remembered, for tradition gives the one thing many shapes. There is an old woman who remembers her, at Derrybrien among the Echtge hills, a vast desolate place, which has changed little since the old poem said, "the stag upon the cold summit of Echtge hears the cry of the wolves," but still mindful of many poems and of the dignity of ancient speech. She says, "The sun and the moon never shone on anybody so handsome, and her skin was so white that it looked blue, and she had two little blushes on her cheeks." And an old wrinkled woman who lives close by Ballylee, and has told me many tales of the Sidhe, says, "I often saw Mary Hynes, she was handsome indeed. She had two bunches of curls beside her cheeks, and they were the colour of silver. I saw Mary Molloy that was drowned in the river beyond, and Mary Guthrie that was in Ardrahan, but she took the sway of them both, a very comely creature. I was at her wake too—she had seen too much of the world. She was a kind creature. One day I was coming home through that field beyond, and I was tired, and who should come out but the Poisin Glegeal (the shining flower), and she gave me a glass of new milk." This old woman meant no more than some beautiful bright colour by the colour of silver, for though I knew an old man—he is dead now—who thought she might know "the cure for all the evils in the world," that the Sidhe knew, she has seen too little gold to know its colour. But a man by the shore at Kinvara, who is too young to remember Mary Hynes, says, "Everybody says there is no one at all to be seen now so handsome; it is said she had beautiful hair, the colour of gold. She was poor, but her clothes every day were the same as Sunday, she had such neatness. And if she went to any kind of a meeting, they would all be killing one another for a sight of her, and there was a great many in love with her, but she died young. It is said that no one that has a song made about them will ever live long."

Those who are much admired are, it is held, taken by the Sidhe, who can use ungoverned feeling for their own ends, so that a father, as an old herb doctor told me once, may give his child into their hands, or a husband his wife. The admired and desired are only safe if one says "God bless them" when one's eyes are upon them. The old woman that sang the song thinks, too, that Mary Hynes was "taken," as the phrase is, "for they have taken many that are not handsome, and why would they not take her? And people came from all parts to look at her, and maybe there were some that did not say 'God bless her.'" An old man who lives by the sea at Duras has as little doubt that she was taken, "for there are some living yet can remember her coming to the pattern[3] there beyond, and she was said to be the handsomest girl in Ireland." She died young because the gods loved her, for the Sidhe are the gods, and it may be that the old saying, which we forget to understand literally, meant her manner of death in old times. These poor countrymen and countrywomen in their beliefs, and in their emotions, are many years nearer to that old Greek world, that set beauty beside the fountain of things, than are our men of learning. She "had seen too much of the world"; but these old men and women, when they tell of her, blame another and not her, and though they can be hard, they grow gentle as the old men of Troy grew gentle when Helen passed by on the walls.

The poet who helped her to so much fame has himself a great fame throughout the west of Ireland. Some think that Raftery was half blind, and say, "I saw Raftery, a dark man, but he had sight enough to see her," or the like, but some think he was wholly blind, as he may have been at the end of his life. Fable makes all things perfect in their kind, and her blind people must never look on the world and the sun. I asked a man I met one day, when I was looking for a pool na mna Sidhe where women of faery have been seen, bow Raftery could have admired Mary Hynes so much f he had been altogether blind? He said, "I think Raftery was altogether blind, but those that are blind have a way of seeing things, and have the power to know more, and to feel more, and to do more, and to guess more than those that have their sight, and a certain wit and a

3 A "pattern," or "patron," is a festival in honour of a saint.

certain wisdom is given to them." Everybody, indeed, will tell you that he was very wise, for was he not only blind but a poet? The weaver whose words about Mary Hynes I have already given, says, "His poetry was the gift of the Almighty, for there are three things that are the gift of the Almighty—poetry and dancing and principles. That is why in the old times an ignorant man coming down from the hillside would be better behaved and have better learning than a man with education you'd meet now, for they got it from God"; and a man at Coole says, "When he put his finger to one part of his head, everything would come to him as if it was written in a book"; and an old pensioner at Kiltartan says, "He was standing under a bush one time, and he talked to it, and it answered him back in Irish. Some say it was the bush that spoke, but it must have been an enchanted voice in it, and it gave him the knowledge of all the things of the world. The bush withered up afterwards, and it is to be seen on the roadside now between this and Rahasine." There is a poem of his about a bush, which I have never seen, and it may have come out of the cauldron of fable in this shape.

A friend of mine met a man once who had been with him when he died, but the people say that he died alone, and one Maurteen Gillane told Dr. Hyde that all night long a light was seen streaming up to heaven from the roof of the house where he lay, and "that was the angels who were with him"; and all night long there was a great light in the hovel, "and that was the angels who were waking him. They gave that honour to him because he was so good a poet, and sang such religious songs." It may be that in a few years Fable, who changes mortalities to immortalities in her cauldron, will have changed Mary Hynes and Raftery to perfect symbols of the sorrow of beauty and of the magnificence and penury of dreams.

1900.

II

When I was in a northern town awhile ago, I had a long talk with a man who had lived in a neighbouring country district when he was a boy. He told me that when a very beautiful girl was born in a family that had not been noted for good looks, her beauty was thought to have come from the Sidhe, and to bring misfortune with it. He went over the names of several beautiful girls that he had known, and said that beauty had never brought happiness to anybody. It was a thing, he said, to be proud of and afraid of. I wish I had written out his words at the time, for they were more picturesque than my memory of them.

1902.

A KNIGHT OF THE SHEEP

Away to the north of Ben Bulben and Cope's mountain lives "a strong farmer," a knight of the sheep they would have called him in the Gaelic days. Proud of his descent from one of the most fighting clans of the Middle Ages, he is a man of force alike in his words and in his deeds. There is but one man that swears like him, and this man lives far away upon the mountain. "Father in Heaven, what have I done to deserve this?" he says when he has lost his pipe; and no man but he who lives on the mountain can rival his language on a fair day over a bargain. He is passionate and abrupt in his movements, and when angry tosses his white beard about with his left hand.

One day I was dining with him when the servant-maid announced a certain Mr. O'Donnell. A sudden silence fell upon the old man and upon his two daughters. At last the eldest daughter said somewhat severely to her father, "Go and ask him to come in and dine." The old man went out, and then came in looking greatly relieved, and said, "He says he will not dine with us." "Go out," said the daughter, "and ask him into the back parlour, and give him some whiskey." Her father, who had just finished his dinner, obeyed sullenly, and I heard the door of the back parlour—a little room where the daughters sat and sewed during the evening—shut to behind the men. The daughter then turned to me and said, "Mr. O'Donnell is the tax-gatherer, and last year he raised our taxes, and my father was very angry, and when he came, brought him into the dairy, and sent the dairy-woman away on a message, and then swore at him a great deal. 'I will teach you, sir,' O'Donnell replied, 'that the law can protect its officers'; but my father reminded him that he had no witness.

At last my father got tired, and sorry too, and said he would show him a short way home. When they were half-way to the main road they came on a man of my father's who was ploughing, and this somehow brought back remembrance of the wrong. He sent the man away on a message, and began to swear at the tax-gatherer again. When I heard of it I was disgusted that he should have made such a fuss over a miserable creature like O'Donnell; and when I heard a few weeks ago that O'Donnell's only son had died and left him heart-broken, I resolved to make my father be kind to him next time he came."

She then went out to see a neighbour, and I sauntered towards the back parlour. When I came to the door I heard angry voices inside. The two men were evidently getting on to the tax again, for I could hear them bandying figures to and fro. I opened the door; at sight of my face the farmer was reminded of his peaceful intentions, and asked me if I knew where the whiskey was. I had seen him put it into the cupboard, and was able therefore to find it and get it out, looking at the thin, grief-struck face of the tax-gatherer. He was rather older than my friend, and very much more feeble and worn, and of a very different type. He was not like him, a robust, successful man, but rather one of those whose feet find no resting-place upon the earth. I recognized one of the children of reverie, and said, "You are doubtless of the stock of the old O'Donnells. I know well the hole in the river where their treasure lies buried under the guard of a serpent with many heads." "Yes, sur," he replied, "I am the last of a line of princes."

We then fell to talking of many commonplace things, and my friend did not once toss up his beard, but was very friendly. At last the gaunt old tax-gatherer got up to go, and my friend said, "I hope we will have a glass together next year." "No, no," was the answer, "I shall be dead next year." "I too have lost sons," said the other in quite a gentle voice. "But your sons were not like my son." And then the two men parted, with an angry flush and bitter hearts, and had I not cast between them some common words or other, might not have parted, but have fallen rather into an angry discussion of the value of their dead sons. If I had not pity for all the children of reverie I should have let them fight it out, and would now have many a wonderful oath to record.

The knight of the sheep would have had the victory, for no soul that wears this garment of blood and clay can surpass him. He was but once beaten; and this is his tale of how it was. He and some farm hands were playing at cards in a small cabin that stood against the end of a big barn. A wicked woman had once lived in this cabin. Suddenly one of the players threw down an ace and began to swear without any cause. His swearing was so dreadful that the others stood up, and my friend said, "All is not right here; there is a spirit in him." They ran to the door that led into the barn to get away as quickly as possible. The wooden bolt would not move, so the knight of the sheep took a saw which stood against the wall near at hand, and sawed through the bolt, and at once the door flew open with a bang, as though some one had been holding it, and they fled through.

AN ENDURING HEART

One day a friend of mine was making a sketch of my Knight of the Sheep. The old man's daughter was sitting by, and, when the conversation drifted to love and lovemaking, she said, "Oh, father, tell him about your love affair." The old man took his pipe out of his mouth, and said, "Nobody ever marries the woman he loves," and then, with a chuckle, "There were fifteen of them I liked better than the woman I married," and he repeated many women's names. He went on to tell how when he was a lad he had worked for his grandfather, his mother's father, and was called (my friend has forgotten why) by his grandfather's name, which we will say was Doran. He had a great friend, whom I shall call John Byrne; and one day he and his friend went to Queenstown to await an emigrant ship, that was to take John Byrne to America. When they were walking along the quay, they saw a girl sitting on a seat, crying miserably, and two men standing up in front of her quarrelling with one another. Doran said, "I think I know what is wrong. That man will be her brother, and that man will be her lover, and the brother is sending her to America to get her away from the lover. How she is crying! but I think I could console her myself." Presently the lover and brother went away, and Doran began to walk up and down before her, saying, "Mild weather, Miss," or the like. She answered him in a little while, and the three began to talk together. The emigrant ship did not arrive for some days; and the three drove about on outside cars very innocently and happily, seeing everything that was to be seen. When at last the ship came, and Doran had to break it to her that he was not going to America, she cried more after him than after the first lover. Doran whispered to Byrne as he went aboard ship, "Now, Byrne, I don't grudge her to you, but don't marry young."

When the story got to this, the farmer's daughter joined In mockingly with, "I suppose you said that for Byrne's good, father." But the old man insisted that he had said it for Byrne's good; and went on to tell how, when he got a letter telling of Byrne's engagement to the girl, he wrote him the same advice. Years passed by, and he heard nothing; and though he was now married, he could not keep from wondering what she was doing. At last he went to America to find out, and though he asked many people for tidings, he could get none. More years went by, and his wife was dead, and he well on in years, and a rich farmer with not a few great matters on his hands. He found an excuse in some vague business to go out to America again, and to begin his search again. One day he fell into talk with an Irishman in a railway carriage, and asked him, as his way was, about emigrants from this place and that, and at last, "Did you ever hear of the miller's daughter from Innis Rath?" and he named the woman he was looking for. "Oh yes," said the other, "she is married to a friend of mine, John MacEwing. She lives at such-and-such a street in Chicago." Doran went to Chicago and knocked at her door. She opened the door herself, and was "not a bit changed." He gave her his real name, which he had taken again after his grandfather's death, and the name of the man he had met in the train. She did not recognize him, but asked him to stay to dinner, saying that her husband would be glad to meet anybody who knew that old friend of his. They talked of many things, but for all their talk, I do not know why, and perhaps he did not know why, he never told her who he was. At dinner he asked her about Byrne, and she put her head down on the table and began to cry, and she cried so he was afraid her husband might be angry. He was afraid to ask what had happened to Byrne, and left soon after, never to see her again.

When the old man had finished the story, he said, "Tell that to Mr. Yeats, he will make a poem about it, perhaps." But the daughter said, "Oh no, father. Nobody could make a poem about a woman like that." Alas! I have never made the poem, perhaps because my own heart, which has loved Helen and all the lovely and fickle women of the world, would be too sore. There are things it is well not to ponder over too much, things that bare words are the best suited for.

1902.

THE SORCERERS

In Ireland we hear but little of the darker powers,[4] and come across any who have seen them even more rarely, for the imagination of the people dwells rather upon the fantastic and capricious, and fantasy and caprice would lose the freedom which is their breath of life, were they to unite them either with evil or with good. And yet the wise are of opinion that wherever man is, the dark powers who would feed his rapacities are there too, no less than the bright beings who store their honey in the cells of his heart, and the twilight beings who flit hither and thither, and that they encompass him with a passionate and melancholy multitude. They hold, too, that he who by long desire or through accident of birth possesses the power of piercing into their hidden abode can see them there, those who were once men or women full of a terrible vehemence, and those who have never lived upon the earth, moving slowly and with a subtler malice. The dark powers cling about us, it is said, day and night, like bats upon an old tree; and that we do not hear more of them is merely because the darker kinds of magic have been but little practised. I have indeed come across very few persons in Ireland who try to communicate with evil powers, and the few I have met keep their purpose and practice wholly hidden from those among whom they live. They are mainly small clerks and the like, and meet for the purpose of their art in a room hung with black hangings. They would not admit me into this room, but finding me not altogether ignorant of the arcane science, showed gladly

---

4 I know better now. We have the dark powers much more than I thought, but not as much as the Scottish, and yet I think the imagination of the people does dwell chiefly upon the fantastic and capricious.

elsewhere what they would do. "Come to us," said their leader, a clerk in a large flour-mill, "and we will show you spirits who will talk to you face to face, and in shapes as solid and heavy as our own."

I had been talking of the power of communicating in states of trance with the angelical and faery beings,—the children of the day and of the twilight—and he had been contending that we should only believe in what we can see and feel when in our ordinary everyday state of mind. "Yes," I said, "I will come to you," or some such words; "but I will not permit myself to become entranced, and will therefore know whether these shapes you talk of are any the more to be touched and felt by the ordinary senses than are those I talk of." I was not denying the power of other beings to take upon themselves a clothing of mortal substance, but only that simple invocations, such as he spoke of, seemed unlikely to do more than cast the mind into trance, and thereby bring it into the presence of the powers of day, twilight, and darkness.

"But," he said, "we have seen them move the furniture hither and thither, and they go at our bidding, and help or harm people who know nothing of them." I am not giving the exact words, but as accurately as I can the substance of our talk.

On the night arranged I turned up about eight, and found the leader sitting alone in almost total darkness in a small back room. He was dressed in a black gown, like an inquisitor's dress in an old drawing, that left nothing of him visible: except his eyes, which peered out through two small round holes. Upon the table in front of him was a brass dish of burning herbs, a large bowl, a skull covered with painted symbols, two crossed daggers, and certain implements shaped like quern stones, which were used to control the elemental powers in some fashion I did not discover. I also put on a black gown, and remember that it did not fit perfectly, and that it interfered with my movements considerably. The sorcerer then took a black cock out of a basket, and cut its throat with one of the daggers, letting the blood fall into the large bowl. He opened a book and began an invocation, which was certainly not English, and had a deep guttural sound. Before he had finished, another of the sorcerers, a man of about twenty-five, came in, and having put on a black gown also, seated himself at my left band. I had the invoker directly in front of me, and soon began to find his eyes, which glittered through the small holes in his hood, affecting me in a curious way. I struggled hard against their influence, and my head began to ache. The invocation continued, and nothing happened for the first few minutes. Then the invoker got up and extinguished the light in the hall, so that no glimmer might come through the slit under the door. There was now no light except from the herbs on the brass dish, and no sound except from the deep guttural murmur of the invocation.

Presently the man at my left swayed himself about, and cried out, "O god! O god!" I asked him what ailed him, but he did not know he had spoken. A moment after he said he could see a great serpent moving about the room, and became considerably excited. I saw nothing with any definite shape, but thought that black clouds were forming about me. I felt I must fall into a trance if I did not struggle against it, and that the influence which was causing this trance was out of harmony with itself, in other words, evil. After a struggle I got rid of the black clouds, and was able to observe with my ordinary senses again. The two sorcerers now began to see black and white columns moving about the room, and finally a man in a monk's habit, and they became greatly puzzled because I did not see these things also, for to them they were as solid as the table before them. The invoker appeared to be gradually increasing in power, and I began to feel as if a tide of darkness was pouring from him and concentrating itself about me; and now too I noticed that the man on my left hand had passed into a death-like trance. With a last great effort I drove off the black clouds; but feeling them to be the only shapes I should see without passing into a trance, and having no great love for them, I asked for lights, and after the needful exorcism returned to the ordinary world.

I said to the more powerful of the two sorcerers—"What would happen if one of your spirits had overpowered me?" "You would go out of this room," he answered, "with his character added to your own." I asked about the origin of his sorcery, but got little of importance, except that he had learned it from his father. He would not tell me more, for he had, it appeared, taken a vow of secrecy.

For some days I could not get over the feeling of having a number of deformed and grotesque figures lingering about me. The Bright Powers are always beautiful and desirable, and the Dim Powers are now beautiful, now quaintly grotesque, but the Dark Powers express their unbalanced natures in shapes of ugliness and horror.

THE DEVIL

My old Mayo woman told me one day that something very bad had come down the road and gone into the house opposite, and though she would not say what it was, I knew quite well. Another day she told me of two friends of hers who had been made love to by one whom they believed to be the devil. One of them was standing by the road-side when he came by on horseback, and asked her to mount up behind him, and go riding. When she would not he vanished. The other was out on the road late at night waiting for her young man, when something came flapping and rolling along the road up to her feet. It had the likeness of a newspaper, and presently it flapped up into her face, and she knew by the size of it that it was the Irish Times. All of a sudden it changed into a young man, who asked her to go walking with him. She would not, and he vanished.

I know of an old man too, on the slopes of Ben Bulben, who found the devil ringing a bell under his bed, and he went off and stole the chapel bell and rang him out. It may be that this, like the others, was not the devil at all, but some poor wood spirit whose cloven feet had got him into trouble.

HAPPY AND UNHAPPY THEOLOGIANS

I

A mayo woman once said to me, "I knew a servant girl who hung herself for the love of God. She was lonely for the priest and her society,[5] and hung herself to the banisters with a scarf. She was no sooner dead than she became white as a lily, and if it had been murder or suicide she would have become black as black. They gave her Christian burial, and the priest said she was no sooner dead than she was with the Lord. So nothing matters that you do for the love of God." I do not wonder at the pleasure she has in telling this story, for she herself loves all holy things with an ardour that brings them quickly to her lips. She told me once that she never hears anything described in a sermon that she does not afterwards see with her eyes. She has described to me the gates of Purgatory as they showed themselves to her eyes, but I remember nothing of the description except that she could not see the souls in trouble but only the gates. Her mind continually dwells on what is pleasant and beautiful. One day she asked me what month and what flower were the most beautiful. When I answered that I did not know, she said, "the month of May, because of the Virgin, and the lily of the valley, because it never sinned, but came pure out of the rocks," and then she asked, "what is the cause of the three cold months of winter?" I did not know even that, and so she said, "the sin of man and the vengeance of God." Christ Himself was not only blessed, but perfect in all manly proportions in her eyes, so much do beauty and holiness go together

---

5 The religious society she had belonged to.

in her thoughts. He alone of all men was exactly six feet high, all others are a little more or a little less.

Her thoughts and her sights of the people of faery are pleasant and beautiful too, and I have never heard her call them the Fallen Angels. They are people like ourselves, only better-looking, and many and many a time she has gone to the window to watch them drive their waggons through the sky, waggon behind waggon in long line, or to the door to hear them singing and dancing in the Forth. They sing chiefly, it seems, a song called "The Distant Waterfall," and though they once knocked her down she never thinks badly of them. She saw them most easily when she was in service in King's County, and one morning a little while ago she said to me, "Last night I was waiting up for the master and it was a quarter-past eleven. I heard a bang right down on the table. 'King's County all over,' says I, and I laughed till I was near dead. It was a warning I was staying too long. They wanted the place to themselves." I told her once of somebody who saw a faery and fainted, and she said, "It could not have been a faery, but some bad thing, nobody could faint at a faery. It was a demon. I was not afraid when they near put me, and the bed under me, out through the roof. I wasn't afraid either when you were at some work and I heard a thing coming flop-flop up the stairs like an eel, and squealing. It went to all the doors. It could not get in where I was. I would have sent it through the universe like a flash of fire. There was a man in my place, a tearing fellow, and he put one of them down. He went out to meet it on the road, but he must have been told the words. But the faeries are the best neighbours. If you do good to them they will do good to you, but they don't like you to be on their path." Another time she said to me, "They are always good to the poor."

II

There is, however, a man in a Galway village who can see nothing but wickedness. Some think him very holy, and others think him a little crazed, but some of his talk reminds one of those old Irish visions of the Three Worlds, which are supposed to have given Dante the plan of the Divine Comedy. But I could not imagine this man seeing Paradise. He is especially angry with the people of faery, and describes the faun-like feet that are so common among them, who are indeed children of Pan, to prove them children of Satan. He will not grant that "they carry away women, though there are many that say so," but he is certain that they are "as thick as the sands of the sea about us, and they tempt poor mortals."

He says, "There is a priest I know of was looking along the ground like as if he was hunting for something, and a voice said to him, 'If you want to see them you'll see enough of them,' and his eyes were opened and he saw the ground thick with them. Singing they do be sometimes, and dancing, but all the time they have cloven feet." Yet he was so scornful of unchristian things for all their dancing and singing that he thinks that "you have only to bid them begone and they will go. It was one night," he says, "after walking back from Kinvara and down by the wood beyond I felt one coming beside me, and I could feel the horse he was riding on and the way he lifted his legs, but they do not make a sound like the hoofs of a horse. So I stopped and turned around and said, very loud, 'Be off!' and he went and never troubled me after. And I knew a man who was dying, and one came on his bed, and he cried out to it, 'Get out of that, you unnatural animal!' and it left him. Fallen angels they are, and after the fall God said, 'Let there be Hell,' and there it was in a moment." An old woman who was sitting by the fire joined in as he said this with "God save us, it's a pity He said the word, and there might have been no Hell the day," but the seer did not notice her words. He went on, "And then he asked the devil what would he take for the souls of all the people. And the devil said nothing would satisfy him but the blood of a virgin's son, so he got that, and then the gates of Hell were opened." He understood the story, it seems, as if it were some riddling old folk tale.

"I have seen Hell myself. I had a sight of it one time in a vision. It had a very high wall around it, all of metal, and an archway, and a straight walk into it, just like what 'ud be leading into a gentleman's orchard, but the edges were not trimmed with box, but with red-hot metal. And inside the wall there were cross-walks, and I'm not sure what there was to the right, but to the left there were five great furnaces, and they full of souls kept there with great chains. So I turned short and went away, and in turning I looked again at the wall, and I could see no end to it.

"And another time I saw Purgatory. It seemed to be in a level place, and no walls around it, but it all one bright blaze, and the souls standing in it. And they suffer near as much as in Hell, only there are no devils with them there, and they have the hope of Heaven.

"And I heard a call to me from there, 'Help me to come out o' this!' And when I looked it was a man I used to know in the army, an Irishman, and from this county, and I believe him to be a descendant of King O'Connor of Athenry.

"So I stretched out my hand first, but then I called out, 'I'd be burned in the flames before I could get within three yards of you.' So then he said, 'Well, help me with your prayers,' and so I do.

"And Father Connellan says the same thing, to help the dead with your prayers, and he's a very clever man to make a sermon, and has a great deal of cures made with the Holy Water he brought back from Lourdes."

1902.

THE LAST GLEEMAN

Michael Moran was born about 1794 off Black Pitts, in the Liberties of Dublin, in Faddle Alley. A fortnight after birth he went stone blind from illness, and became thereby a blessing to his parents, who were soon able to send him to rhyme and beg at street corners and at the bridges over the Liffey. They may well have wished that their quiver were full of such as he, for, free from the interruption of sight, his mind became a perfect echoing chamber, where every movement of the day and every change of public passion whispered itself into rhyme or quaint saying. By the time he had grown to manhood he was the admitted rector of all the ballad-mongers of the Liberties. Madden, the weaver, Kearney, the blind fiddler from Wicklow, Martin from Meath, M'Bride from heaven knows where, and that M'Grane, who in after days, when the true Moran was no more, strutted in borrowed plumes, or rather in borrowed rags, and gave out that there had never been any Moran but himself, and many another, did homage before him, and held him chief of all their tribe. Nor despite his blindness did he find any difficulty in getting a wife, but rather was able to pick and choose, for he was just that mixture of ragamuffin and of genius which is dear to the heart of woman, who, perhaps because she is wholly conventional herself, loves the unexpected, the crooked, the bewildering. Nor did he lack, despite his rags, many excellent things, for it is remembered that he ever loved caper sauce, going so far indeed in his honest indignation at its absence upon one occasion as to fling a leg of mutton at his wife. He was not, however, much to look at, with his coarse frieze coat with its cape and scalloped edge, his old corduroy trousers and great brogues, and his stout stick made fast to his wrist by a thong of leather: and he would have been a woeful shock to the gleeman MacConglinne, could that friend of kings have beheld him in prophetic vision from the pillar stone at Cork. And yet though the short cloak and the leather wallet were no more, he was a true gleeman, being alike poet, jester, and newsman of the people. In the morning when he had finished his breakfast, his wife or some neighbour would read the newspaper to him, and read on and on until he interrupted with, "That'll do—I have me meditations"; and from these meditations would come the day's store of jest and rhyme. He had the whole Middle Ages under his frieze coat.

He had not, however, MacConglinne's hatred of the Church and clergy, for when the fruit of his meditations did not ripen well, or when the crowd called for something more solid, he would recite or sing a metrical tale or ballad of saint or martyr or of Biblical adventure. He would stand at a street corner, and when a crowd had gathered would begin in some such fashion as follows (I copy the record of one who knew him)—"Gather round me, boys, gather round me. Boys, am I standin' in puddle? am I standin' in wet?" Thereon several boys would cry, "Ali, no! yez not! yer in a nice dry place. Go on with St. Mary; go on with Moses"—each calling for his favourite tale. Then Moran, with a suspicious wriggle of his body and a clutch at his rags, would burst out with "All me buzzim friends are turned backbiters"; and after a final "If yez don't drop your coddin' and diversion I'll lave some of yez a case," by way of warning to the boys, begin his recitation, or perhaps still delay, to ask, "Is there a crowd round me now? Any blackguard heretic around me?" The best-known of his religious tales was St. Mary of Egypt, a long poem of exceeding solemnity, condensed from the much longer work of a certain Bishop Coyle. It told how a fast woman of Egypt, Mary by name, followed pilgrims to Jerusalem for no good purpose, and then, turning penitent on finding herself withheld from entering the Temple by supernatural interference, fled to the desert and spent the remainder of her life in solitary penance. When at last she was at the point of death, God sent

Bishop Zozimus to hear her confession, give her the last sacrament, and with the help of a lion, whom He sent also, dig her grave. The poem has the intolerable cadence of the eighteenth century, but was so popular and so often called for that Moran was soon nicknamed Zozimus, and by that name is he remembered. He had also a poem of his own called Moses, which went a little nearer poetry without going very near. But he could ill brook solemnity, and before long parodied his own verses in the following ragamuffin fashion:

> In Egypt's land, contagious to the Nile,
> King Pharoah's daughter went to bathe in style.
> She tuk her dip, then walked unto the land,
> To dry her royal pelt she ran along the strand.
> A bulrush tripped her, whereupon she saw
> A smiling babby in a wad o' straw.
> She tuk it up, and said with accents mild,
> "'Tare-and-agers, girls, which av yez owns the child?"

His humorous rhymes were, however, more often quips and cranks at the expense of his contemporaries. It was his delight, for instance, to remind a certain shoemaker, noted alike for display of wealth and for personal uncleanness, of his inconsiderable origin in a song of which but the first stanza has come down to us:

> At the dirty end of Dirty Lane,
> Liv'd a dirty cobbler, Dick Maclane;
> His wife was in the old king's reign
>   A stout brave orange-woman.
> On Essex Bridge she strained her throat,
> And six-a-penny was her note.
> But Dickey wore a bran-new coat,
>   He got among the yeomen.

He was a bigot, like his clan,
And in the streets he wildly sang,
O Roly, toly, toly raid, with his old jade.

He had troubles of divers kinds, and numerous interlopers to face and put down. Once an officious peeler arrested him as a vagabond, but was triumphantly routed amid the laughter of the court, when Moran reminded his worship of the precedent set by Homer, who was also, he declared, a poet, and a blind man, and a beggarman. He had to face a more serious difficulty as his fame grew. Various imitators started up upon all sides. A certain actor, for instance, made as many guineas as Moran did shillings by mimicking his sayings and his songs and his getup upon the stage. One night this actor was at supper with some friends, when dispute arose as to whether his mimicry was overdone or not. It was agreed to settle it by an appeal to the mob. A forty-shilling supper at a famous coffeehouse was to be the wager. The actor took up his station at Essex Bridge, a great haunt of Moran's, and soon gathered a small crowd. He had scarce got through "In Egypt's land, contagious to the Nile," when Moran himself came up, followed by another crowd. The crowds met in great excitement and laughter. "Good Christians," cried the pretender, "is it possible that any man would mock the poor dark man like that?"

"Who's that? It's some imposhterer," replied Moran.

"Begone, you wretch! it's you'ze the imposhterer. Don't you fear the light of heaven being struck from your eyes for mocking the poor dark man?"

"Saints and angels, is there no protection against this? You're a most inhuman-blaguard to try to deprive me of my honest bread this way," replied poor Moran.

"And you, you wretch, won't let me go on with the beautiful poem. Christian people, in your charity won't you beat this man away? he's taking advantage of my darkness."

The pretender, seeing that he was having the best of it, thanked the people for their sympathy and protection, and went on with the poem, Moran listening for a time in bewildered silence. After a while Moran protested again with:

"Is it possible that none of yez can know me? Don't yez see it's myself; and that's some one else?"

"Before I can proceed any further in this lovely story," interrupted the pretender, "I call on yez to contribute your charitable donations to help me to go on."

"Have you no sowl to be saved, you mocker of heaven?" cried Moran, Put completely beside himself by this last injury—"Would you rob the poor as well as desave the world? O, was ever such wickedness known?"

"I leave it to yourselves, my friends," said the pretender, "to give to the real dark man, that you all know so well, and save me from that schemer," and with that he collected some pennies and half-pence. While he was doing so, Moran started his Mary of Egypt, but the indignant crowd seizing his stick were about to belabour him, when they fell back bewildered anew by his close resemblance to himself. The pretender now called to them to "just give him a grip of that villain, and he'd soon let him know who the imposhterer was!" They led him over to Moran, but instead of closing with him he thrust a few shillings into his hand, and turning to the crowd explained to them he was indeed but an actor, and that he had just gained a wager, and so departed amid much enthusiasm, to eat the supper he had won.

In April 1846 word was sent to the priest that Michael Moran was dying. He found him at 15 (now 14 1/2) Patrick Street, on a straw bed, in a room full of ragged ballad-singers come to cheer his last moments. After his death the ballad-singers, with many fiddles and the like, came again and gave him a fine wake, each adding to the merriment whatever he knew in the way of rann, tale, old saw, or quaint rhyme. He had had his day, had said his prayers and made his confession, and why should they not give him a hearty send-off? The funeral took place the next day. A good party of his admirers and friends got into the hearse with the coffin, for the day was wet and nasty. They had not gone far when one of them burst out with "It's cruel cowld, isn't it?" "Garra'," replied another, "we'll all be as stiff as the corpse when we get to the berrin-ground." "Bad cess to him," said a third; "I wish he'd held out another month until the weather got dacent." A man called Carroll thereupon produced a half-pint of whiskey, and they all drank to the soul of the departed. Unhappily, however, the hearse was over-weighted, and they had not reached the cemetery before the spring broke, and the bottle with it.

Moran must have felt strange and out of place in that other kingdom he was entering, perhaps while his friends were drinking in his honour. Let us hope that some kindly middle region was found for him, where he can call dishevelled angels about him with some new and more rhythmical form of his old

> Gather round me, boys, will yez
> Gather round me?
> And hear what I have to say
> Before ould Salley brings me
> My bread and jug of tay;

and fling outrageous quips and cranks at cherubim and seraphim. Perhaps he may have found and gathered, ragamuffin though he be, the Lily of High Truth, the Rose of Far-sought Beauty, for whose lack so many of the writers of Ireland, whether famous or forgotten, have been futile as the blown froth upon the shore.

REGINA, REGINA PIGMEORUM, VENI

One night a middle-aged man, who had lived all his life far from the noise of cab-wheels, a young girl, a relation of his, who was reported to be enough of a seer to catch a glimpse of unaccountable lights moving over the fields among the cattle, and myself, were walking along a far western sandy shore. We talked of the Forgetful People as the faery people are sometimes called, and came in the midst of our talk to a notable haunt of theirs, a shallow cave amidst black rocks, with its reflection under it in the wet sea sand. I asked the young girl if she could see anything, for I had quite a number of things to ask the Forgetful People. She stood still for a few minutes, and I saw that she was passing into a kind of waking trance, in which the cold sea breeze no longer troubled her, nor the dull boom of the sea distracted her attention. I then called aloud the names of the great faeries, and in a moment or two she said that she could hear music far inside the rocks, and then a sound of confused talking, and of people stamping their feet as if to applaud some unseen performer. Up to this my other friend had been walking to and fro some yards off, but now he passed close to us, and as he did so said suddenly that we were going to be interrupted, for he heard the laughter of children somewhere beyond the rocks. We were, however, quite alone. The spirits of the place had begun to cast their influence over him also. In a moment he was corroborated by the girl, who said that bursts of laughter had begun to mingle with the music, the confused talking, and the noise of feet. She next saw a bright light streaming out of the cave, which seemed to have grown much deeper, and a quantity of little people,[6] in various coloured dresses, red predominating, dancing to a tune which she did not recognize.

I then bade her call out to the queen of the little people to come and talk with us. There was, however, no answer to her command. I therefore repeated the words aloud myself, and in a moment a very beautiful tall woman came out of the cave. I too had by this time fallen into a kind of trance, in which what we call the unreal had begun to take upon itself a masterful reality, and was able to see the faint gleam of golden ornaments, the shadowy blossom of dim hair. I then bade the girl tell this tall queen to marshal her followers according to their natural divisions, that we might see them. I found as before that I had to repeat the command myself. The creatures then came out of the cave, and drew themselves up, if I remember rightly, in four bands. One of these bands carried quicken boughs in their hands, and another had necklaces made apparently of serpents' scales, but their dress I cannot remember, for I was quite absorbed in that gleaming woman. I asked her to tell the seer whether these caves were the greatest faery haunts in the neighbourhood. Her lips moved, but the answer was inaudible. I bade the seer lay her hand upon the breast of the queen, and after that she heard every word quite distinctly. No, this was not the greatest faery haunt, for there was a greater one a little further ahead. I then asked her whether it was true that she and her people carried away mortals, and if so, whether they put another soul in the place of the one they had taken? "We change the bodies," was her answer. "Are any of you ever born into mortal life?" "Yes." "Do I know any who were among your people before birth?" "You do." "Who are they?" "It would not be lawful for you to know." I then asked whether she and her people were not "dramatizations of our moods"? "She does not understand," said my friend, "but says that her

6 The people and faeries in Ireland are sometimes as big as we are, sometimes bigger, and sometimes, as I have been told, about three feet high. The Old Mayo woman I so often quote, thinks that it is something in our eyes that makes them seem big or little.

people are much like human beings, and do most of the things human beings do." I asked her other questions, as to her nature, and her purpose in the universe, but only seemed to puzzle her. At last she appeared to lose patience, for she wrote this message for me upon the sands—the sands of vision, not the grating sands under our feet—"Be careful, and do not seek to know too much about us." Seeing that I had offended her, I thanked her for what she had shown and told, and let her depart again into her cave. In a little while the young girl awoke out of her trance, and felt again the cold wind of the world, and began to shiver.

I tell these things as accurately as I can, and with no theories to blur the history. Theories are poor things at the best, and the bulk of mine have perished long ago. I love better than any theory the sound of the Gate of Ivory, turning upon its hinges, and hold that he alone who has passed the rose-strewn threshold can catch the far glimmer of the Gate of Horn. It were perhaps well for us all if we would but raise the cry Lilly the astrologer raised in Windsor Forest, "Regina, Regina Pigmeorum, Veni," and remember with him, that God visiteth His children in dreams. Tall, glimmering queen, come near, and let me see again the shadowy blossom of thy dim hair.

"AND FAIR, FIERCE WOMEN"

One day a woman that I know came face to face with heroic beauty, that highest beauty which Blake says changes least from youth to age, a beauty which has been fading out of the arts, since that decadence we call progress, set voluptuous beauty in its place. She was standing at the window, looking over to Knocknarea where Queen Maive is thought to be buried, when she saw, as she has told me, "the finest woman you ever saw travelling right across from the mountain and straight to her." The woman had a sword by her side and a dagger lifted up in her hand, and was dressed in white, with bare arms and feet. She looked "very strong, but not wicked," that is, not cruel. The old woman had seen the Irish giant, and "though he was a fine man," he was nothing to this woman, "for he was round, and could not have stepped out so soldierly"; "she was like Mrs.——" a stately lady of the neighbourhood, "but she had no stomach on her, and was slight and broad in the shoulders, and was handsomer than any one you ever saw; she looked about thirty." The old woman covered her eyes with her hands, and when she uncovered them the apparition had vanished. The neighbours were "wild with her," she told me, because she did not wait to find out if there was a message, for they were sure it was Queen Maive, who often shows herself to the pilots. I asked the old woman if she had seen others like Queen Maive, and she said, "Some of them have their hair down, but they look quite different, like the sleepy-looking ladies one sees in the papers. Those with their hair up are like this one. The others have long white dresses, but those with their hair up have short dresses, so that you can see their legs right up to the calf." After some careful questioning I found that they wore what might very well be a kind of buskin; she went on, "They are fine and dashing looking, like the men one sees riding their horses in twos and threes on the slopes of the mountains with their swords swinging." She repeated over and over, "There is no such race living now, none so finely proportioned," or the like, and then said, "The present Queen[7] is a nice, pleasant-looking woman, but she is not like her. What makes me think so little of the ladies is that I see none as they be," meaning as the spirits. "When I think of her and of the ladies now, they are like little children running about without knowing how to put their clothes on right. Is it the ladies? Why, I would not call them women at all." The other day a friend of mine questioned an old woman in a Galway workhouse about Queen Maive, and was told that "Queen Maive was handsome, and overcame all her enemies with a bawl stick, for the hazel is blessed, and the best weapon that can be got. You might walk the world with it," but she grew "very disagreeable in the end—oh very disagreeable. Best not to be talking about it. Best leave it between the book and the hearer." My friend thought the old woman had got some scandal about Fergus son of Roy and Maive in her head.

And I myself met once with a young man in the Burren Hills who remembered an old poet who made his poems in Irish and had met when he was young, the young man said, one who called herself Maive, and said she was a queen "among them," and asked him if he would have money or pleasure. He said he would have pleasure, and she gave him her love for a time, and then went from him, and ever after he was very mournful. The young man had often heard him sing the poem of lamentation that he made, but could only remember that it was "very mournful," and that he called her "beauty of all beauties."

1902.

---

7   Queen Victoria.

ENCHANTED WOODS

I

Last summer, whenever I had finished my day's work, I used to go wandering in certain roomy woods, and there I would often meet an old countryman, and talk to him about his work and about the woods, and once or twice a friend came with me to whom he would open his heart more readily than to me, He had spent all his life lopping away the witch elm and the hazel and the privet and the hornbeam from the paths, and had thought much about the natural and supernatural creatures of the wood. He has heard the hedgehog—"grainne oge," he calls him—"grunting like a Christian," and is certain that he steals apples by rolling about under an apple tree until there is an apple sticking to every quill. He is certain too that the cats, of whom there are many in the woods, have a language of their own—some kind of old Irish. He says, "Cats were serpents, and they were made into cats at the time of some great change in the world. That is why they are hard to kill, and why it is dangerous to meddle with them. If you annoy a cat it might claw or bite you in a way that would put poison in you, and that would be the serpent's tooth." Sometimes he thinks they change into wild cats, and then a nail grows on the end of their tails; but these wild cats are not the same as the marten cats, who have been always in the woods. The foxes were once tame, as the cats are now, but they ran away and became wild. He talks of all wild creatures except squirrels—whom he hates—with what seems an affectionate interest, though at times his eyes will twinkle with pleasure as he remembers how he made hedgehogs unroll themselves when he was a boy, by putting a wisp of burning straw under them.

I am not certain that he distinguishes between the natural and supernatural very clearly. He told me the other day that foxes and cats like, above all, to be in the "forths" and lisses after nightfall; and he will certainly pass from some story about a fox to a story about a spirit with less change of voice than when he is going to speak about a marten cat—a rare beast now-a-days. Many years ago he used to work in the garden, and once they put him to sleep in a garden-house where there was a loft full of apples, and all night he could hear people rattling plates and knives and forks over his head in the loft. Once, at any rate, be has seen an unearthly sight in the woods. He says, "One time I was out cutting timber over in Inchy, and about eight o'clock one morning when I got there I saw a girl picking nuts, with her hair hanging down over her shoulders, brown hair, and she had a good, clean face, and she was tall and nothing on her head, and her dress no way gaudy but simple, and when she felt me coming she gathered herself up and was gone as if the earth had swallowed her up. And I followed her and looked for her, but I never could see her again from that day to this, never again." He used the word clean as we would use words like fresh or comely.

Others too have seen spirits in the Enchanted Woods. A labourer told us of what a friend of his had seen in a part of the woods that is called Shanwalla, from some old village that was before the weed. He said, "One evening I parted from Lawrence Mangan in the yard, and he went away through the path in Shanwalla, an' bid me goodnight. And two hours after, there he was back again in the yard, an' bid me light a candle that was in the stable. An' he told me that when he got into Shanwalla, a little fellow about as high as his knee, but having a head as big as a man's body, came beside him and led him out of the path an' round about, and at last it brought him to the lime-kiln, and then it vanished and left him."

A woman told me of a sight that she and others had seen by a certain deep pool in the river. She said, "I came over the stile from the chapel, and others along with me; and a great blast of wind came and two trees were bent and broken and fell into the river, and the splash of water out of it went up to the skies. And those that were with me saw many figures, but myself I only saw one, sitting there by the bank where the trees fell. Dark clothes he had on, and he was headless."

A man told me that one day, when he was a boy, he and another boy went to catch a horse in a certain field, full of boulders and bushes of hazel and creeping juniper and rock-roses, that is where the lake side is for a little clear of the woods. He said to the boy that was with him, "I bet a button that if I fling a pebble on to that bush it will stay on it," meaning that the bush was so matted the pebble would not be able to go through it. So he took up "a pebble of cow-dung, and as soon as it hit the bush there came out of it the most beautiful music that ever was heard." They ran away, and when they had gone about two hundred yards they looked back and saw a woman dressed in white, walking round and round the bush. "First it had the form of a woman, and then of a man, and it was going round the bush."

II

I often entangle myself in argument more complicated than even those paths of Inchy as to what is the true nature of apparitions, but at other times I say as Socrates said when they told him a learned opinion about a nymph of the Illissus, "The common opinion is enough for me." I believe when I am in the mood that all nature is full of people whom we cannot see, and that some of these are ugly or grotesque, and some wicked or foolish, but very many beautiful beyond any one we have ever seen, and that these are not far away when we are walking in pleasant and quiet places. Even when I was a boy I could never walk in a wood without feeling that at any moment I might find before me somebody or something I had long looked for without knowing what I looked for. And now I will at times explore every little nook of some poor coppice with almost anxious footsteps, so deep a hold has this imagination upon me. You too meet with a like imagination, doubtless, somewhere, wherever your ruling stars will have it, Saturn driving you to the woods, or the Moon, it may be, to the edges of the sea. I will not of a certainty believe that there is nothing in the sunset, where our forefathers imagined the dead following their shepherd the sun, or nothing but some vague presence as little moving as nothing. If beauty is not a gateway out of the net we were taken in at our birth, it will not long be beauty, and we will find it better to sit at home by the fire and fatten a lazy body or to run hither and thither in some foolish sport than to look at the finest show that light and shadow ever made among green leaves. I say to myself, when I am well out of that thicket of argument, that they are surely there, the divine people, for only we who have neither simplicity nor wisdom have denied them, and the simple of all times and the wise men of ancient times have seen them and even spoken to them. They live out their passionate lives not far off, as I think, and we shall be among them when we die if we but keep our natures simple and passionate. May it not even be that death shall unite us to all romance, and that some day we shall fight dragons among blue hills, or come to that whereof all romance is but

> Foreshadowings mingled with the images
> Of man's misdeeds in greater days than these,

as the old men thought in The Earthly Paradise when they were in good spirits.

1902

MIRACULOUS CREATURES

There are marten cats and badgers and foxes in the Enchanted Woods, but there are of a certainty mightier creatures, and the lake hides what neither net nor fine can take. These creatures are of the race of the white stag that flits in and out of the tales of Arthur, and of the evil pig that slew Diarmuid where Ben Bulben mixes with the sea wind. They are the wizard creatures of hope and fear, they are of them that fly and of them that follow among the thickets that are about the Gates of Death. A man I know remembers that his father was one night in the wood Of Inchy, "where the lads of Gort used to be stealing rods. He was sitting by the wall, and the dog beside him, and he heard something come running from Owbawn Weir, and he could see nothing, but the sound of its feet on the ground was like the sound of the feet of a deer. And when it passed him, the dog got between him and the wall and scratched at it there as if it was afraid, but still he could see nothing but only hear the sound of hoofs. So when it was passed he turned and came away home. Another time," the man says, "my father told me he was in a boat out on the lake with two or three men from Gort, and one of them had an eel-spear, and he thrust it into the water, and it hit something, and the man fainted and they had to carry him out of the boat to land, and when he came to himself he said that what he struck was like a calf, but whatever it was, it was not fish!" A friend of mine is convinced that these terrible creatures, so common in lakes, were set there in old times by subtle enchanters to watch over the gates of wisdom. He thinks that if we sent our spirits down into the water we would make them of one substance with strange moods Of ecstasy and power, and go out it may be to the conquest of the world. We

241

would, however, he believes, have first to outface and perhaps overthrow strange images full of a more powerful life than if they were really alive. It may be that we shall look at them without fear when we have endured the last adventure, that is death.

1902.

ARISTOTLE OF THE BOOKS

The friend who can get the wood-cutter to talk more readily than he will to anybody else went lately to see his old wife. She lives in a cottage not far from the edge of the woods, and is as full of old talk as her husband. This time she began to talk of Goban, the legendary mason, and his wisdom, but said presently, "Aristotle of the Books, too, was very wise, and he had a great deal of experience, but did not the bees get the better of him in the end? He wanted to know how they packed the comb, and he wasted the better part of a fortnight watching them, and he could not see them doing it. Then he made a hive with a glass cover on it and put it over them, and he thought to see. But when he went and put his eyes to the glass, they had it all covered with wax so that it was as black as the pot; and he was as blind as before. He said he was never rightly kilt till then. They had him that time surely!"

1902.

THE SWINE OF THE GODS

A few years ago a friend of mine told me of something that happened to him when he was a. young man and out drilling with some Connaught Fenians. They were but a car-full, and drove along a hillside until they came to a quiet place. They left the car and went further up the hill with their rifles, and drilled for a while. As they were coming down again they saw a very thin, long-legged pig of the old Irish sort, and the pig began to follow them. One of them cried out as a joke that it was a fairy pig, and they all began to run to keep up the joke. The pig ran too, and presently, how nobody knew, this mock terror became real terror, and they ran as for their lives. When they got to the car they made the horse gallop as fast as possible, but the pig still followed. Then one of them put up his rifle to fire, but when he looked along the barrel he could see nothing. Presently they turned a corner and came to a village. They told the people of the village what had happened, and the people of the village took pitchforks and spades and the like, and went along the road with them to drive the pig away. When they turned the comer they could not find anything.

1902.

A VOICE

One day I was walking over a bit of marshy ground close to Inchy Wood when I felt, all of a sudden, and only for a second, an emotion which I said to myself was the root of Christian mysticism. There had swept over me a sense of weakness, of dependence on a great personal Being somewhere far off yet near at hand. No thought of mine had prepared me for this emotion, for I had been pre-occupied with Aengus and Edain, and with Mannanan, son of the sea. That night I awoke lying upon my back and hearing a voice speaking above me and saying, "No human soul is like any other human soul, and therefore the love of God for any human soul is infinite, for no other soul can satisfy the same need in God." A few nights after this I awoke to see the loveliest people I have ever seen. A young man and a young girl dressed in olive-green raiment, cut like old Greek raiment, were standing at my bedside. I looked at the girl and noticed that her dress was gathered about her neck into a kind of chain, or perhaps into some kind of stiff embroidery which represented ivy-leaves. But what filled me with wonder was the miraculous mildness of her face. There are no such faces now. It was beautiful, as few faces are beautiful, but it had neither, one would think, the light that is in desire or in hope or in fear or in speculation. It was peaceful like the faces of animals, or like mountain pools at evening, so peaceful that it was a little sad. I thought for a moment that she might be the beloved of Aengus, but how could that hunted, alluring, happy, immortal wretch have a face like this? Doubtless she was from among the children of the Moon, but who among them I shall never know.

1902.

KIDNAPPERS

A little north of the town of Sligo, on the southern side of Ben Bulben, some hundreds of feet above the plain, is a small white square in the limestone. No mortal has ever touched it with his hand; no sheep or goat has ever browsed grass beside it. There is no more inaccessible place upon the earth, and few more encircled by awe to the deep considering. It is the door of faery-land. In the middle of night it swings open, and the unearthly troop rushes out. All night the gay rabble sweep to and fro across the land, invisible to all, unless perhaps where, in some more than commonly "gentle" place—Drumcliff or Drum-a-hair—the nightcapped heads of faery-doctors may be thrust from their doors to see what mischief the "gentry" are doing. To their trained eyes and ears the fields are covered by red-hatted riders, and the air is full of shrill voices—a sound like whistling, as an ancient Scottish seer has recorded, and wholly different from the talk of the angels, who "speak much in the throat, like the Irish," as Lilly, the astrologer, has wisely said. If there be a new-born baby or new-wed bride in the neighbourhood, the nightcapped "doctors" will peer with more than common care, for the unearthly troop do not always return empty-handed. Sometimes a new-wed bride or a new-born baby goes with them into their mountains; the door swings to behind, and the new-born or the new-wed moves henceforth in the bloodless land of Faery; happy enough, but doomed to melt out at the last judgment like bright vapour, for the soul cannot live without sorrow. Through this door of white stone, and the other doors of that land where geabheadh tu an sonas aer pighin ("you can buy joy for a penny"), have gone kings, queens, and princes, but so greatly has the power of Faery dwindled, that there are none but peasants in these sad chronicles of mine.

Somewhere about the beginning of last century appeared at the western corner of Market Street, Sligo, where the butcher's shop now is, not a palace, as in Keats's Lamia, but an apothecary's shop, ruled over by a certain unaccountable Dr. Opendon. Where he came from, none ever knew. There also was in Sligo, in those days, a woman, Ormsby by name, whose husband had fallen mysteriously sick. The doctors could make nothing of him. Nothing seemed wrong with him, yet weaker and weaker he grew. Away went the wife to Dr. Opendon. She was shown into the shop parlour. A black cat was sitting straight up before the fire. She had just time to see that the side-board was covered with fruit, and to say to herself, "Fruit must be wholesome when the doctor has so much," before Dr. Opendon came in. He was dressed all in black, the same as the cat, and his wife walked behind him dressed in black likewise. She gave him a guinea, and got a little bottle in return. Her husband recovered that time. Meanwhile the black doctor cured many people; but one day a rich patient died, and cat, wife, and doctor all vanished the night after. In a year the man Ormsby fell sick once more. Now he was a goodlooking man, and his wife felt sure the "gentry" were coveting him. She went and called on the "faery-doctor" at Cairnsfoot. As soon as he had heard her tale, he went behind the back door and began muttering, muttering, muttering-making spells. Her husband got well this time also. But after a while he sickened again, the fatal third time, and away went she once more to Cairnsfoot, and out went the faery-doctor behind his back door and began muttering, but soon he came in and told her it was no use— her husband would die; and sure enough the man died, and ever after when she spoke of him Mrs. Ormsby shook her head saying she knew well where he was, and it wasn't in heaven or hell or purgatory either. She probably believed that a log of wood was left behind in his place, but so bewitched that it seemed the dead body of her husband.

She is dead now herself, but many still living remember her. She was, I believe, for a time a servant or else a kind of pensioner of some relations of my own.

Sometimes those who are carried off are allowed after many years—seven usually—a final glimpse of their friends. Many years ago a woman vanished suddenly from a Sligo garden where she was walking with her husband. When her son, who was then a baby, had grown up he received word in some way, not handed down, that his mother was glamoured by faeries, and imprisoned for the time in a house in Glasgow and longing to see him. Glasgow in those days of sailing-ships seemed to the peasant mind almost over the edge of the known world, yet he, being a dutiful son, started away. For a long time he walked the streets of Glasgow; at last down in a cellar he saw his mother working. She was happy, she said, and had the best of good eating, and would he not eat? and therewith laid all kinds of food on the table; but he, knowing well that she was trying to cast on him the glamour by giving him faery food, that she might keep him with her, refused and came home to his people in Sligo.

Some five miles southward of Sligo is a gloomy and tree-bordered pond, a great gathering-place of water-fowl, called, because of its form, the Heart Lake. It is haunted by stranger things than heron, snipe, or wild duck. Out of this lake, as from the white square stone in Ben Bulben, issues an unearthly troop. Once men began to drain it; suddenly one of them raised a cry that he saw his house in flames. They turned round, and every man there saw his own cottage burning. They hurried home to find it was but faery glamour. To this hour on the border of the lake is shown a half-dug trench—the signet of their impiety. A little way from this lake I heard a beautiful and mournful history of faery kidnapping. I heard it from a little old woman in a white cap, who sings to herself in Gaelic, and moves from one foot to the other as though she remembered the dancing of her youth.

A young man going at nightfall to the house of his just married bride, met in the way a jolly company, and with them his bride. They were faeries, and had stolen her as a wife for the chief of their band. To him they seemed only a company of merry mortals. His bride, when she saw her old love, bade him welcome, but was most fearful lest be should eat the faery food, and so be glamoured out of the earth into that bloodless dim nation, wherefore she set him down to play cards with three of the cavalcade; and he played on, realizing nothing until he saw the chief of the band carrying his bride away in his arms. Immediately he started up, and knew that they were faeries; for slowly all that jolly company melted into shadow and night. He hurried to the house of his beloved. As he drew near came to him the cry of the keeners. She had died some time before he came. Some noteless Gaelic poet had made this into a forgotten ballad, some odd verses of which my white-capped friend remembered and sang for me.

Sometimes one hears of stolen people acting as good genii to the living, as in this tale, heard also close by the haunted pond, of John Kirwan of Castle Hacket. The Kirwans[8] are a family much rumoured of in peasant stories, and believed to be the descendants of a man and a spirit. They have ever been famous for beauty, and I have read that the mother of the present Lord Cloncurry was of their tribe.

John Kirwan was a great horse-racing man, and once landed in Liverpool with a fine horse, going racing somewhere in middle England. That evening, as he walked by the docks, a slip of a boy came up and asked where he was stabling his horse. In such and such a place, he answered. "Don't put him there," said the slip of a boy; "that stable will be burnt to-night." He took his horse elsewhere, and sure enough the stable was burnt down. Next day the boy came and asked as reward to ride as his

8 I have since heard that it was not the Kirwans, but their predecessors at Castle Hacket, the Hackets themselves, I think, who were descended from a man and a spirit, and were notable for beauty. I imagine that the mother of Lord Cloncurry was descended from the Hackets. It may well be that all through these stories the name of Kirwan has taken the place of the older name. Legend mixes everything together in her cauldron.

jockey in the coming race, and then was gone. The race-time came round. At the last moment the boy ran forward and mounted, saying, "If I strike him with the whip in my left hand I will lose, but if in my right hand bet all you are worth." For, said Paddy Flynn, who told me the tale, "the left arm is good for nothing. I might go on making the sign of the cross with it, and all that, come Christmas, and a Banshee, or such like, would no more mind than if it was that broom." Well, the slip of a boy struck the horse with his right hand, and John Kirwan cleared the field out. When the race was over, "What can I do for you now?" said he. "Nothing but this," said the boy: "my mother has a cottage on your land-they stole me from the cradle. Be good to her, John Kirwan, and wherever your horses go I will watch that no ill follows them; but you will never see me more." With that he made himself air, and vanished.

Sometimes animals are carried off—apparently drowned animals more than others. In Claremorris, Galway, Paddy Flynn told me, lived a poor widow with one cow and its calf. The cow fell into the river, and was washed away. There was a man thereabouts who went to a red-haired woman—for such are supposed to be wise in these things—and she told him to take the calf down to the edge of the river, and hide himself and watch. He did as she had told him, and as evening came on the calf began to low, and after a while the cow came along the edge of the river and commenced suckling it. Then, as he had been told, he caught the cow's tail. Away they went at a great pace across hedges and ditches, till they came to a royalty (a name for the little circular ditches, commonly called raths or forts, that Ireland is covered with since Pagan times). Therein he saw walking or sitting all the people who had died out of his village in his time. A woman was sitting on the edge with a child on her knees, and she called out to him to mind what the red-haired woman had told him, and he remembered she had said, Bleed the cow. So he stuck his knife into the cow and drew blood. That broke the spell, and he was able to turn her homeward. "Do not forget the spancel," said the woman with the child on her knees; "take the inside one." There were three spancels on a bush; he took one, and the cow was driven safely home to the widow.

There is hardly a valley or mountainside where folk cannot tell you of some one pillaged from amongst them. Two or three miles from the Heart Lake lives an old woman who was stolen away in her youth. After seven years she was brought home again for some reason or other, but she had no toes left. She had danced them off. Many near the white stone door in Ben Bulben have been stolen away.

It is far easier to be sensible in cities than in many country places I could tell you of. When one walks on those grey roads at evening by the scented elder-bushes of the white cottages, watching the faint mountains gathering the clouds upon their heads, one all too readily discovers, beyond the thin cobweb veil of the senses, those creatures, the goblins, hurrying from the white square stone door to the north, or from the Heart Lake in the south.

THE UNTIRING ONES

It is one of the great troubles of life that we cannot have any unmixed emotions. There is always something in our enemy that we like, and something in our sweetheart that we dislike. It is this entanglement of moods which makes us old, and puckers our brows and deepens the furrows about our eyes. If we could love and hate with as good heart as the faeries do, we might grow to be long-lived like them. But until that day their untiring joys and sorrows must ever be one-half of their fascination. Love with them never grows weary, nor can the circles of the stars tire out their dancing feet. The Donegal peasants remember this when they bend over the spade, or sit full of the heaviness of the fields beside the griddle at nightfall, and they tell stories about it that it may not be forgotten. A short while ago, they say, two faeries, little creatures, one like a young man, one like a young woman, came to a farmer's house, and spent the night sweeping the hearth and setting all tidy. The next night they came again, and while the farmer was away, brought all the furniture up-stairs into one room, and having arranged it round the walls, for the greater grandeur it seems, they began to dance. They danced on and on, and days and days went by, and all the country-side came to look at them, but still their feet never tired. The farmer did not dare to live at home the while; and after three months he made up his mind to stand it no more, and went and told them that the priest was coming. The little creatures when they heard this went back to their own country, and there their joy shall last as long as the points of the rushes are brown, the people say, and that is until God shall burn up the world with a kiss.

But it is not merely faeries who know untiring days, for there have been men and women who, falling under their enchantment, have attained, perhaps by the right of their God-given spirits, an even more than faery abundance of life and feeling. It seems that when mortals have gone amid those poor happy leaves of the Imperishable Rose of Beauty, blown hither and thither by the winds that awakened the stars, the dim kingdom has acknowledged their birthright, perhaps a little sadly, and given them of its best. Such a mortal was born long ago at a village in the south of Ireland. She lay asleep in a cradle, and her mother sat by rocking her, when a woman of the Sidhe (the faeries) came in, and said that the child was chosen to be the bride of the prince of the dim kingdom, but that as it would never do for his wife to grow old and die while he was still in the first ardour of his love, she would be gifted with a faery life. The mother was to take the glowing log out of the fire and bury it in the garden, and her child would live as long as it remained unconsumed. The mother buried the log, and the child grew up, became a beauty, and married the prince of the faeries, who came to her at nightfall. After seven hundred years the prince died, and another prince ruled in his stead and married the beautiful peasant girl in his turn; and after another seven hundred years he died also, and another prince and another husband came in his stead, and so on until she had had seven husbands. At last one day the priest of the parish called upon her, and told her that she was a scandal to the whole neighbourhood with her seven husbands and her long life. She was very sorry, she said, but she was not to blame, and then she told him about the log, and he went straight out and dug until he found it, and then they burned it, and she died, and was buried like a Christian, and everybody was pleased. Such a mortal too was Clooth-na-bare,[9] who went all over the world seeking a lake deep enough to drown her faery

---

9 Doubtless Clooth-na-bare should be Cailleac Bare, which would mean the old Woman Bare. Bare or Bere or Verah or Dera or Dhera was a very famous person, perhaps the mother of the Gods herself. A friend of mine found her, as he thinks frequenting Lough Leath, or the Grey Lake on a mountain of the

life, of which she had grown weary, leaping from hill to lake and lake to hill, and setting up a cairn of stones wherever her feet lighted, until at last she found the deepest water in the world in little Lough Ia, on the top of the Birds' Mountain at Sligo.

The two little creatures may well dance on, and the woman of the log and Clooth-na-bare sleep in peace, for they have known untrammelled hate and unmixed love, and have never wearied themselves with "yes" and "no," or entangled their feet with the sorry net of "maybe" and "perhaps." The great winds came and took them up into themselves.

Fews. Perhaps Lough Ia is my mishearing, or the storyteller's mispronunciation of Lough Leath, for there are many Lough Leaths.

EARTH, FIRE AND WATER

Some French writer that I read when I was a boy, said that the desert went into the heart of the Jews in their wanderings and made them what they are. I cannot remember by what argument he proved them to be even yet the indestructible children of earth, but it may well be that the elements have their children. If we knew the Fire Worshippers better we might find that their centuries of pious observance have been rewarded, and that the fire has given them a little of its nature; and I am certain that the water, the water of the seas and of lakes and of mist and rain, has all but made the Irish after its image. Images form themselves in our minds perpetually as if they were reflected in some pool. We gave ourselves up in old times to mythology, and saw the Gods everywhere. We talked to them face to face, and the stories of that communion are so many that I think they outnumber all the like stories of all the rest of Europe. Even to-day our country people speak with the dead and with some who perhaps have never died as we understand death; and even our educated people pass without great difficulty into the condition of quiet that is the condition of vision. We can make our minds so like still water that beings gather about us that they may see, it may be, their own images, and so live for a moment with a clearer, perhaps even with a fiercer life because of our quiet. Did not the wise Porphyry think that all souls come to be born because of water, and that "even the generation of images in the mind is from water"?

1902.

255

THE OLD TOWN

I fell, one night some fifteen years ago, into what seemed the power of faery.

I had gone with a young man and his sister—friends and relations of my own—to pick stories out of an old countryman; and we were coming home talking over what he had told us. It was dark, and our imaginations were excited by his stories of apparitions, and this may have brought us, unknown to us, to the threshold, between sleeping and waking, where Sphinxes and Chimaeras sit open-eyed and where there are always murmurings and whisperings. I cannot think that what we saw was an imagination of the waking mind. We had come under some trees that made the road very dark, when the girl saw a bright light moving slowly across the road. Her brother and myself saw nothing, and did not see anything until we had walked for about half-an-hour along the edge of the river and down a narrow lane to some fields where there was a ruined church covered with ivy, and the foundations of what was called "the Old Town," which had been burned down, it was said, in Cromwell's day. We had stood for some few minutes, so far as I can recollect, looking over the fields full of stones and brambles and elder-bushes, when I saw a small bright light on the horizon, as it seemed, mounting up slowly towards the sky; then we saw other faint lights for a minute or two, and at last a bright flame like the flame of a torch moving rapidly over the river. We saw it all in such a dream, and it seems all so unreal, that I have never written of it until now, and hardly ever spoken of it, and even when thinking, because of some unreasoning impulse, I have avoided giving it weight in the argument. Perhaps I have felt that my recollections of things seen when the sense of reality was weakened must be untrustworthy. A few months ago, however, I talked it over with my two friends, and compared their somewhat meagre recollections with my own. That sense of unreality was all the more wonderful because the next day I heard sounds as unaccountable as were those lights, and without any emotion of unreality, and I remember them with perfect distinctness and confidence. The girl was sitting reading under a large old-fashioned mirror, and I was reading and writing a couple of yards away, when I heard a sound as if a shower of peas had been thrown against the mirror, and while I was looking at it I heard the sound again, and presently, while I was alone in the room, I heard a sound as if something much bigger than a pea had struck the wainscoting beside my head. And after that for some days came other sights and sounds, not to me but to the girl, her brother, and the servants. Now it was a bright light, now it was letters of fire that vanished before they could be read, now it was a heavy foot moving about in the seemingly empty house. One wonders whether creatures who live, the country people believe, wherever men and women have lived in earlier times, followed us from the ruins of the old town? or did they come from the banks of the river by the trees where the first light had shone for a moment?

1902.

THE MAN AND HIS BOOTS

There was a doubter in Donegal, and he would not hear of ghosts or sheogues, and there was a house in Donegal that had been haunted as long as man could remember, and this is the story of how the house got the better of the man. The man came into the house and lighted a fire in the room under the haunted one, and took off his boots and set them On the hearth, and stretched out his feet and warmed him self. For a time he prospered in his unbelief; but a little while after the night had fallen, and everything had got very dark, one of his boots began to move. It got up off the floor and gave a kind of slow jump towards the door, and then the other boot did the same, and after that the first boot jumped again. And thereupon it struck the man that an invisible being had got into his boots, and was now going away in them. When the boots reached the door they went up-stairs slowly, and then the man heard them go tramp, tramp round the haunted room over his head. A few minutes passed, and he could hear them again upon the stairs, and after that in the passage outside, and then one of them came in at the door, and the other gave a jump past it and came in too. They jumped along towards him, and then one got up and hit him, and afterwards the other hit him, and then again the first hit him, and so on, until they drove him out of the room, and finally out of the house. In this way he was kicked out by his own boots, and Donegal was avenged upon its doubter. It is not recorded whether the invisible being was a ghost or one of the Sidhe, but the fantastic nature of the vengeance is like the work of the Sidhe who live in the heart of fantasy.

A COWARD

One day I was at the house of my friend the strong farmer, who lives beyond Ben Bulben and Cope's mountain, and met there a young lad who seemed to be disliked by the two daughters. I asked why they disliked him, and was; told he was a coward. This interested me, for some whom robust children of nature take to be cowards are but men and women with a nervous system too finely made for their life and work. I looked at the lad; but no, that pink-and-white face and strong body had nothing of undue sensibility. After a little he told me his story. He had lived a wild and reckless life, until one day, two years before, he was coming home late at night, and suddenly fell himself sinking in, as it were, upon the ghostly world. For a moment he saw the face of a dead brother rise up before him, and then he turned and ran. He did not stop till he came to a cottage nearly a mile down the road. He flung himself against the door with so much of violence that he broke the thick wooden bolt and fell upon the floor. From that day he gave up his wild life, but was a hopeless coward. Nothing could ever bring him to look, either by day or night, upon the spot where he had seen the face, and he often went two miles round to avoid it; nor could, he said, "the prettiest girl in the country" persuade him to see her home after a party if he were alone. He feared everything, for he had looked at the face no man can see unchanged-the imponderable face of a spirit.

THE THREE O'BYRNES AND
THE EVIL FAERIES

In the dim kingdom there is a great abundance of all excellent things. There is more love there than upon the earth; there is more dancing there than upon the earth; and there is more treasure there than upon the earth. In the beginning the earth was perhaps made to fulfil the desire of man, but now it has got old and fallen into decay. What wonder if we try and pilfer the treasures of that other kingdom!

A friend was once at a village near Sleive League. One day he was straying about a rath called "Cashel Nore." A man with a haggard face and unkempt hair, and clothes falling in pieces, came into the rath and began digging. My friend turned to a peasant who was working near and asked who the man was. "That is the third O'Byrne," was the answer. A few days after he learned this story: A great quantity of treasure had been buried in the rath in pagan times, and a number of evil faeries set to guard it; but some day it was to be found and belong to the family of the O'Byrnes. Before that day three O'Byrnes must find it and die. Two had already done so. The first had dug and dug until at last he had got a glimpse of the stone coffin that contained it, but immediately a thing like a huge hairy dog came down the mountain and tore him to pieces. The next morning the treasure had again vanished deep into the earth. The second O'Byrne came and dug and dug until he found the coffer, and lifted the lid and saw the gold shining within. He saw some horrible sight the next moment, and went raving mad and soon died. The treasure again sank out of sight. The third O'Byrne is now digging. He believes that he will die in some terrible way the moment he finds the treasure, but that the spell will be broken, and the O'Byrne family made rich for ever, as they were of old.

A peasant of the neighbourhood once saw the treasure. He found the shin-bone of a hare lying on the grass. He took it up; there was a hole in it; he looked through the hole, and saw the gold heaped up under the ground. He hurried home to bring a spade, but when he got to the rath again he could not find the spot where he had seen it.

DRUMCLIFF AND ROSSES

Drumcliff and Rosses were, are, and ever shall be, please Heaven! places of unearthly resort. I have lived near by them and in them, time after time, and have gathered thus many a crumb of faery lore. Drumcliff is a wide green valley, lying at the foot of Ben Bulben, the mountain in whose side the square white door swings open at nightfall to loose the faery riders on the world. The great St. Columba himself, the builder of many of the old ruins in the valley, climbed the mountains on one notable day to get near heaven with his prayers. Rosses is a little sea-dividing, sandy plain, covered with short grass, like a green tablecloth, and lying in the foam midway between the round cairn-headed Knocknarea and "Ben Bulben, famous for hawks":

> But for Benbulben and Knocknarea
> Many a poor sailor'd be cast away,

as the rhyme goes.

At the northern corner of Rosses is a little promontory of sand and rocks and grass: a mournful, haunted place. No wise peasant would fall asleep under its low cliff, for he who sleeps here may wake "silly," the "good people" having carried off his soul. There is no more ready shortcut to the dim kingdom than this plovery headland, for, covered and smothered now from sight by mounds of sand, a long cave goes thither "full of gold and silver, and the most beautiful parlours and drawing-rooms." Once, before the sand covered it, a dog strayed in, and was heard yelping helplessly deep underground in a fort far inland. These forts or raths, made before modern history had begun, cover all Rosses and all Columkille. The one where the dog yelped has, like most others, an underground beehive chamber in the midst. Once when I was poking about there, an unusually intelligent and "reading" peasant who had come with me, and waited outside, knelt down by the opening, and whispered in a timid voice, "Are you all right, sir?" I had been some little while underground, and he feared I had been carried off like the dog.

No wonder he was afraid, for the fort has long been circled by ill-boding rumours. It is on the ridge of a small hill, on whose northern slope lie a few stray cottages. One night a farmer's young son came from one of them and saw the fort all flaming, and ran towards it, but the "glamour" fell on him, and he sprang on to a fence, cross-legged, and commenced beating it with a stick, for he imagined the fence was a horse, and that all night long he went on the most wonderful ride through the country. In the morning he was still beating his fence, and they carried him home, where he remained a simpleton for three years before he came to himself again. A little later a farmer tried to level the fort. His cows and horses died, and an manner of trouble overtook him, and finally he himself was led home, and left useless with "his head on his knees by the fire to the day of his death."

A few hundred yards southwards of the northern angle of Rosses is another angle having also its cave, though this one is not covered with sand. About twenty years ago a brig was wrecked near by, and three or four fishermen were put to watch the deserted hulk through the darkness. At midnight they saw sitting on a stone at the cave's mouth two red-capped fiddlers fiddling with all their might. The men fled. A great crowd of villagers rushed down to the cave to see the fiddlers, but the creatures had gone.

To the wise peasant the green hills and woods round him are full of never-fading mystery. When the aged countrywoman stands at her door in the evening, and, in her own words, "looks at the mountains and thinks of the goodness of God," God is all the nearer, because the pagan powers are not far: because northward in Ben Bulben, famous for hawks, the white square door swings open at sundown, and those wild unchristian riders rush forth upon the fields, while southward the White Lady, who is doubtless Maive herself, wanders under the broad cloud nightcap of Knocknarea. How may she doubt these things, even though the priest shakes his head at her? Did not a herd-boy, no long while since, see the White Lady? She passed so close that the skirt of her dress touched him. "He fell down, and was dead three days." But this is merely the small gossip of faerydom—the little stitches that join this world and the other.

One night as I sat eating Mrs. H—'s soda-bread, her husband told me a longish story, much the best of all I heard in Rosses. Many a poor man from Fin M'Cool to our own days has had some such adventure to tell of, for those creatures, the "good people," love to repeat themselves. At any rate the story-tellers do. "In the times when we used to travel by the canal," he said, "I was coming down from Dublin. When we came to Mullingar the canal ended, and I began to walk, and stiff and fatigued I was after the slowness. I had some friends with me, and now and then we walked, now and then we rode in a cart. So on till we saw some girls milking cows, and stopped to joke with them. After a while we asked them for a drink of milk. 'We have nothing to put it in here,' they said, 'but come to the house with us.' We went home with them, and sat round the fire talking. After a while the others went, and left me, loath to stir from the good fire. I asked the girls for something to eat. There was a pot on the fire, and they took the meat out and put it on a plate, and told me to eat only the meat that came off the head. When I had eaten, the girls went out, and I did not see them again. It grew darker and darker, and there I still sat, loath as ever to leave the good fire, and after a while two men came in, carrying between them a corpse. When I saw them, coming I hid behind the door. Says one to the other, putting the corpse on the spit, 'Who'll turn the spit? Says the other, 'Michael H—, come out of that and turn the meat.' I came out all of a tremble, and began turning the spit. 'Michael H——,' says the one who spoke first, 'if you let it burn we'll have to put you on the spit instead'; and on that they went out. I sat there trembling and turning the corpse till towards midnight. The men came again, and the one said it was burnt, and the other said it was done right. But having fallen out over it, they both said they would do me no harm that time; and, sitting by the fire, one of them cried out: 'Michael H——, can you tell me a story?' 'Divil a one,' said I. On which he caught me by the shoulder, and put me out like a shot. It was a wild blowing night. Never in all my born days did I see such a night-the darkest night that ever came out of the heavens. I did not know where I was for the life of me. So when one of the men came after me and touched me on the shoulder, with a 'Michael H——, can you tell a story now?' 'I can,' says I. In he brought me; and putting me by the fire, says: 'Begin.' 'I have no story but the one,' says I, 'that I was sitting here, and you two men brought in a corpse and put it on the spit, and set me turning it.' 'That will do,' says he; 'ye may go in there and lie down on the bed.' And I went, nothing loath; and in the morning where was I but in the middle of a green field!"

"Drumcliff" is a great place for omens. Before a prosperous fishing season a herring-barrel appears in the midst of a storm-cloud; and at a place called Columkille's Strand, a place of marsh and mire, an ancient boat, with St. Columba himself, comes floating in from sea on a moonlight night: a portent of a brave harvesting. They have their dread portents too. Some few seasons ago a fisherman saw, far on the horizon, renowned Hy Brazel, where he who touches shall find no more labour or care, nor cynic laughter, but shall go walking about under shadiest boscage, and enjoy the conversation of Cuchullin and his heroes. A vision of Hy Brazel forebodes national troubles.

Drumcliff and Rosses are chokeful of ghosts. By bog, road, rath, hillside, sea-border they gather in all shapes: headless women, men in armour, shadow hares, fire-tongued hounds, whistling seals, and so on. A whistling seal sank a ship the other day. At Drumcliff there is a very ancient graveyard. The Annals of the Four Masters have this verse about a soldier named Denadhach, who died in 871: "A pious soldier of the race of Con lies under hazel crosses at Drumcliff." Not very long ago an old woman, turning to go into the churchyard at night to pray, saw standing before her a man in armour, who asked her where she was going. It was the "pious soldier of the race of Con," says local wisdom, still keeping watch, with his ancient piety, over the graveyard. Again, the custom is still common hereabouts of sprinkling the doorstep with the blood of a chicken on the death of a very young child, thus (as belief is) drawing into the blood the evil spirits from the too weak soul. Blood is a great gatherer of evil spirits. To cut your hand on a stone on going into a fort is said to be very dangerous.

There is no more curious ghost in Drumcliff or Rosses than the snipe-ghost. There is a bush behind a house in a village that I know well: for excellent reasons I do not say whether in Drumcliff or Rosses or on the slope of Ben Bulben, or even on the plain round Knocknarea. There is a history concerning the house and the bush. A man once lived there who found on the quay of Sligo a package containing three hundred pounds in notes. It was dropped by a foreign sea captain. This my man knew, but said nothing. It was money for freight, and the sea captain, not daring to face his owners, committed suicide in mid-ocean. Shortly afterwards my man died. His soul could not rest. At any rate, strange sounds were heard round his house, though that had grown and prospered since the freight money. The wife was often seen by those still alive out in the garden praying at the bush I have spoken of, for the shade of the dead man appeared there at times. The bush remains to this day: once portion of a hedge, it now stands by itself, for no one dare put spade or pruning-knife about it. As to the strange sounds and voices, they did not cease till a few years ago, when, during some repairs, a snipe flew out of the solid plaster and away; the troubled ghost, say the neighbours, of the note-finder was at last dislodged.

My forebears and relations have lived near Rosses and Drumcliff these many years. A few miles northward I am wholly a stranger, and can find nothing. When I ask for stories of the faeries, my answer is some such as was given me by a woman who lives near a white stone fort—one of the few stone ones in Ireland—under the seaward angle of Ben Bulben: "They always mind their own affairs and I always mind mine": for it is dangerous to talk of the creatures. Only friendship for yourself or knowledge of your forebears will loosen these cautious tongues. My friend, "the sweet Harp-String" (I give no more than his Irish name for fear of gaugers), has the science of unpacking the stubbornest heart, but then he supplies the potheen-makers with grain from his own fields. Besides, he is descended from a noted Gaelic magician who raised the "dhoul" in Great Eliza's century, and he has a kind of prescriptive right to hear tell of all kind of other-world creatures. They are almost relations of his, if all people say concerning the parentage of magicians be true.

THE THICK SKULL OF THE FORTUNATE

I

Once a number of Icelandic peasantry found a very thick skull in the cemetery where the poet Egil was buried. Its great thickness made them feel certain it was the skull of a great man, doubtless of Egil himself. To be doubly sure they put it on a wall and hit it hard blows with a hammer. It got white where the blows fell but did not break, and they were convinced that it was in truth the skull of the poet, and worthy of every honour. In Ireland we have much kinship with the Icelanders, or "Danes" as we call them and all other dwellers in the Scandinavian countries. In some of our mountainous and barren places, and in our seaboard villages, we still test each other in much the same way the Icelanders tested the head of Egil. We may have acquired the custom from those ancient Danish pirates, whose descendants the people of Rosses tell me still remember every field and hillock in Ireland which once belonged to their forebears, and are able to describe Rosses itself as well as any native. There is one seaboard district known as Roughley, where the men are never known to shave or trim their wild red beards, and where there is a fight ever on foot. I have seen them at a boat-race fall foul of each other, and after much loud Gaelic, strike each other with oars. The first boat had gone aground, and by dint of hitting out with the long oars kept the second boat from passing, only to give the victory to the third. One day the Sligo people say a man from Roughley was tried in Sligo for breaking a skull in a row, and made the defence not unknown in Ireland, that some heads are so thin you cannot be responsible for them. Having turned with a look of passionate contempt towards the solicitor who was prosecuting, and cried, "that little fellow's skull if ye were to hit it would go like an egg-shell," he beamed upon the judge, and said in a wheedling voice, "but a man might wallop away at your lordship's for a fortnight."

II

I wrote all this years ago, out of what were even then old memories. I was in Roughley the other day, and found it much like other desolate places. I may have been thinking of Moughorow, a much wilder place, for the memories of one's childhood are brittle things to lean upon.

1902.

THE RELIGION OF A SAILOR

A sea captain when he stands upon the bridge, or looks out from his deck-house, thinks much about God and about the world. Away in the valley yonder among the corn and the poppies men may well forget all things except the warmth of the sun upon the face, and the kind shadow under the hedge; but he who journeys through storm and darkness must needs think and think. One July a couple of years ago I took my supper with a Captain Moran on board the S.S. Margaret, that had put into a western river from I know not where. I found him a man of many notions all flavoured with his personality, as is the way with sailors. He talked in his queer sea manner of God and the world, and up through all his words broke the hard energy of his calling.

"Sur," said he, "did you ever hear tell of the sea captain's prayer?"

"No," said I; "what is it?"

"It is," he replied, "'O Lord, give me a stiff upper lip.'"

"And what does that mean?"

"It means," he said, "that when they come to me some night and wake me up, and say, 'Captain, we're going down,' that I won't make a fool o' meself. Why, sur, we war in mid Atlantic, and I standin' on the bridge, when the third mate comes up to me looking mortial bad. Says he, 'Captain, all's up with us.' Says I, 'Didn't you know when you joined that a certain percentage go down every year?' 'Yes, sur,' says he; and says I, 'Arn't you paid to go down?' 'Yes, sur,' says he; and says I, 'Then go down like a man, and be damned to you!'"

CONCERNING THE NEARNESS TOGETHER OF HEAVEN, EARTH, AND PURGATORY

In Ireland this world and the world we go to after death are not far apart. I have heard of a ghost that was many years in a tree and many years in the archway of a bridge, and my old Mayo woman says, "There is a bush up at my own place, and the people do be saying that there are two souls doing their penance under it. When the wind blows one way the one has shelter, and when it blows from the north the other has the shelter. It is twisted over with the way they be rooting under it for shelter. I don't believe it, but there is many a one would not pass by it at night." Indeed there are times when the worlds are so near together that it seems as if our earthly chattels were no more than the shadows of things beyond. A lady I knew once saw a village child running about with a long trailing petticoat upon her, and asked the creature why she did not have it cut short. "It was my grandmother's," said the child; "would you have her going about yonder with her petticoat up to her knees, and she dead but four days?" I have read a story of a woman whose ghost haunted her people because they had made her grave-clothes so short that the fires of purgatory burned her knees. The peasantry expect to have beyond the grave houses much like their earthly homes, only there the thatch will never grow leaky, nor the white walls lose their lustre, nor shall the dairy be at any time empty of good milk and butter. But now and then a landlord or an agent or a gauger will go by begging his bread, to show how God divides the righteous from the unrighteous.

1892 and 1902.

271

THE EATERS OF PRECIOUS STONES

Sometimes when I have been shut off from common interests, and have for a little forgotten to be restless, I get waking dreams, now faint and shadow-like, now vivid and solid-looking, like the material world under my feet. Whether they be faint or vivid, they are ever beyond the power of my will to alter in any way. They have their own will, and sweep hither and thither, and change according to its commands. One day I saw faintly an immense pit of blackness, round which went a circular parapet, and on this parapet sat innumerable apes eating precious stones out of the palms of their hands. The stones glittered green and crimson, and the apes devoured them with an insatiable hunger. I knew that I saw the Celtic Hell, and my own Hell, the Hell of the artist, and that all who sought after beautiful and wonderful things with too avid a thirst, lost peace and form and became shapeless and common. I have seen into other people's hells also, and saw in one an infernal Peter, who had a black face and white lips, and who weighed on a curious double scales not only the evil deeds committed, but the good deeds left undone, of certain invisible shades. I could see the scales go up and down, but I could not see the shades who were, I knew, crowding about him. I saw on another occasion a quantity of demons of all kinds of shapes—fish-like, serpent-like, ape-like, and dog-like—sitting about a black pit such as that in my own Hell, and looking at a moon—like reflection of the Heavens which shone up from the depths of the pit.

OUR LADY OF THE HILLS

When we were children we did not say at such a distance from the post-office, or so far from the butcher's or the grocer's, but measured things by the covered well in the wood, or by the burrow of the fox in the hill. We belonged then to God and to His works, and to things come down from the ancient days. We would not have been greatly surprised had we met the shining feet of an angel among the white mushrooms upon the mountains, for we knew in those days immense despair, unfathomed love—every eternal mood,—but now the draw-net is about our feet. A few miles eastward of Lough Gill, a young Protestant girl, who was both pretty herself and prettily dressed in blue and white, wandered up among those mountain mushrooms, and I have a letter of hers telling how she met a troop of children, and became a portion of their dream. When they first saw her they threw themselves face down in a bed of rushes, as if in a great fear; but after a little other children came about them, and they got up and followed her almost bravely. She noticed their fear, and presently stood still and held out her arms. A little girl threw herself into them with the cry, "Ah, you are the Virgin out o' the picture!" "No," said another, coming near also, "she is a sky faery, for she has the colour of the sky." "No," said a third, "she is the faery out of the foxglove grown big." The other children, however, would have it that she was indeed the Virgin, for she wore the Virgin's colours. Her good Protestant heart was greatly troubled, and she got the children to sit down about her, and tried to explain who she was, but they would have none of her explanation. Finding explanation of no avail, she asked had they ever heard of Christ? "Yes," said one; "but we do not like Him, for He would kill us if it were not for the Virgin." "Tell Him to be good to me," whispered another into her ear. "We would not let me near Him, for dad says I am a divil," burst out a third.

She talked to them a long time about Christ and the apostles, but was finally interrupted by an elderly woman with a stick, who, taking her to be some adventurous hunter for converts, drove the children away, despite their explanation that here was the great Queen of Heaven come to walk upon the mountain and be kind to them. When the children had gone she went on her way, and had walked about half-a-mile, when the child who was called "a divil" jumped down from the high ditch by the lane, and said she would believe her "an ordinary lady" if she had "two skirts," for "ladies always had two skirts." The "two skirts" were shown, and the child went away crestfallen, but a few minutes later jumped down again from the ditch, and cried angrily, "Dad's a divil, mum's a divil, and I'm a divil, and you are only an ordinary lady," and having flung a handful of mud and pebbles ran away sobbing. When my pretty Protestant had come to her own home she found that she had dropped the tassels of her parasol. A year later she was by chance upon the mountain, but wearing now a plain black dress, and met the child who had first called her the Virgin out o' the picture, and saw the tassels hanging about the child's neck, and said, "I am the lady you met last year, who told you about Christ." "No, you are not! no, you are not! no, you are not!" was the passionate reply. And after all, it was not my pretty Protestant, but Mary, Star of the Sea, still walking in sadness and in beauty upon many a mountain and by many a shore, who cast those tassels at the feet of the child. It is indeed fitting that man pray to her who is the mother of peace, the mother of dreams, and the mother of purity, to leave them yet a little hour to do good and evil in, and to watch old Time telling the rosary of the stars.

THE GOLDEN AGE

A while ago I was in the train, and getting near Sligo. The last time
I had been there something was troubling me, and I had longed for a
message from those beings or bodiless moods, or whatever they be, who
inhabit the world of spirits. The message came, for one night I saw with
blinding distinctness a black animal, half weasel, half dog, moving along
the top of a stone wall, and presently the black animal vanished, and
from the other side came a white weasel-like dog, his pink flesh shining
through his white hair and all in a blaze of light; and I remembered a
pleasant belief about two faery dogs who go about representing day and
night, good and evil, and was comforted by the excellent omen. But now
I longed for a message of another kind, and chance, if chance there
is, brought it, for a man got into the carriage and began to play on a
fiddle made apparently of an old blacking-box, and though I am quite
unmusical the sounds filled me with the strangest emotions. I seemed to
hear a voice of lamentation out of the Golden Age. It told me that we are
imperfect, incomplete, and no more like a beautiful woven web, but like a
bundle of cords knotted together and flung into a comer. It said that the
world was once all perfect and kindly, and that still the kindly and perfect
world existed, but buried like a mass of roses under many spadefuls of
earth. The faeries and the more innocent of the spirits dwelt within it,
and lamented over our fallen world in the lamentation of the wind-tossed
reeds, in the song of the birds, in the moan of the waves, and in the sweet
cry of the fiddle. It said that with us the beautiful are not clever and the
clever are not beautiful, and that the best of our moments are marred
by a little vulgarity, or by a pin-prick out of sad recollection, and that the

275

fiddle must ever lament about it all. It said that if only they who live in the Golden Age could die we might be happy, for the sad voices would be still; but alas! alas! they must sing and we must weep until the Eternal gates swing open.

We were now getting into the big glass-roofed terminus, and the fiddler put away his old blacking-box and held out his hat for a copper, and then opened the door and was gone.

A REMONSTRANCE WITH SCOTSMEN FOR HAVING SOURED THE DISPOSITION OF THEIR GHOSTS AND FAERIES

Not only in Ireland is faery belief still extant. It was only the other day I heard of a Scottish farmer who believed that the lake in front of his house was haunted by a water-horse. He was afraid of it, and dragged the lake with nets, and then tried to pump it empty. It would have been a bad thing for the water-horse had he found him. An Irish peasant would have long since come to terms with the creature. For in Ireland there is something of timid affection between men and spirits. They only ill-treat each other in reason. Each admits the other side to have feelings. There are points beyond which neither will go. No Irish peasant would treat a captured faery as did the man Campbell tells of. He caught a kelpie, and tied her behind him on his horse. She was fierce, but he kept her quiet by driving an awl and a needle into her. They came to a river, and she grew very restless, fearing to cross the water. Again he drove the awl and needle into her. She cried out, "Pierce me with the awl, but keep that slender, hair-like slave (the needle) out of me." They came to an inn. He turned the light of a lantern on her; immediately she dropped down like a falling star, and changed into a lump of jelly. She was dead. Nor would they treat the faeries as one is treated in an old Highland poem. A faery loved a little child who used to cut turf at the side of a faery hill. Every day the faery put out his hand from the hill with an enchanted knife. The child used to cut the turf with the knife. It did not take long, the knife being charmed. Her brothers wondered why she was done so quickly. At last they resolved to watch, and find out who helped her. They saw the small hand come out of the earth, and the little child take from it the knife. When the turf was all cut, they saw her make three taps on the ground with the handle. The small hand came out of the hill. Snatching the knife from the child, they cut the hand off with a blow. The faery was never again seen. He drew his bleeding arm into the earth, thinking, as it is recorded, he had lost his hand through the treachery of the child.

In Scotland you are too theological, too gloomy. You have made even the Devil religious. "Where do you live, good-wyf, and how is the minister?" he said to the witch when he met her on the high-road, as it came out in the trial. You have burnt all the witches. In Ireland we have left them alone. To be sure, the "loyal minority" knocked out the eye of one with a cabbage-stump on the 31st of March, 1711, in the town of Carrickfergus. But then the "loyal minority" is half Scottish. You have discovered the faeries to be pagan and wicked. You would like to have them all up before the magistrate. In Ireland warlike mortals have gone amongst them, and helped them in their battles, and they in turn have taught men great skill with herbs, and permitted some few to hear their tunes. Carolan slept upon a faery rath. Ever after their tunes ran in his head, and made him the great musician he was. In Scotland you have denounced them from the pulpit. In Ireland they have been permitted by the priests to consult them on the state of their souls. Unhappily the priests have decided that they have no souls, that they will dry up like so much bright vapour at the last day; but more in sadness than in anger they have said it. The Catholic religion likes to keep on good terms with its neighbours.

These two different ways of looking at things have influenced in each country the whole world of sprites and goblins. For their gay and graceful doings you must go to Ireland; for their deeds of terror to Scotland. Our Irish faery terrors have about them something of make-believe. When a peasant strays into an enchanted hovel, and is made to turn a corpse all night on a spit before the fire, we do not feel anxious; we know he will wake in the midst of a green field, the dew on his old coat. In Scotland it is altogether different. You have soured the naturally excellent disposition of ghosts and goblins. The piper M'Crimmon, of the Hebrides, shouldered his pipes, and marched into a sea cavern, playing loudly, and followed by his dog. For a long time the people could hear the pipes. He must have gone nearly a mile, when they heard the sound of a struggle. Then the piping ceased suddenly. Some time went by, and then his dog came out of the cavern completely flayed, too weak even to howl. Nothing else ever came out of the cavern. Then there is the tale of the man who dived into a lake where treasure was thought to be. He saw a great coffer of iron. Close to the coffer lay a monster, who warned him to return whence he came. He rose to the surface; but the bystanders, when they heard he had seen the treasure, persuaded him to dive again. He dived. In a little while his heart and liver floated up, reddening the water. No man ever saw the rest of his body.

These water-goblins and water-monsters are common in Scottish folk-lore. We have them too, but take them much less dreadfully. Our tales turn all their doings to favour and to prettiness, or hopelessly humorize the creatures. A hole in the Sligo river is haunted by one of these monsters. He is ardently believed in by many, but that does not prevent the peasantry playing with the subject, and surrounding it with conscious fantasies. When I was a small boy I fished one day for congers in the monster hole. Returning home, a great eel on my shoulder, his head flapping down in front, his tail sweeping the ground behind, I met a fisherman of my acquaintance. I began a tale of an immense conger, three times larger than the one I carried, that had broken my line and escaped. "That was him," said the fisherman. "Did you ever hear how he made my brother emigrate? My brother was a diver, you know, and grubbed stones for the Harbour Board. One day the beast comes up to him, and says, 'What are you after?' 'Stones, sur,' says he. 'Don't you think you had better be going?' 'Yes, sur,' says he. And that's why my brother emigrated. The people said it was because he got poor, but that's not true."

You—you will make no terms with the spirits of fire and earth and air and water. You have made the Darkness your enemy. We—we exchange civilities with the world beyond.

WAR

When there was a rumour of war with France a while ago, I met a poor Sligo woman, a soldier's widow, that I know, and I read her a sentence out of a letter I had just had from London: "The people here are mad for war, but France seems inclined to take things peacefully," or some like sentence. Her mind ran a good deal on war, which she imagined partly from what she had heard from soldiers, and partly from tradition of the rebellion of '98, but the word London doubled her interest, for she knew there were a great many people in London, and she herself had once lived in "a congested district." "There are too many over one another in London. They are getting tired of the world. It is killed they want to be. It will be no matter; but sure the French want nothing but peace and quietness. The people here don't mind the war coming. They could not be worse than they are. They may as well die soldierly before God. Sure they will get quarters in heaven." Then she began to say that it would be a hard thing to see children tossed about on bayonets, and I knew her mind was running on traditions of the great rebellion. She said presently, "I never knew a man that was in a battle that liked to speak of it after. They'd sooner be throwing hay down from a hayrick." She told me how she and her neighbours used to be sitting over the fire when she was a girl, talking of the war that was coming, and now she was afraid it was coming again, for she had dreamed that all the bay was "stranded and covered with seaweed." I asked her if it was in the Fenian times that she had been so much afraid of war coming. But she cried out, "Never had I such fun and pleasure as in the Fenian times. I was in a house where some of the officers used to be staying, and in the daytime I would be walking after the soldiers' band, and at night I'd be going down to the end of the garden watching a soldier, with his red coat on him, drilling the Fenians in the field behind the house. One night the boys tied the liver of an old horse, that had been dead three weeks, to the knocker, and I found it when I opened the door in the morning." And presently our talk of war shifted, as it had a way of doing, to the battle of the Black Pig, which seems to her a battle between Ireland and England, but to me an Armageddon which shall quench all things in the Ancestral Darkness again, and from this to sayings about war and vengeance. "Do you know," she said, "what the curse of the Four Fathers is? They put the man-child on the spear, and somebody said to them, 'You will be cursed in the fourth generation after you,' and that is why disease or anything always comes in the fourth generation."

1902.

THE QUEEN AND THE FOOL

I have heard one Hearne, a witch-doctor, who is on the border of Clare and Galway, say that in "every household" of faery "there is a queen and a fool," and that if you are "touched" by either you never recover, though you may from the touch of any other in faery. He said of the fool that he was "maybe the wisest of all," and spoke of him as dressed like one of the "mummers that used to be going about the country." Since then a friend has gathered me some few stories of him, and I have heard that he is known, too, in the highlands. I remember seeing a long, lank, ragged man sitting by the hearth in the cottage of an old miller not far from where I am now writing, and being told that he was a fool; and I find from the stories that my friend has gathered that he is believed to go to faery in his sleep; but whether he becomes an Amadan-na-Breena, a fool of the forth, and is attached to a household there, I cannot tell. It was an old woman that I know well, and who has been in faery herself, that spoke of him. She said, "There are fools amongst them, and the fools we see, like that Amadan of Ballylee, go away with them at night, and so do the woman fools that we call Oinseachs (apes)." A woman who is related to the witch-doctor on the border of Clare, and who can Cure people and cattle by spells, said, "There are some cures I can't do. I can't help any one that has got a stroke from the queen or the fool of the forth. I knew of a woman that saw the queen one time, and she looked like any Christian. I never heard of any that saw the fool but one woman that was walking near Gort, and she called out, 'There's the fool of the forth coming after me.' So her friends that were with her called out, though they could see nothing, and I suppose he went away at that, for she got no harm. He was like a big strong man, she said, and half naked, and that is all she said about him. I have never seen any myself, but I am a cousin of Hearne, and my uncle was away twenty-one years." The wife of the old miller said, "It is said they are mostly good neighbours, but the stroke of the fool is what there is no cure for; any one that gets that is gone. The Amadan-na-Breena we call him!" And an old woman who lives in the Bog of Kiltartan, and is very poor, said, "It is true enough, there is no cure for the stroke of the Amadan-na-Breena. There was an old man I knew long ago, he had a tape, and he could tell what diseases you had with measuring you; and he knew many things. And he said to me one time, 'What month of the year is the worst?' and I said, 'The month of May, of course.' 'It is not,' he said; 'but the month of June, for that's the month that the Amadan gives his stroke!' They say he looks like any other man, but he's leathan (wide), and not smart. I knew a boy one time got a great fright, for a lamb looked over the wall at him with a beard on it, and he knew it was the Amadan, for it was the month of June. And they brought him to that man I was telling about, that had the tape, and when he saw him he said, 'Send for the priest, and get a Mass said over him.' And so they did, and what would you say but he's living yet and has a family! A certain Regan said, 'They, the other sort of people, might be passing you close here and they might touch you. But any that gets the touch of the Amadan-na-Breena is done for.' It's true enough that it's in the month of June he's most likely to give the touch. I knew one that got it, and he told me about it himself. He was a boy I knew well, and he told me that one night a gentleman came to him, that had been his land-lord, and that was dead. And he told him to come along with him, for he wanted him to fight another man. And when he went he found two great troops of them, and the other troop had a living man with them too, and he was put to fight him. And they had a great fight, and he got the better of the other man, and then the troop on his side gave a great shout, and he was left home again. But about three years after that he was cutting bushes in a wood and he saw the Amadan coming at him. He

284

had a big vessel in his arms, and it was shining, so that the boy could see nothing else; but he put it behind his back then and came running, and the boy said he looked wild and wide, like the side of the hill. And the boy ran, and he threw the vessel after him, and it broke with a great noise, and whatever came out of it, his head was gone there and then. He lived for a while after, and used to tell us many things, but his wits were gone. He thought they mightn't have liked him to beat the other man, and he used to be afraid something would come on him." And an old woman in a Galway workhouse, who had some little knowledge of Queen Maive, said the other day, "The Amadan-na-Breena changes his shape every two days. Sometimes he comes like a youngster, and then he'll come like the worst of beasts, trying to give the touch he used to be. I heard it said of late he was shot, but I think myself it would be hard to shoot him."

I knew a man who was trying to bring before his mind's eye an image of Aengus, the old Irish god of love and poetry and ecstasy, who changed four of his kisses into birds, and suddenly the image of a man with a cap and bells rushed before his mind's eye, and grew vivid and spoke and called itself "Aengus' messenger." And I knew another man, a truly great seer, who saw a white fool in a visionary garden, where there was a tree with peacocks' feathers instead of leaves, and flowers that opened to show little human faces when the white fool had touched them with his coxcomb, and he saw at another time a white fool sitting by a pool and smiling and watching the images of many fair women floating up from the pool.

What else can death be but the beginning of wisdom and power and beauty? and foolishness may be a kind of death. I cannot think it wonderful that many should see a fool with a shining vessel of some enchantment or wisdom or dream too powerful for mortal brains in "every household of them." It is natural, too, that there should be a queen to every household of them, and that one should hear little of their kings, for women come more easily than men to that wisdom which ancient peoples, and all wild peoples even now, think the only wisdom. The self, which is the foundation of our knowledge, is broken in pieces

285

by foolishness, and is forgotten in the sudden emotions of women, and therefore fools may get, and women do get of a certainty, glimpses of much that sanctity finds at the end of its painful journey. The man who saw the white fool said of a certain woman, not a peasant woman, "If I had her power of vision I would know all the wisdom of the gods, and her visions do not interest her." And I know of another woman, also not a peasant woman, who would pass in sleep into countries of an unearthly beauty, and who never cared for anything but to be busy about her house and her children; and presently an herb doctor cured her, as he called it. Wisdom and beauty and power may sometimes, as I think, come to those who die every day they live, though their dying may not be like the dying Shakespeare spoke of. There is a war between the living and the dead, and the Irish stories keep harping upon it. They will have it that when the potatoes or the wheat or any other of the fruits of the earth decay, they ripen in faery, and that our dreams lose their wisdom when the sap rises in the trees, and that our dreams can make the trees wither, and that one hears the bleating of the lambs of faery in November, and that blind eyes can see more than other eyes. Because the soul always believes in these, or in like things, the cell and the wilderness shall never be long empty, or lovers come into the world who will not understand the verse—

> Heardst thou not sweet words among
> That heaven-resounding minstrelsy?
> Heardst thou not that those who die
> Awake in a world of ecstasy?
> How love, when limbs are interwoven,
> And sleep, when the night of life is cloven,
> And thought to the world's dim boundaries clinging,
> And music when one's beloved is singing,
> Is death?

1901.

THE FRIENDS OF THE
PEOPLE OF FAERY

Those that see the people of faery most often, and so have the most of their wisdom, are often very poor, but often, too, they are thought to have a strength beyond that of man, as though one came, when one has passed the threshold of trance, to those sweet waters where Maeldun saw the dishevelled eagles bathe and become young again.

There was an old Martin Roland, who lived near a bog a little out of Gort, who saw them often from his young days, and always towards the end of his life, though I would hardly call him their friend. He told me a few months before his death that "they" would not let him sleep at night with crying things at him in Irish, and with playing their pipes. He had asked a friend of his what he should do, and the friend had told him to buy a flute, and play on it when they began to shout or to play on their pipes, and maybe they would give up annoying him; and he did, and they always went out into the field when he began to play. He showed me the pipe, and blew through it, and made a noise, but he did not know how to play; and then he showed me where he had pulled his chimney down, because one of them used to sit up on it and play on the pipes. A friend of his and mine went to see him a little time ago, for she heard that "three of them" had told him he was to die. He said they had gone away after warning him, and that the children (children they had "taken," I suppose) who used to come with them, and play about the house with them, had "gone to some other place," because "they found the house too cold for them, maybe"; and he died a week after he had said these things.

His neighbours were not certain that he really saw anything in his old age, but they were all certain that he saw things when he was a young man. His brother said, "Old he is, and it's all in his brain the things he sees. If he was a young man we might believe in him." But he was improvident, and never got on with his brothers. A neighbour said, "The poor man, they say they are mostly in his head now, but sure he was a fine fresh man twenty years ago the night he saw them linked in two lots, like young slips of girls walking together. It was the night they took away Fallon's little girl." And she told how Fallon's little girl had met a woman "with red hair that was as bright as silver," who took her away. Another neighbour, who was herself "clouted over the ear" by one of them for going into a fort where they were, said, "I believe it's mostly in his head they are; and when he stood in the door last night I said, 'The wind does be always in my ears, and the sound of it never stops,' to make him think it was the same with him; but he says, 'I hear them singing and making music all the time, and one of them is after bringing out a little flute, and it's on it he's playing to them.' And this I know, that when he pulled down the chimney where he said the piper used to be sitting and playing, he lifted up stones, and he an old man, that I could not have lifted when I was young and strong."

A friend has sent me from Ulster an account of one who was on terms of true friendship with the people of faery. It has been taken down accurately, for my friend, who had heard the old woman's story some time before I heard of it, got her to tell it over again, and wrote it out at once. She began by telling the old woman that she did not like being in the house alone because of the ghosts and fairies; and the old woman said, "There's nothing to be frightened about in faeries, miss. Many's the time I talked to a woman myself that was a faery, or something of the sort, and no less and more than mortal anyhow. She used to come about your grandfather's house—your mother's grandfather, that is—in my young days. But you'll have heard all about her." My friend said that she had heard about her, but a long time before, and she wanted to hear about her again; and the old woman went on, "Well dear, the very first time ever I heard word of her coming about was when your uncle—that is, your mother's uncle—Joseph married, and building a house for his wife, for he brought her first to his father's, up at the house by the Lough. My father and us were living nigh hand to where the new house was to be built, to overlook the men at their work. My father was a weaver, and brought his looms and all there into a cottage that was close by. The foundations were marked out, and the building stones lying about, but the masons had not come yet; and one day I was standing with my mother foment the house, when we sees a smart wee woman coming up the field over the burn to us. I was a bit of a girl at the time, playing about and sporting myself, but I mind her as well as if I saw her there now!" My friend asked how the woman was dressed, and the old woman said, "It was a gray cloak she had on, with a green cashmere skirt and a black silk handkercher tied round her head, like the country women did use to wear in them times." My friend asked, "How wee was she?" And the old woman said, "Well now, she wasn't wee at all when I think of it, for all we called her the Wee Woman. She was bigger than many a one, and yet not tall as you would say. She was like a woman about thirty, brown-haired and round in the face. She was like Miss Betty, your grandmother's sister, and Betty was like none of the rest, not like your grandmother, nor any of them. She was round and fresh in the face, and she never was married, and she never would take any man; and we used to say that the Wee Woman—her being like Betty—was, maybe, one of their own people that had been took off before she grew to her full height, and for that she was always following us and warning and foretelling. This time she walks straight over to where my mother was standing. 'Go over to the Lough this minute!'—ordering her like that—'Go over to the Lough, and tell Joseph that he must change the foundation of this house to where I'll show you fornent the thornbush. That is where it is to be built, if he is to have luck and prosperity, so do what I'm telling ye this minute.' The house was being built on 'the path' I suppose—the path used by the people of faery in their journeys, and my mother brings Joseph down and shows him, and he changes the foundations, the way he was bid, but didn't bring it exactly to where was pointed, and the end of that was, when he come to the house, his own wife lost her life with an accident that come to a horse that hadn't room to turn right with a harrow between the bush and the wall. The Wee Woman was queer and angry when next she come, and says to us, 'He didn't do as I bid him, but he'll see what he'll see.'" My friend asked where the woman came from this time, and if she was dressed as before, and the woman said, "Always the same way, up the field beyant the burn. It was a thin sort of shawl she had about her in summer, and a cloak about her in winter; and many and many a time she came, and always it was good advice she was giving to my mother, and warning her what not to do if she would have good luck. There was none of the other children of us ever seen her unless me; but I used to be glad when I seen her coming up the bum, and would run out and catch her by the hand and the cloak, and call to my mother, 'Here's the Wee Woman!' No man body ever seen her. My father used to be wanting to, and was angry with my mother and me, thinking we were telling lies and talking foolish like. And so one day when she had come, and was sitting by the fireside talking to my mother, I slips out to the field where he was digging. 'Come up,' says I, 'if ye want to see her. She's sitting at the fireside now, talking to mother.' So in he comes with me and looks round angry like and sees nothing, and he up with a broom that was near hand and hits me a crig with it. 'Take that now!' says he, 'for making a fool of me!' and away with him as fast as he could, and queer and angry with me. The Wee Woman says to me then, 'Ye got that now for bringing people to see me. No man body ever seen me, and none ever will.'

"There was one day, though, she gave him a queer fright anyway, whether he had seen her or not. He was in among the cattle when it happened, and he comes up to the house all trembling like. 'Don't let me hear you say another word of your Wee Woman. I have got enough of her this time.' Another time, all the same, he was up Gortin to sell horses, and before he went off, in steps the Wee Woman and says she to my mother, holding out a sort of a weed, 'Your man is gone up by Gortin, and there's a bad fright waiting him coming home, but take this and sew it in his coat, and he'll get no harm by it.' My mother takes the herb, but thinks to herself, 'Sure there's nothing in it,' and throws it on the floor, and lo and behold, and sure enough! coming home from Gortin, my father got as bad a fright as ever he got in his life. What it was I don't right mind, but anyway he was badly damaged by it. My mother was in a queer way, frightened of the Wee Woman, after what she done, and sure enough the next time she was angry. 'Ye didn't believe me,' she said, 'and ye threw the herb I gave ye in the fire, and I went far enough for it.' There was another time she came and told how William Hearne was dead in America. 'Go over,' she says, 'to the Lough, and say that William is dead, and he died happy, and this was the last Bible chapter ever he read,' and with that she gave the verse and chapter. 'Go,' she says, 'and tell them to read them at the next class meeting, and that I held his head while he died.' And sure enough word came after that how William had died on the day she named. And, doing as she did about the chapter and hymn, they never had such a prayer-meeting as that. One day she and me and my mother was standing talking, and she was warning her about something, when she says of a sudden, 'Here comes Miss Letty in all her finery, and it's time for me to be off.' And with that she gave a swirl round on her feet, and raises up in the air, and round and round she goes, and up and up, as if it was a winding stairs she went up, only far swifter. She went up and up, till she was no bigger than a bird up against the clouds, singing and singing the whole time the loveliest music I ever heard in my life from that day to this. It wasn't a hymn she was singing, but poetry, lovely poetry, and me and my mother stands gaping up, and all of a tremble. 'What is she at all, mother?' says I. 'Is it an angel she is, or a faery woman, or what?' With that up come Miss Letty, that was your grandmother, dear, but Miss Letty she was then, and no word of her being anything else, and she wondered to see us gaping up that way, till me and my mother told her of it. She went on gay-dressed then, and was lovely looking. She was up the lane where none of us could see her coming forward when the Wee Woman rose up in that queer way, saying, 'Here comes Miss Letty in all her finery.' Who knows to what far country she went, or to see whom dying?

"It was never after dark she came, but daylight always, as far as I mind, but wanst, and that was on a Hallow Eve night. My mother was by the fire, making ready the supper; she had a duck down and some apples. In slips the Wee Woman, 'I'm come to pass my Hallow Eve with you,' says she. 'That's right,' says my mother, and thinks to herself, 'I can give her her supper nicely.' Down she sits by the fire a while. 'Now I'll tell you where you'll bring my supper,' says she. 'In the room beyond there beside the loom—set a chair in and a plate.' 'When ye're spending the night, mayn't ye as well sit by the table and eat with the rest of us?' 'Do what you're bid, and set whatever you give me in the room beyant. I'll eat there and nowhere else.' So my mother sets her a plate of duck and some apples, whatever was going, in where she bid, and we got to our supper and she to hers; and when we rose I went in, and there, lo and behold ye, was her supper-plate a bit ate of each portion, and she clean gone!"

1897.

DREAMS THAT HAVE NO MORAL

The friend who heard about Maive and the hazel-stick went to the workhouse another day. She found the old people cold and wretched, "like flies in winter," she said; but they forgot the cold when they began to talk. A man had just left them who had played cards in a rath with the people of faery, who had played "very fair"; and one old man had seen an enchanted black pig one night, and there were two old people my friend had heard quarrelling as to whether Raftery or Callanan was the better poet. One had said of Raftery, "He was a big man, and his songs have gone through the whole world. I remember him well. He had a voice like the wind"; but the other was certain "that you would stand in the snow to listen to Callanan." Presently an old man began to tell my friend a story, and all listened delightedly, bursting into laughter now and then. The story, which I am going to tell just as it was told, was one of those old rambling moralless tales, which are the delight of the poor and the hard driven, wherever life is left in its natural simplicity. They tell of a time when nothing had consequences, when even if you were killed, if only you had a good heart, somebody would bring you to life again with a touch of a rod, and when if you were a prince and happened to look exactly like your brother, you might go to bed with his queen, and have only a little quarrel afterwards. We too, if we were so weak and poor that everything threatened us with misfortune, would remember, if foolish people left us alone, every old dream that has been strong enough to fling the weight of the world from its shoulders.

There was a king one time who was very much put out because he had no son, and he went at last to consult his chief adviser. And the chief adviser said, "It's easy enough managed if you do as I tell you. Let you send some one," says he, "to such a place to catch a fish. And when the fish is brought in, give it to the queen, your wife, to eat."

So the king sent as he was told, and the fish was caught and brought in, and he gave it to the cook, and bade her put it before the fire, but to be careful with it, and not to let any blob or blister rise on it. But it is impossible to cook a fish before the fire without the skin of it rising in some place or other, and so there came a blob on the skin, and the cook put her finger on it to smooth it down, and then she put her finger into her mouth to cool it, and so she got a taste of the fish. And then it was sent up to the queen, and she ate it, and what was left of it was thrown out into the yard, and there was a mare in the yard and a greyhound, and they ate the bits that were thrown out.

And before a year was out, the queen had a young son, and the cook had a young son, and the mare had two foals, and the greyhound had two pups.

And the two young sons were sent out for a while to some place to be cared, and when they came back they adviser and said, "Tell me some way that I can know were so much like one another no person could know which was the queen's son and which was the cook's. And the queen was vexed at that, and she went to the chief which is my own son, for I don't like to be giving the same eating and drinking to the cook's son as to my own." "It is easy to know that," said the chief adviser, "if you will do as I tell you. Go you outside, and stand at the door they will be coming in by, and when they see you, your own son will bow his head, but the cook's son will only laugh."

So she did that, and when her own son bowed his head, her servants put a mark on him that she would know him again. And when they were all sitting at their dinner after that, she said to Jack, that was the cook's son, "It is time for you to go away out of this, for you are not my son." And her own son, that we will call Bill, said, "Do not send him away, are we not brothers?" But Jack said, "I would have been long ago out of this

294

house if I knew it was not my own father and mother owned it." And for all Bill could say to him, he would not stop. But before he went, they were by the well that was in the garden, and he said to Bill, "If harm ever happens to me, that water on the top of the well will be blood, and the water below will be honey."

Then he took one of the pups, and one of the two horses, that was foaled after the mare eating the fish, and the wind that was after him could not catch him, and he caught the wind that was before him. And he went on till he came to a weaver's house, and he asked him for a lodging, and he gave it to him. And then he went on till he came to a king's house, and he sent in at the door to ask, "Did he want a servant?" "All I want," said the king, "is a boy that will drive out the cows to the field every morning, and bring them in at night to be milked." "I will do that for you," said Jack; so the king engaged him.

In the morning Jack was sent out with the four-and-twenty cows, and the place he was told to drive them to had not a blade of grass in it for them, but was full of stones. So Jack looked about for some place where there would be better grass, and after a while he saw a field with good green grass in it, and it belonging to a giant. So he knocked down a bit of the wall and drove them in, and he went up himself into an apple-tree and began to eat the apples. Then the giant came into the field. "Fee-faw-fum," says he, "I smell the blood of an Irishman. I see you where you are, up in the tree," he said; "you are too big for one mouthful, and too small for two mouthfuls, and I don't know what I'll do with you if I don't grind you up and make snuff for my nose." "As you are strong, be merciful," says Jack up in the tree. "Come down out of that, you little dwarf," said the giant, "or I'll tear you and the tree asunder." So Jack came down. "Would you sooner be driving red-hot knives into one another's hearts," said the giant, "or would you sooner be fighting one another on red-hot flags?" "Fighting on red-hot flags is what I'm used to at home," said Jack, "and your dirty feet will be sinking in them and my feet will be rising." So then they began the fight. The ground that was hard they made soft, and the ground that was soft they made hard, and they made spring wells come up through the green flags. They were like that all through the day, no one getting the upper hand of the other, and at last a little bird came and sat on the bush and said to Jack, "If you don't make an end of him by sunset, he'll make an end of you." Then Jack put out his strength, and he brought the giant down on his knees. "Give me my life," says the giant, "and I'll give you the three best gifts." "What are those?" said Jack. "A sword that nothing can stand against, and a suit that when you put it on, you will see everybody, and nobody will see you, and a pair of shoes that will make you ran faster than the wind blows." "Where are they to be found?" said Jack. "In that red door you see there in the hill." So Jack went and got them out. "Where will I try the sword?" says he. "Try it on that ugly black stump of a tree," says the giant. "I see nothing blacker or uglier than your own head," says Jack. And with that he made one stroke, and cut off the giant's head that it went into the air, and he caught it on the sword as it was coming down, and made two halves of it. "It is well for you I did not join the body again," said the head, "or you would have never been able to strike it off again." "I did not give you the chance of that," said Jack. And he brought away the great suit with him.

So he brought the cows home at evening, and every one wondered at all the milk they gave that night. And when the king was sitting at dinner with the princess, his daughter, and the rest, he said, "I think I only hear two roars from beyond to-night in place of three."

The next morning Jack went out again with the cows, and he saw another field full of grass, and he knocked down the wall and let the cows in. All happened the same as the day before, but the giant that came this time had two heads, and they fought together, and the little bird came and spoke to Jack as before. And when Jack had brought the giant down, he said, "Give me my life, and I'll give you the best thing I have." "What is that?" says Jack. "It's a suit that you can put on, and you will see every one but no one can see you." "Where is it?" said Jack. "It's inside that little red door at the side of the hill." So Jack went and brought out the

suit. And then he cut off the giant's two heads, and caught them coming down and made four halves of them. And they said it was well for him he had not given them time to join the body.

That night when the cows came home they gave so much milk that all the vessels that could be found were filled up.

The next morning Jack went out again, and all happened as before, and the giant this time had four heads, and Jack made eight halves of them. And the giant had told him to go to a little blue door in the side of the hill, and there he got a pair of shoes that when you put them on would go faster than the wind.

That night the cows gave so much milk that there were not vessels enough to hold it, and it was given to tenants and to poor people passing the road, and the rest was thrown out at the windows. I was passing that way myself, and I got a drink of it.

That night the king said to Jack, "Why is it the cows are giving so much milk these days? Are you bringing them to any other grass?" "I am not," said Jack, "but I have a good stick, and whenever they would stop still or lie down, I give them blows of it, that they jump and leap over walls and stones and ditches; that's the way to make cows give plenty of milk."

And that night at the dinner, the king said, "I hear no roars at all."

The next morning, the king and the princess were watching at the window to see what would Jack do when he got to the field. And Jack knew they were there, and he got a stick, and began to batter the cows, that they went leaping and jumping over stones, and walls, and ditches. "There is no lie in what Jack said," said the king then.

Now there was a great serpent at that time used to come every seven years, and he had to get a kines daughter to eat, unless she would have some good man to fight for her. And it was the princess at the place Jack was had to be given to it that time, and the king had been feeding a bully underground for seven years, and you may believe he got the best of everything, to be ready to fight it.

And when the time came, the princess went out, and the bully with her down to the shore, and when they got there what did he do, but to tie the princess to a tree, the way the serpent would be able to swallow her easy with no delay, and he himself went and hid up in an ivy-tree. And Jack knew what was going on, for the princess had told him about it, and had asked would he help her, but he said he would not. But he came out now, and he put on the suit he had taken from the first giant, and he came by the place the princess was, but she didn't know him. "Is that right for a princess to be tied to a tree?" said Jack. "It is not, indeed," said she, and she told him what had happened, and how the serpent was coming to take her. "If you will let me sleep for awhile with my head in your lap," said Jack, "you could wake me when it is coming." So he did that, and she awakened him when she saw the serpent coming, and Jack got up and fought with it, and drove it back into the sea. And then he cut the rope that fastened her, and he went away. The bully came down then out of the tree, and he brought the princess to where the king was, and he said, "I got a friend of mine to come and fight the serpent to-day, where I was a little timorous after being so long shut up underground, but I'll do the fighting myself to-morrow."

The next day they went out again, and the same thing happened, the bully tied up the princess where the serpent could come at her fair and easy, and went up himself to hide in the ivy-tree. Then Jack put on the suit he had taken from the second giant, and he walked out, and the princess did not know him, but she told him all that had happened yesterday, and how some young gentleman she did not know had come and saved her. So Jack asked might he lie down and take a sleep with his head in her lap, the way she could awake him. And an happened the same way as the day before. And the bully gave her up to the king, and said he had brought another of his friends to fight for her that day.

The next day she was brought down to the shore as before, and a great many people gathered to see the serpent that was coming to bring the king's daughter away. And Jack brought out the suit of clothes he had brought away from the third giant, and she did not know him, and they talked as before. But when he was asleep this time, she thought she would make sure of being able to find him again, and she took out her scissors and cut off a piece of his hair, and made a little packet of it and put it away. And she did another thing, she took off one of the shoes that was on his feet.

And when she saw the serpent coming she woke him, and he said, "This time I will put the serpent in a way that he will eat no more king's daughters." So he took out the sword he had got from the giant, and he put it in at the back of the serpent's neck, the way blood and water came spouting out that went for fifty miles inland, and made an end of him. And then he made off, and no one saw what way he went, and the bully brought the princess to the king, and claimed to have saved her, and it is he who was made much of, and was the right-hand man after that.

But when the feast was made ready for the wedding, the princess took out the bit of hair she had, and she said she would marry no one but the man whose hair would match that, and she showed the shoe and said that she would marry no one whose foot would not fit that shoe as well. And the bully tried to put on the shoe, but so much as his toe would not go into it, and as to his hair, it didn't match at all to the bit of hair she had cut from the man that saved her.

So then the king gave a great ball, to bring all the chief men of the country together to try would the shoe fit any of them. And they were all going to carpenters and joiners getting bits of their feet cut off to try could they wear the shoe, but it was no use, not one of them could get it on.

Then the king went to his chief adviser and asked what could he do. And the chief adviser bade him to give another ball, and this time he said, "Give it to poor as well as rich."

So the ball was given, and many came flocking to it, but the shoe would not fit any one of them. And the chief adviser said, "Is every one here that belongs to the house?" "They are all here," said the king, "except the boy that minds the cows, and I would not like him to be coming up here."

Jack was below in the yard at the time, and he heard what the king said, and he was very angry, and he went and got his sword and came running up the stairs to strike off the king's head, but the man that kept the gate met him on the stairs before he could get to the king, and quieted him down, and when he got to the top of the stairs and the princess saw him, she gave a cry and ran into his arms. And they tried the shoe and it fitted him, and his hair matched to the piece that had been cut off. So then they were married, and a great feast was given for three days and three nights.

And at the end of that time, one morning there came a deer outside the window, with bells on it, and they ringing. And it called out, "Here is the hunt, where is the huntsman and the hound?" So when Jack heard that he got up and took his horse and his hound and went hunting the deer. When it was in the hollow he was on the hill, and when it was on the hill he was in the hollow, and that went on all through the day, and when night fell it went into a wood. And Jack went into the wood after it, and all he could see was a mud-wall cabin, and he went in, and there he saw an old woman, about two hundred years old, and she sitting over the fire. "Did you see a deer pass this way?" says Jack. "I did not," says she, "but it's too late now for you to be following a deer, let you stop the night here." "What will I do with my horse and my hound?" said Jack. "Here are two ribs of hair," says she, "and let you tie them up with them." So Jack went out and tied up the horse and the hound, and when he came in again the old woman said, "You killed my three sons, and I'm going to kill you now," and she put on a pair of boxing-gloves, each one of them nine stone weight, and the nails in them fifteen inches long. Then they began to fight, and Jack was getting the worst of it. "Help, hound!" he cried out, then "Squeeze hair," cried out the old woman, and the rib of hair that was about the hound's neck squeezed him to death. "Help, horse!" Jack called out, then, "Squeeze hair," called out the old woman, and the rib of hair that was about the horse's neck began to tighten and squeeze him to death. Then the old woman made an end of Jack and threw him outside the door.

To go back now to Bill. He was out in the garden one day, and he took a look at the well, and what did he see but the water at the top was blood, and what was underneath was honey. So he went into the house again, and he said to his mother, "I will never eat a second meal at the same table, or sleep a second night in the same bed, till I know what is happening to Jack."

So he took the other horse and hound then, and set off, over the hills where cock never crows and horn never sounds, and the devil never blows his bugle. And at last he came to the weaver's house, and when he went in, the weaver says, "You are welcome, and I can give you better treatment than I did the last time you came in to me," for she thought it was Jack who was there, they were so much like one another. "That is good," said Bill to himself, "my brother has been here." And he gave the weaver the full of a basin of gold in the morning before he left.

Then he went on till he came to the king's house, and when he was at the door the princess came running down the stairs, and said, "Welcome to you back again." And all the people said, "It is a wonder you have gone hunting three days after your marriage, and to stop so long away." So he stopped that night with the princess, and she thought it was her own husband all the time.

And in the morning the deer came, and bells ringing on her, under the windows, and called out, "The hunt is here, where are the huntsmen and the hounds?" Then Bill got up and got his horse and his hound, and followed her over hills and hollows till they came to the wood, and there he saw nothing but the mud-wall cabin and the old woman sitting by the fire, and she bade him stop the night there, and gave him two ribs of hair to tie his horse and his hound with. But Bill was wittier than Jack was, and before he went out, he threw the ribs of hair into the fire secretly. When he came in the old woman said, "Your brother killed my three sons, and

I killed him, and I'll kill you along with him." And she put her gloves on, and they began the fight, and then Bill called out, "Help, horse." "Squeeze hair," called the old woman; "I can't squeeze, I'm in the fire," said the hair. And the horse came in and gave her a blow of his hoof. "Help, hound," said Bill then. "Squeeze, hair," said the old woman; "I can't, I'm in the fire," said the second hair. Then the bound put his teeth in her, and Bill brought her down, and she cried for mercy. "Give me my life," she said, "and I'll tell you where you'll get your brother again, and his hound and horse." "Where's that?" said Bill. "Do you see that rod over the fire?" said she; "take it down and go outside the door where you'll see three green stones, and strike them with the rod, for they are your brother, and his horse and hound, and they'll come to life again." "I will, but I'll make a green stone of you first," said Bill, and he cut off her head with his sword.

Then he went out and struck the stones, and sure enough there were Jack, and his horse and hound, alive and well. And they began striking other stones around, and men came from them, that had been turned to stones, hundreds and thousands of them.

Then they set out for home, but on the way they had some dispute or some argument together, for Jack was not well pleased to hear he had spent the night with his wife, and Bill got angry, and he struck Jack with the rod, and turned him to a green stone. And he went home, but the princess saw he had something on his mind, and he said then, "I have killed my brother." And he went back then and brought him to life, and they lived happy ever after, and they had children by the basketful, and threw them out by the shovelful. I was passing one time myself, and they called me in and gave me a cup of tea.

1902.

BY THE ROADSIDE

Last night I went to a wide place on the Kiltartan road to listen to some Irish songs. While I waited for the singers an old man sang about that country beauty who died so many years ago, and spoke of a singer he had known who sang so beautifully that no horse would pass him, but must turn its head and cock its ears to listen. Presently a score of men and boys and girls, with shawls over their beads, gathered under the trees to listen. Somebody sang Sa Muirnin Diles, and then somebody else Jimmy Mo Milestor, mournful songs of separation, of death, and of exile. Then some of the men stood up and began to dance, while another lilted the measure they danced to, and then somebody sang Eiblin a Ruin, that glad song of meeting which has always moved me more than other songs, because the lover who made it sang it to his sweetheart under the shadow of a mountain I looked at every day through my childhood. The voices melted into the twilight and were mixed into the trees, and when I thought of the words they too melted away, and were mixed with the generations of men. Now it was a phrase, now it was an attitude of mind, an emotional form, that had carried my memory to older verses, or even to forgotten mythologies. I was carried so far that it was as though I came to one of the four rivers, and followed it under the wall of Paradise to the roots of the trees of knowledge and of life. There is no song or story handed down among the cottages that has not words and thoughts to carry one as far, for though one can know but a little of their ascent, one knows that they ascend like medieval genealogies through unbroken dignities to the beginning of the world. Folk art is, indeed, the oldest of the aristocracies of thought, and because it refuses what is passing and trivial, the merely clever and pretty, as certainly as the vulgar and insincere, and because it has gathered into itself the simplest and most unforgetable thoughts of the generations, it is the soil where all great art is rooted. Wherever it is spoken by the fireside, or sung by the roadside, or carved upon the lintel, appreciation of the arts that a single mind gives unity and design to, spreads quickly when its hour is come.

In a society that has cast out imaginative tradition, only a few people—three or four thousand out of millions—favoured by their own characters and by happy circumstance, and only then after much labour, have understanding of imaginative things, and yet "the imagination is the man himself." The churches in the Middle Age won all the arts into their service because men understood that when imagination is impoverished, a principal voice—some would say the only voice—for the awakening of wise hope and durable faith, and understanding charity, can speak but in broken words, if it does not fall silent. And so it has always seemed to me that we, who would re-awaken imaginative tradition by making old songs live again, or by gathering old stories into books, take part in the quarrel of Galilee. Those who are Irish and would spread foreign ways, which, for all but a few, are ways of spiritual poverty, take part also. Their part is with those who were of Jewry, and yet cried out, "If thou let this man go thou art not Caesar's friend."

1901.

INTO THE TWILIGHT

Out-worn heart, in a time out-worn,
Come clear of the nets of wrong and right;
Laugh, heart, again in the gray twilight;
Sigh, heart, again in the dew of the morn.
Thy mother Eire is always young,
Dew ever shining and twilight gray,
Though hope fall from thee or love decay
Burning in fires of a slanderous tongue.
Come, heart, where hill is heaped upon hill,
For there the mystical brotherhood
Of hollow wood and the hilly wood
And the changing moon work out their will.
And God stands winding his lonely horn;
And Time and World are ever in flight,
And love is less kind than the gray twilight,
And hope is less dear than the dew of the morn.

THE LAND OF HEART'S DESIRE

LITTLE BLUE BOOK NO. 335

Edited by E. Haldeman-Julius

PERSONS

MAURTEEN BRUIN.
SHAWN BRUIN.
FATHER HART.
BRIDGET BRUIN.
MAIRE BRUIN.
A FAERY CHILD.

*The scene is laid in the Barony of Kilmacowen in
the county of Sligo, and the time is the
end of Eighteenth Century. The
characters are supposed to
speak in Gaelic.*

The kitchen of MAURTEEN BRAIN'S *house. An open grate with a turf
fire is at the left side of the room, with a table in front of it. There is a door leading
to the open air at the back, and another door a little to its left, leading into an inner
room. There is a window, a settle, and a large dresser on the right side of the room,
and a great bowl of primroses on the sill of the window.* MAURTEEN BRUIN,
FATHER HART; *and* BRIDGET BRUIN *are sitting at the table.* SHAWN
BRUIN *is setting the table for supper.* MAIRE BRUIN *sits on the settle reading
a yellow manuscript.*

BRIDGET BRUIN.
>Because I bade her go and feed the calves,
>She took that old book down out of the thatch
>And has been doubled over it all day.
>We would be deafened by her groans and moans
>Had she to work as some do, Father Hart,
>Get up at dawn like me, and mend and scour;
>Or ride abroad in the boisterous night like you,
>The pyx and blessed bread under your arm.

SHAWN BRUIN.
>You are too cross.

BRIDGET BRUIN.
>The young side with the young.

MAURTEEN BRUIN.
>She quarrels with my wife a bit at times,
>And is too deep just now in the old book;
>But do not blame her greatly; she will grow
>As quiet as a puff-ball in a tree
>When but the moons of marriage dawn and die
>For half a score of times.

FATHER HART
>   Their hearts are wild
>As be the hearts of birds, till children come.

BRIDGET BRUIN.
>She would not mind the griddle, milk the cow,
>Or even lay the knives and spread the cloth.

310

FATHER HART.

    I never saw her read a book before:
    What may it be?

MAURTEEN BRUIN.

               I do not rightly know:
    It has been in the thatch for fifty years.
    My father told me my grandfather wrote it,
    Killed a red heifer and bound it with the hide.
    But draw your chair this way—supper is spread;
    And little good he got out of the book,
    Because it filled his house with roaming bards,
    And roaming ballad-makers and the like,
    And wasted all his goods.—Here is the wine;
    The griddle bread's beside you, Father Hart.
    Colleen, what have you got there in the book
    That you must leave the bread to cool? Had I,
    Or had my father, read or written books
    There were no stockings full of silver and gold
    To come, when I am dead, to Shawn and you.

FATHER HART.

    You should not fill your head with foolish dreams.
    What are you reading?

MAIRE BRUIN.

            How a Princess Edene,
    A daughter of a King of Ireland, heard
    A voice singing on a May eve like this,
    And followed, half awake and half asleep,
    Until she came into the land of faery,

Where nobody gets old and godly and grave,
Where nobody gets old and crafty and wise,
Where nobody gets old and bitter of tongue;
And she is still there, busied with a dance.
Deep in the dewy shadow of a wood,
Or where stars walk upon a mountain top.

MAURTEEN BRUIN.
Persuade the colleen to put by the book:
My grandfather would mutter just such things,
And he was no judge of a dog or horse,
And any idle boy could blarney him.
Just speak your mind.

FATHER HART.
                        Put it away, my colleen.
God spreads the heavens above us like great wings,
And gives a little round of deeds and days,
And then come the wrecked angels and set snares,
And bait them with light hopes and heavy dreams,
Until the heart is puffed with pride and goes,
Half shuddering and half joyous, from God's peace;
And it was some wrecked angel, blind tears,
Who flattered Edene's heart with merry words.
My colleen, I have seen some other girls
Restless and ill at ease, but years went by
And they grew like their neighbours and were glad
In minding children, working at the churn,
And gossiping of weddings and of wakes;
For life moves out of a red flare of dreams
Into a common light of common hours,
Until old age bring the red flare again.

312

SHAWN BRUIN.

Yet do not blame her greatly, Father Hart, For she is dull while I am in the fields, And mother's tongue were harder still to bear, But for her fancies: this is May Eve too, When the good people post about the world, And surely one may think of them to-night. Maire, have you the primroses to fling Before the door to make a golden path For them to bring good luck into the house. Remember, they may steal new-married brides Upon May Eve.

MAIRE BRUIN *(going over to the window and taking the flowers from the bowl.)*

Here are the primroses.

[She goes to the door and strews the primroses outside.

FATHER HART.

You do well, daughter, because God permits
Great power to the good people on May Eve.

MAURTEEN BRUIN.

They can work all their will with primroses—
Change them to golden money, or little flames
To burn up those who do them any wrong.

MAIRE BRUIN.

I had no sooner flung them by the door
Than the wind cried and hurried them away.

BRIDGET BRUIN.

May God have mercy on us!

MAIRE BRUIN.

The good people
Will not be lucky to the house this year,
But I am glad that I was courteous to them,
For are not they, likewise, children of God?

FATHER HART.
No, child; they are the children of the fiend,
And they have power until the end of Time,
When God shall fight with them a great pitched battle
And hack them into pieces.

MAIRE BRUIN.

He will smile,
Father, perhaps, and open his great door,

FATHER HART.
Did but the lawless angels see that door
They would fall, slain by everlasting peace;
And when such angels knock upon our doors
Who goes with them must drive through the same storm.

[*A knock at the door.* MAIRE BRUIN *opens it and then goes to the dresser and fills a porringer with milk and hands it through the door and takes it back empty and closes the door.*

MAIRE BRUIN.
A little queer old woman cloaked in green
Who came to beg a porringer of milk.

BRIDGET BRUIN.

 The good people go asking milk and fire
 Upon May Eve—Woe on the house that gives
 For they have power upon it for a year.
 I knew you would bring evil on the house

MAURTEEN BRUIN.

 Who was she?

MAIRE BRUIN.

 Both the tongue and face were strange.

MAURTEEN BRUIN.

 Some strangers came last week to Clover Hill;
 She must be one of them.

BRIDGET BRUIN.

 I am afraid.

MAURTEEN BRUIN.

 The priest will keep all harm out of the house.

FATHER HART.

 The Cross will keep all harm out of the house
 While it hangs there.

MAURTEEN BRUIN.

 Come, sit beside me, colleen,
 And cut away your dreams of discontent,
 For I would have you light up my last days
 Like a bright torch of pine, and when I die

I will make you the wealthiest hereabout;
For hid away where nobody can find
I have a stocking full of silver and gold.

BRIDGET BRUIN.
You are the fool of every pretty face,
And I must pinch and pare that my son's wife
May have all kinds of ribbons for her head.

MAURTEEN BRUIN.
Do not be cross; she is a right good girl!
The butter's by your elbow, Father Hart.
My colleen, have not Fate and Time and Change
Done well for me and for old Bridget there?
We have a hundred acres of good land,
And sit beside each other at the fire,
The wise priest of our parish to our right,
And you and our dear son to left of us.
To sit beside the board and drink good wine
And watch the turf smoke coiling from the fire
And feel content and wisdom in your heart,
This is the best of life; when we are young
We long to tread a way none trod before,
But find the excellent old way through love
And through the care of children to the hour
For bidding Fate and Time and Change good-bye.

[A *knock at the door.* MAIRE BRUIN *opens it and then takes a sod of turf out of the hearth in the tongs and passes it through the door and closes the door and remains standing by it.*

MAIRE BRUIN.

 A little queer old man in a green coat,
 Who asked a burning sod to light his pipe.

BRIDGET BRUIN.

 You have now given milk and fire and brought
 For all you know, evil upon the house.
 Before you married you were idle and fine,
 And went about with ribbons on your head;
 And now you are a good-for-nothing wife.

SHAWN BRUIN.

 Be quiet, mother!

MAURTEEN BRUIN.

 You are much too cross!

MAIRE BRUIN.

 What do I care if I have given this house,
 Where I must hear all day a bitter tongue,
 Into the power of faeries!

BRIDGET BRUIN.

                    You know, well
 How calling the good people by that name
 Or talking of them over much at all
 May bring all kinds of evil on the house.

MAIRE BRUIN.

 Come, faeries, take me out of this dull house!
 Let me have all the freedom I have lost—

Work when I will and idle when I will!
Faeries, came take me out of this dull world,
For I would ride with you upon the wind,
Run on the top of the dishevelled tide,
And dance upon the mountains like a flame!

FATHER HART.
You cannot know the meaning of your words!

MAIRE BRUIN.
Father, I am right weary of four tongues:
A tongue that is too crafty and too wise,
A tongue that is too godly and too grave,
A tongue that is more bitter than the tide,
And a kind tongue too full of drowsy love,
Of drowsy love and my captivity.

[SHAWN BRUIN *comes over to her and leads her to the settle.*

SHAWN BRUIN.
Do not blame me: I often lie awake
Thinking that all things trouble your bright head—
How beautiful it is—such broad pale brows
Under a cloudy blossoming of hair!
Sit down beside me here—these are too old,
And have forgotten they were ever young.

MAIRE BRUIN.
O, you are the great door-post of this house,
And I the red nasturtium climbing up.

[She takes SHAWN'S hand but looks shyly at the priest and lets it go.

FATHER HART.
    Good daughter, take his hand—by love alone
    God binds us to Himself and to the hearth
    And shuts us from the waste beyond His peace,
    From maddening freedom and bewildering light.

SHAWN BRUIN.
    Would that the world were mine to give it you
    With every quiet hearth and barren waste,
    The maddening freedom of its woods and tides,
    And the bewildering lights upon its hills.

MAIRE BRUIN.
    Then I would take and break it in my hands
    To see you smile watching it crumble away.

SHAWN BRUIN.
    Then I would mould a world of fire and dew
    With no one bitter, grave, or over wise,
    And nothing marred or old to do you wrong.
    And crowd the enraptured quiet of the sky
    With candles burning to your lonely face.

MAIRE BRUIN.
    Your looks are all the candles that I need.

SHAWN BRUIN.
    Once a fly dancing in a beam o' the sun,
    Or the light wind blowing out of the dawn,

Could fill your heart with dreams none other knew,
But now the indissoluble sacrament
Has mixed your heart that was most proud and cold
With my warm heart for ever; and sun and moor,
Must fade and heaven be rolled up like a scroll;
But your white spirit still walk by my spirit.
For not a power in earth and heaven and hell
Can break this bond binding heart unto heart.

[A VOICE *sings in the distance.*

MAIRE BRUIN.
Did you hear something call? O, guard me close,
Because I have said wicked things to-night.

A VOICE *(close to the door)*.
The wind blows out of the gates of the day,
   The wind blows over the lonely of heart
And the lonely of heart is withered away,
   While the faeries dance in a place apart,
Shaking their milk-white feet in a ring,
   Tossing their milk-white arms in the air;
For they hear the wind laugh, and murmur, and sing
   Of a land where even the old are fair,
And even the wise are merry of tongue;
   But I heard a reed of Coolaney say,
'When the wind has laughed and murmured and sung,
   The lonely of heart must wither away!'

MAURTEEN BRUIN.

    I am right happy, and would make all else
    Be happy too. I hear a child outside,
    And will go bring her in out of the cold.

    [He opens the door. A CHILD *dressed in a green jacket with a red cap comes into the house.*

THE CHILD.

    I tire of winds and waters and pale lights!

MAURTEEN BRUIN.

    You are most welcome. It is cold out there,
    Who'd think to face such cold on a May Eve.

THE CHILD.

    And when I tire of this warm little house,
    There is one here who must away, away,
    To where the woods, the stars, and the white streams
    Are holding a continual festival.

MAURTEEN BRUIN.

    O listen to her dreamy and strange talk,
    Come to the fire.

THE CHILD.

             I'll sit upon your knee,
    For I have run from where the winds are born,
    And long-to rest my feet a little while.

    [She sits upon his knee.

BRIDGET BRUIN.

How pretty you are!

MAURTEEN BRUIN.

Your hair is wet with dew!

BRIDGET BRUIN.

I'll chafe your poor chilled feet.

MAURTEEN BRUIN.

You must have come
A long long way, for I have never seen
Your pretty face, and must be tired and hungry;
Here is some bread and wine.

THE CHILD.

They are both nasty.
Old mother, have you nothing nice for me?

BRIDGET BRUIN.

I have some honey!

[*She goes into the next room.*

MAURTEEN BRUIN.

You are a dear child;
The mother was quite cross before you came.

[BRIDGET *returns with the honey, and goes to the dresser and fills a
porringer with milk.*

BRIDGET BRUIN.

    She is the child of gentle people; look
    At her white hands and at her pretty dress.
    I've brought you some new milk, but wait awhile
    And I will put it by the fire to warm,
    For things well fitted for poor folk like us
    Would never please a high-born child like you.

THE CHILD.

    Old mother, my old mother, the green dawn
    Brightens above while you blow up the fire;
    And evening finds you spreading the white cloth.
    The young may lie in bed and dream and hope,
    But you work on because your heart is old.

BRIDGET BRUIN.

    The young are idle.

THE CHILD.

               Old father, you are wise,
    And all the years have gathered in your heart
    To whisper of the wonders that are gone.
    The young must sigh through many a dream and hope,
    But you are wise because your heart is old.

MAURTEEN BRUIN.

    O, who would think to find so young a child
    Loving old age and wisdom.

      [BRIDGET *gives her more bread and honey.*

THE CHILD.
    No more, mother.

MAURTEEN BRUIN.
    What a small bite; The milk is ready now;
    What a small sip!

THE CHILD.
                    Put on my shoes, old mother,
    For I would like to dance now I have dined.
    The reeds are dancing by Coolaney lake,
    And I would like to dance until the reeds
    And the loud wind, the white wave on the shore,
    And all the stars have danced themselves to sleep.

    [BRIDGET *having put on her shoes, she gets off the old man's knees and is*
    about to dance, but suddenly sees the crucifix and shrieks and covers her eyes.

What is that ugly thing on the black cross?

FATHER HART.
    You cannot know how naughty your words are!
    That is Our Blessed Lord!

THE CHILD.
    Hide it away!

BRIDGET BRUIN.
    I have begun to be afraid again!

324

THE CHILD.
Hide it away!

MAURTEEN BRUIN.
That would be wickedness!

BRIDGET BRUIN.
That would be sacrilege!

THE CHILD
The tortured thing!
Hide it away.

MAURTEEN BRUIN.
Her parents are to blame.

FATHER HART.
That is the image of the Son of God.

[The CHILD *puts her arm round his neck lovingly and kisses him.*

THE CHILD.
Hide it away! Hide it away!

MAURTEEN BRUIN.
No! no!

FATHER HART.
Because you are so young and little a child
I will go take it down.

THE CHILD.
Hide it away,
And cover it out of sight and out of mind.
       FATHER HART *(*takes it down and carries it towards the inner
       room).
Since you have come into this barony
I will instruct you in our blessed faith:
Being a clever child you will soon learn.

       *(*To the others.)

We must be tender with all budding things,
Our Maker let no thought of Calvary
Trouble the morning stars in their first song.

       [Puts the crucifix in the inner room.

THE CHILD.
       O, what a nice, smooth floor to dance upon!
       The wind is blowing on the waving reeds,
       The wind is blowing on the heart of man.

       [She dances, swaying about like the reeds.

MAIRE *(to* SHAWN BRUIN).
       Just now when she came near I thought I heard
       Other small steps beating upon the floor,
       And a faint music blowing in the wind—
       Invisible pipes giving her feet the time.

SHAWN BRUIN.
   I heard no step but hers.

MAIRE BRUIN.
                  Look to the bolt!
   Because the unholy powers are abroad.

MAURTEEN BRUIN *(to the* CHILD).
   Come over here, and if you promise me
   Not to talk wickedly of holy things
   I'll give you something.

THE CHILD.
   Bring it me, old father!

   [MAURTEEN BRUIN *goes into the next room.*

FATHER HART.
   I will have queen cakes when you come to me!

   [MAURTEEN BRUIN *returns and lays a piece of money on the table.
   The* CHILD *makes a gesture of refusal.*

MAURTEEN BRUIN.
   It will buy lots of toys; see how it glitters!

THE CHILD.
   Come, tell me, do you love me?

MAURTEEN BRUIN.
   I love you!

THE CHILD.
> Ah! but you love this fireside!

FATHER HART.
> I love you.

THE CHILD.
> But you love Him above.

BRIDGET BRUIN.
> She is blaspheming.

THE CHILD *(to* MAIRE).
> And do you likewise love me?

MAIRE BRUIN.
> I don't know.

THE CHILD.
> You love that great tall fellow over there:
> Yet I could make you ride upon the winds,
> Run on the top of the dishevelled tide,
> And dance upon the mountains like a flame!

MAIRE BRUIN.
> Queen of the Angels and kind Saints defend us!
> Some dreadful fate has fallen: before she came
> The wind cried out and took the primroses.
> And I gave milk and fire, and when she came
> She made you hide the blessed crucifix;

She wears, too, the green jacket and red cap
Of the unholy creatures of the Raths.

FATHER HART.
You fear because of her wild, pretty prates;
She knows no better.

(To the CHILD) Child, how old are you?

THE CHILD.
My own dear people live a long, long time,
So I am young; but measure by your years
And I am older than the eagle cock
Who blinks and blinks on Ballydawley Hill,
And he's the oldest thing under the moon.
At times I merely care to dance and dance—
At times grow wiser than the eagle cock.

FATHER HART.
What are you?

THE CHILD.
                    I am of the faery people.
I sent my messengers for milk and fire,
And then I heard one call to me and came.

[*They all except* MAIRE BRUIN *gather about the priest for protection.*
MAIRE BRUIN *stays on the settle as if in a trance of terror. The* CHILD
*takes primroses from the great bowl and begins to strew them between herself
and the priest and about* MAIRE BRUIN. *During the following dialogue*

SHAWN BRUIN *goes more than once to the brink of the primroses, but shrinks back to the others timidly.*

FATHER HART.
I will confront this mighty spirit alone.
[They cling to him and hold him back.

THE CHILD *(while she strews the primroses.)*
No one whose heart is heavy with human tears
Can cross these little cressets of the wood.

FATHER HART.
Be not afraid, the Father is with us,
And all the nine angelic hierarchies,
The Holy Martyrs and the Innocents,
The adoring Magi in their coats of mail,
And He who died and rose on the third day,
And Mary with her seven times wounded heart.

[The CHILD ceases strewing the primroses, and kneels upon the settle beside
    MAIRE *and puts her arms about her neck.*

Cry daughter to the Angels and the Saints.

THE CHILD.
You shall go with me, newly-married bride,
And gaze upon a merrier multitude:
White-armed Nuala and Ardroe the Wise,
Feacra of the hurtling foam, and him
Who is the ruler of the western host,
Finvarra, and their Land of Heart's Desire,

Where beauty has no ebb, decay no flood,
But joy is wisdom, Time an endless song.
I kiss you and the world begins to fade.

FATHER HART.
Daughter, I call you unto home and love!

THE CHILD.
Stay, and come with me, newly-married bride,
For, if you hear him, you grow like the rest:
Bear children, cook, be mindful of the churn,
And wrangle over butter, fowl, and eggs,
And sit at last there, old and bitter of tongue,
Watching the white stars war upon your hopes.

FATHER HART.
Daughter, I point you out the way to heaven!

THE CHILD.
But I can lead you, newly-married bride,
Where nobody gets old and crafty and wise,
Where nobody gets old and godly and grave,
Where nobody gets old and bitter of tongue,
And where kind tongues bring no captivity,
For we are only true to the far lights
We follow singing, over valley and hill.

FATHER HART.
By the dear name of the one crucified,
I bid you, Maire Bruin, come to me.

THE CHILD.

I keep you in the name of your own heart!

[She leaves the settle, and stooping takes up a mass of primroses and kisses them.

We have great power to-night, dear golden folk
For he took down and hid the crucifix.
And my invisible brethren fill the house;
I hear their footsteps going up and down.
O, they shall soon rule all the hearts of men
And own all lands; last night they merrily danced
About his chapel belfrey! *(To* MAIRE.) Come away,
I hear my brethren bidding us away!

FATHER HART.

I will go fetch the crucifix again.

[They hang about him in terror and prevent him from moving.

BRIDGET BRUIN.

The enchanted flowers will kill us if you go.

MAURTEEN BRUIN.

They turn the flowers to little twisted flames.

SHAWN BRUIN.

The little twisted flames burn up the heart.

THE CHILD.

I hear them call us, newly-married bride.

MAIRE BRUIN.
I will go with you.

FATHER HART.
She is lost, alas,

THE CHILD (*standing by the door*).
Then, follow but the heavy body of clay,
And clinging mortal hope must fall from you;
For we who ride the winds, run on the waves,
And dance upon the mountains, are more light
Than dewdrops on the banners of the dawn.

MAIRE BRUIN.
Then take my soul.

[SHAWN BRUIN *goes over to her.*

SHAWN BRUIN.
              Beloved, do not leave me!
What will my life be if you go with her?
Remember when I met you by the well
And took your hand in mine and spoke of love.

MAIRE BRUIN.
Dear face! Dear voice!

THE CHILD.
Come, newly-married bride!

MAIRE BRUIN.

    I always loved her world—and yet—and yet
    I think that I would stay if I could stay.

    [Sinks into his arms.

THE CHILD *(from the door).*

    White bird, white bird, come with me, little bird!

MAIRE BRUIN.

    She calls my soul!

THE CHILD.

    Come with me, little bird!

MAIRE BRUIN.

    I can hear songs and dancing!

SHAWN BRUIN.

    Stay with me!

MAIRE BRUIN.

    Dear, I would stay—and yet and yet—

THE CHILD.

               White bird!
    Come, little bird with crest of gold!

MAIRE BRUIN *(very softly).*

    And yet—

THE CHILD.
Come, little bird with silver feet!

SHAWN BRUIN.
Dead, dead!

FATHER HART.
Thus do the evil spirits snatch their prey
Almost out of the very hand of God;
And day by day their power is more and more,
And men and women leave old paths, for pride
Comes knocking with thin knuckles on the heart.

A VOICE *sings outside*—
The wind blows out of the gates of the day,
    The wind blows over the lonely of heart,
And the lonely of heart is withered away,
    While the faeries dance in a place apart,
Shaking their milk-white feet in a ring,
    Tossing their milk-white arms in the air;
For they hear the wind laugh and murmur and sing
    Of a land where even the old are fair,
And even the wise are merry of tongue;
    But I heard a reed of Coolaney say,
'When the wind has laughed and murmured and sung,
    The lonely of heart must wither away.'

[The song is taken up by many voices, who sing loudly, as if in triumph. Some of the voices seem to come from within the house.

335

CPSIA information can be obtained
at www.ICGtesting.com
Printed in the USA
BVHW051737290123
657387BV00003B/53